Mirror of Language

MIRROR

OF

LANGUAGE

The Debate on Bilingualism

KENJI HAKUTA

Basic Books, Inc., Publishers

NEW YORK

Grateful acknowledgement is given to Aida Comulada, Marguerite Leopold (for Werner F. Leopold), and Ralph Robinett for permission to discuss their work, and to the following sources:

New York Times Letters to the Editor, copyright © 1974/76/81 by The New York Times Company. Reprinted by permission.

Northwestern University Press, *Speech Development of a Bilingual Child: A Linguist's Record,* by Werner F. Leopold, vols. 1–4.

Language Shift: Social Determinants of Linguistic Change in Bilingual Austria, By Susan Gal: Copyright 1979 by Susan Gal. Used by permission of Academic Press and the author.

Library of Congress Cataloging-in-Publication Data

Hakuta, Kenji.
    Mirror of language.

    Bibliography: p. 242
    Includes index.
    1. Bilingualism.   2. Language acquisition.   I.   Title.
P115.H34   1985   404'.2   85–45313
ISBN   0–465–04636–3   (cloth)
ISBN   0–465–04637–1   (paper)

Copyright © 1986 by Basic Books, Inc.
Printed in the United States of America
Designed by Vincent Torre
87 88 89 90 MPC 9 8 7 6 5 4 3 2 1

FOR

Aida, Kay, Isa, Lisette, Mary,

Millie, Pat, and Wanda

Contents

Contents

Preface

I WROTE THIS BOOK for two reasons. First, I was moved by the sheer accumulation of inquiries I have had about bilingualism. Parents, students, professionals, politicians, and people who are simply curious about language have asked me for information that was at once scientifically nontechnical and intellectually sophisticated.

Many parents want to know if it is wise to raise their children with more than one language—a choice that arises when the parents use more than one language at home, when a daytime babysitter uses another language, or when the family goes abroad for an extended stay. Many professionals, such as teachers and policy makers, have to make decisions about educating children who have grown up using a different language at home. Should the home language be used in instruction at all? Should it be maintained even after the child successfully masters the language used in school? How should proficiency in the two languages be defined and evaluated? In our cosmopolitan world, such questions are being asked with increasing frequency, particularly as American public interest in foreign languages is rekindled by concern over the dangers of monolingualism in causing cultural and economic isolation and in crippling national intelligence and security (Simon 1980). Professionals want a basic grasp of the concepts of bilingualism to aid them in formulating the best curriculum for particular

---

children or the best policy for the nation at large. I have tried to outline the pieces of the research puzzle in a way that they would find useful in making such decisions.

Second, I wrote this as an appeal to my colleagues in the social and behavioral sciences. Because the study of bilingualism cuts across several traditional academic disciplines—psychology, linguistics, sociology, anthropology, and education, among them—it is particularly susceptible to the narrowness and fragmentation that beset so much of our work. I hope this book serves as a reminder of the breadth of the research agenda of bilingualism and, more generally, of the need to study research problems of all kinds in their widest contexts. Of course, students in a variety of disciplines will also, I hope, profit from this book as an introduction to the research area and as an inspiration to conduct their own investigations of bilingualism.

Many individuals and institutions have contributed generously to the preparation of this book. For comments and discussion about various portions of the manuscript, I would like to thank Muriel Bell, Lois Bloom, Carol Feldman, Bernardo Ferdman, Sylvia Galambos, Kathleen Galotti, Michael Green, William Kessen, Lloyd Komatsu, Mary McGroarty, Joan Miller, John Schumann, and Marilyn Vihman. I owe an extended thanks to Nancy Goodban and Catherine Snow, who tackled the manuscript in its entirety. I would also like especially to thank Aida Comulada, the late Werner F. Leopold, and Ralph Robinett for allowing me to draw on our conversations.

I started this book while I was a Fellow at the Center for Advanced Study in the Behavioral Sciences in Palo Alto from 1982 to 1983. The Center provided the ideal setting for thinking and writing about the issues in their broad contexts. Its staff librarians, Bruce Harley and Margaret Amara, tirelessly accommodated my embarrassingly large number of requests for source materials. I am also grateful to the Exxon Education Foundation, the Alfred P. Sloan Foundation, and the Spencer Foundation for their financial support for my fellowship year.

My own research projects discussed in various parts of this book have been funded by grants from the National Institute of Education, the National Science Foundation, and the Spencer Foundation.

Finally, I thank my editor, Judith Greissman of Basic Books, who has been my vigilant but cheerful disciplinarian. Her combination of friendliness, sharp editorial instincts, and ability to balance the perspectives of the reader and author is rare. I also thank Nina Gunzenhauser for her incisive copyediting, which extended beyond grammar and helped sharpen my thinking.

Mirror of Language

Chapter 1

Introduction

LANGUAGE has always been at the center of scholarly and theological debates about the very definition of humanness. In recent times, the debates have generally been shaped by more specialized concerns, such as the nature of language acquisition, the role of language in thought processes, and the relationship between language and social identity. For social scientists who conduct such inquiries, the person who is bilingual* represents an intriguing case.

To the extent that mental and social systems are affected by specific features of languages, a bilingual person must have two parallel systems, one for each language, that must at the same time be interrelated. The bilingual presents a packaging puzzle, as it were, in which two language-bounded mental and social systems must be housed in a single mind. This book is concerned with the delicate pattern of coexistence, cooperation, and competition formed by the two languages of the bilingual. The languages leave their own imprints on the linguistic, psychological, and social experiences of the bilingual. A compari-

---

*Although the discussion throughout this book refers to *bilinguals,* the points made apply equally well to multilingualism and to non-oral-aural languages such as American Sign Language.

son of the patterns will tell us about the role of language in these domains of experience, and in this sense bilingualism is the mirror of language.

The definition of a bilingual in this book is deliberately open-ended. It begins where "the speaker of one language can produce complete meaningful utterances in the other language" (Haugen 1953, 7). This broad definition is preferable to a narrow one that might include only those with native-like control of two languages. Native-like control is difficult to define, and very few people who would generally be considered bilingual have anything resembling native-like control of both languages. More important, the broad definition incorporates a developmental perspective, bringing the entire process of second-language acquisition into the domain of bilingualism. The study of bilingualism should include not only the study of the bilingual person but also the circumstances surrounding the creation of bilingualism and its maintenance or attrition.

The definitional problems make it fruitless to estimate the proportion of the world's population that is bilingual. Mackey (1967), in a classic essay, argues that "bilingualism, far from being exceptional, is a problem which affects the majority of the world's population" (p. 11). He notes, for example, that there are about thirty times as many languages as there are countries, implying that to the extent that countries attempt to maintain linguistic unity (such as through education in one national language), there will be bilingualism.

Mackey further argues that the dominance of certain languages invites bilingualism. Specifically, a few languages are spoken by large segments of the world's population, putting pressure on speakers of the numerically weak languages to learn the predominant languages. About half the world's population are native speakers of languages from the Indo-European family, which includes English, Hindi, Urdu, Spanish, Russian, German, French, Italian, Portuguese, and Bengali. But these languages make up only 5 percent of the total. Other numerically powerful languages—such as Mandarin, with five hundred million speakers—strengthen the pattern. Ultimately, Mackey estimates, "70 per cent of the world's population [will use] less than 12 per cent of the world's languages" (p. 15).

Mackey also notes that dynamic forces of history contribute to bilingualism: the movement of peoples through immigration or migrant labor, invasion and colonialism, and other upheavals all contribute to making bilingualism a far more prevalent phenomenon than might commonly be believed. For example, there are an estimated fourteen to fifteen million migrant workers in Western Europe (Rist 1979). In West Germany and France, more than 10 percent of the labor force consists of foreign workers, mostly from countries in the Mediterranean region. Contrary to popular belief, these workers have little prospect of returning to their native countries. There are now five million immigrant children in the industrialized countries of Western Europe, and one estimate suggests that "a third of the young European population in the year 2000 is going to have immigrant background" (Skutnabb-Kangas 1978, 228).

The United States census of 1980 provides some estimates of the size of the bilingual population within this country (Waggoner 1984). Some 34.6 million persons—15.3 percent of the total U.S. population—were identified as "language minority," that is, members of families in which non-English languages (predominantly Spanish, French, German, Italian, and Polish) are spoken. Of these, 4.5 million are school-aged children who speak their native (non-English) language at home. These numbers do not exactly correspond to the number of bilingual people in the United States, of course, but they do suggest that a significant proportion of the U.S. population confronts the various aspects of bilingualism dealt with in this book.

These numbers are given only by way of example, for an entire book could be written on the language statistics of countries around the world (Kloss [1974] has compiled such a reference source of language statistics). The point is that bilingualism is not the exception to the rule of monolingualism. In fact, it is highly likely that a Martian landing at a random location on earth would conclude, after observing the linguistic environment, that the inhabitants are bilingual.

An Ecology of Bilingualism

The subject of bilingualism, then, is of very real concern to a substantial number of people whose lives involve the use of two or more languages. It does not exist merely to satisfy the strange appetites of social scientists. By way of introducing these concerns, which form the subject matter of this book, let me describe the experiences of Aida Comulada, a friend of mine who encounters the many faces of bilingualism every day.

Aida is the principal of the Garfield School, an elementary school in a low-income area of Bridgeport, Connecticut. Her school has a substantial proportion of children from homes where a language other than English is spoken. About 70 percent of her pupils come from Spanish-speaking homes, another 10 percent from Laotian homes. She also gets an occasional single speaker of a language; for example, at this writing there is one child from an Arabic-speaking home. The amount of English the children know when they arrive at Aida's school varies widely. Some students come with a good working knowledge of English as well as of their native language; others have limited ability in both. Still others, indeed the majority, have very limited ability in English but normal skills in their native language. The parents of these children are well aware of the importance of English for survival in this society, and they see the teaching of English as a major responsibility of the schools.

The Spanish-speaking students have available to them special "bilingual" classes if their English is limited. In these classes, students receive instruction primarily in Spanish, with English phased in progressively as the students learn their second language. The Laotian students have no such programs because of the problem of finding certified teachers in their language. They do have a Laotian "resource aide" in the school, who teaches math in Laotian and who is generally available in the English as a Second Language (ESL) classes for Laotian students.

The Spanish-speaking students (mainly Puerto Rican) and the Laotian students are learning English under very different circumstances, the major one being immigration status. The Laotians are refugees, from agricultural backgrounds, and they are in the English-speaking milieu to stay. Their chances of returning to their homeland are minuscule, and they are determined to learn the language. The Puerto Ricans, on the other hand, are not immigrants. They are Americans, and they can (and do) return to Puerto Rico, where Spanish is the official language. They are not under the same extreme pressure as the Laotians. Aida likens the Laotians to the Costa Rican and Colombian children she taught in Norwalk many years ago, whose parents were also doggedly determined to have their children learn English, as only those who have no other option can be.

Aida is well aware of the stigma that society attaches to students identified as "bilingual." Bilingualism in the United States is seen as a transitional stage into fully assimilated English monolingualism. Historically, it has been associated with low-income, low-status persons who are educationally at risk. Bilingual education, which exists in various forms nationwide as a remedy for the educational problems of these students, is regarded with suspicion by some sectors of the public. It is seen by some to foster separationist tendencies, of the sort evidenced in officially bilingual countries such as Canada and Belgium. As the principal of a school that has a bilingual program, Aida is

7

constantly in the position of defending the program. And her previous experience has given her ample practice in advocating bilingual education. As supervisor of the Bilingual Program for the New Haven school district, the third largest in Connecticut, and as president of the Connecticut Association for Bilingual and Bicultural Education, an organization of teachers and administrators in bilingual education programs, she heard just about every kind of accusation about the program from the press, from school board members, from the community. It was accused of failing to teach the children English, of using unqualified teachers whose jobs made them the sole beneficiaries of bilingual education, of creating students who were proficient in neither Spanish nor English, of segregating students from the mainstream of American life, of confusing children's intellectual and personality development. Although these arguments are not supported by research, they pointed to the cold realities of an environment hostile to bilingual education. Particularly strong heat came from the generation of older immigrants who themselves had gone through the old "sink-or-swim" method of learning English, in which they were simply thrown into regular classes and expected to learn English. "I did it," the line went. "Why can't they?"

As supervisor of the bilingual program in New Haven, Aida came to witness firsthand the patterns of language use in the bilingual community of Puerto Ricans. The constant flow of people in both directions between New Haven and Puerto Rico served to maintain Spanish in the community. Yet there seemed to be a danger of loss of the language among the longer-term residents. In this group, particularly among the children, English was the dominant language and seemed to have attained this status at the expense of Spanish.

The community's bilingualism could be described as subtractive, rather than additive; the second language replaced the first. High school courses in Spanish as a foreign language were evidence of the loss. In those classes were Puerto Rican students struggling to relearn the native language they had lost. Worse, these students represented the ones most driven to regain their Spanish; for each one, there were several others who avoided Spanish for various reasons, allowing the language to disappear from their lives. There was little that the bilingual program could do to help maintain Spanish in this community, much to Aida's regret, since by law it could serve only as a transitional program for students with limited English.

Aida was also faced with practical problems in supervising the program. To recruit teachers who could teach in Spanish, she often resorted to bringing teachers in directly from Puerto Rico. Her own house frequently served as a temporary home for newly arrived teachers as they adjusted to life on the English-speaking mainland. Naturally, there were differences in the ease with which they adapted to the new environment. Since the bilingual program often used pairs of monolingual teachers (one in English, the other in Spanish), the teachers from Puerto Rico sometimes had limited English. They themselves, as adults, had to go through the process of learning English, with varying degrees of success.

Aida has also witnessed the bilingual development of her own children and other relatives. She has two daughters, now teenagers, who grew up using both languages at home and who have maintained their Spanish despite the strength of their adaptation to the strongly English-oriented environment. Aida does not think that raising her children bilingually had any negative effects on their development. Rather, she sees their bilingualism as an enrichment that allows them to sample more broadly the opportunities presented by a diverse world. Neither she nor her daughters would have it any other way.

Aida's bilingual saga shows why an odyssey into the intricacies of bilingualism cannot stop at language. Bilingualism, in addition to being a linguistic concept, refers to a constellation of tensions having to do with a multitude of psychological, societal, and political realities.

An Overview of the Book

In the United States, bilingualism is a term with meanings beyond the use of more than one language. As Aida knows well, the bilingual child in the American classroom commonly evokes the image of a child who speaks English poorly, has difficulty in school, and is in need of remediation. This image has a relatively long history, dating back to the turn of the century. In chapter 2, I dig into this history to reveal the origins of the controversy over the intelligence of bilinguals. For decades researchers debated not about whether bilingual children in American schools were intellectually inferior—that was considered to have been "proved"—but about whether they were so because they were of poor genetic stock or because they were confused by the attempt to use two languages. The complex story ends with a twist, as we will see in reviewing more contemporary research with middle-class bilinguals, showing that bilingualism can indeed enhance the cognitive development of children.

In chapter 2, I also emphasize the importance of understanding the perspectives of researchers, a theme repeated throughout the book. I used to believe that "when the facts are in, the data will speak for themselves." Now I am (a bit) wiser. The facts are always seen from the point of view of a theory, either an explicit scientific theory or, more subtly, an implicit theory about human beings and about language. This point underscores the second, perhaps more subtle reason why the word *mirror* appears in the title of this book. The story of bilingualism is in part about the changing perspectives of social scientists, changes that occur not only as a function of trends in the profession but as a function of trends in society as a whole.

Returning to Aida, we have seen that she brought up her children in a home environment where Spanish and English were both used. To borrow from Swain's (1972) clever dissertation title, the children grew up with bilingualism as a first language. Different disciplinary perspectives on this process are the focus of chapter 3, in which the works of the linguist Werner Leopold are contrasted with those of the psychologist Madorah Smith. Leopold focused on the details of the development, separation, and interaction of the two languages simultaneously learned by his daughter Hildegard. In contrast, Smith concentrated on differences between individual children, including the differences between bilingual and monolingual children, rather than on the qualitative characteristics of their language. I discuss the differences and commonalities in their approaches to understanding early bilingualism in children.

Between the late 1950s and early 1960s, scholarly interest shifted, for a number of reasons, from an interest in the description of behaviors toward the postulation of complex structures in the mind. This new "mentalism," described in chapters 3 and 4, led to speculations about abstract mental processes and the drawing of hypothetical maps of the bilingual mind. This research enables us to ask questions about the way knowledge acquired in one language transfers to the other language. In Aida's bilingual education classes, for example, children learn subject matter in Spanish and transfer that knowledge to English. They do not have to learn the same subject twice, once in each language. Another important question is whether the conditions under which a person learns two languages can cause different outcomes in terms of mental structure. Are Aida's daughters, who learned two languages simultaneously in the home, different from children such as Aida's Laotian students, who learn the second language only at school age? And if so, how are they different? In chapter 4, I critically examine the various ways in which the qualities of the bilingual mind have been characterized.

Chapter 5 is a linguistic view of how children learn a second language. How do Aida's Puerto Rican and Laotian students learn English, for example? An important issue here is whether the first language of the children makes a difference in the way in which they acquire English. Do the Spanish and Laotian systems already resident in these children exert different influences on how the children perceive English? If they do, it might be important to make the second-language curriculum sensitive to these realities. Another important question involves individual differences. Some children seem to learn a second language more quickly than others. What might account for these variations among children?

A comparison of second-language acquisition in adults with that observed in children is the topic of chapter 6. Once again in Aida's territory, we look at the similarities and differences in the ways the children in her bilingual program and the teachers whom she recruited from Puerto Rico acquired English. The popular conception is that second-language learning is radically different for adults and for children, a myth that we put to rest. In fact, the more important question is what accounts for the tremendous variation among different adult second-language learners. Aida noticed, for example, that teachers arriving in New Haven from Puerto Rico showed widely differing rates of learning English and adjusting to new cultural conditions. In this chapter, I discuss the roles of language aptitude, personality, attitudes, and social setting in accounting for observed differences in adult second-language acquisition.

Chapter 7 is about the characteristics of bilingual communities. Aida observed, for example, that the community in New Haven seems to be moving toward English at the expense of Spanish. The rate at which immigrant languages have been displaced by English in the United States is truly remarkable, and we explore the reasons for this mass extinction. In an effort to give perspective, I characterize a number of different bilingual communities, with a focus on the complexities involved in describing how languages are used in communities. Particularly important is the question of under what conditions a community stabilizes into bilingualism and under what conditions one language atrophies and the community moves toward monolingualism. Looming large in this picture are the cultural and social values attached to particular languages and the clashes that are regularly observed as a result of competing values.

When competing languages and values exist in a society, bilingual education is in many ways the most salient issue, and that is the topic of chapter 8. I have already outlined the controversies over bilingual education that constantly confront Aida, and there are many. The heated emotions raised by bilingual education have led to much misunderstanding, and one goal of the chapter is to clear up some misconceptions. It appears, however, that the conflicts run much deeper than can be resolved by objective inquiry and clarification. There are emotional and political realities underlying the controversy over bilingual education that no amount of scientific investigation will smooth over. They need to be addressed before popular support for bilingual education can be mobilized. The chapter serves an integrative role for the book, for it contains most of the issues raised by the previous chapters. In the final chapter, I offer some capsule conclusions and outline the enduring tension points in bilingualism that are certain to be found in future debates on the topic.

Chapter 2

Bilingualism and Intelligence

"YOU KNOW, I've always wondered. Is it good or bad for children to be bilingual?" This is the question I am most frequently asked. It comes up in my office with students and colleagues; at cocktail parties and during dinner conversations; at professional meetings of scholars and school teachers. My questioners often know of a child whose learning problems have been attributed to bilingualism. They have heard that using two languages in early childhood creates a split personality, a linguistic Jekyll and Hyde. They have also heard that bilingualism is a good thing, that it enriches the intellect, creates a multidimensional view of the world. "Tell me," they demand, "what is the truth?"

It is no wonder that the average person is confused, for scholars have made both claims: bilingualism is bad; bilingualism is good. George Thompson (1952), in a widely used American textbook on child psychology, wrote:

There can be no doubt that the child reared in a bilingual environment is handicapped in his language growth. One can debate the issue as to whether speech facility in two languages is worth the consequent retardation in the common language of the realm. (P. 367)

On the other hand, Canadian researchers Elizabeth Peal and Wallace Lambert (1962) triumphantly drew a contrasting picture of the bilingual as

a youngster whose wider experiences in two cultures have given him advantages which a monolingual does not enjoy. Intellectually his experience with two language systems seems to have left him with a mental flexibility, a superiority in concept formation, a more diversified set of mental abilities. . . . In contrast, the monolingual appears to have a more unitary structure of intelligence which he must use for all types of intellectual tasks. (P. 20)

The primary objective of this chapter will be to look at the literature on "good" and "bad" bilingualism with respect to an elusive psychological construct called "intelligence." Since the turn of the century, psychologists have tried to develop objective instruments for measuring this construct, and researchers have used the performance of bilinguals on such measures as an indication of whether bilingualism is good or bad.

An overview of the hundreds of studies that compare the performance of bilinguals with monolinguals on various measures of intelligence reveals that research in the first half of this century was guided by the question of whether or not bilingualism has a negative effect on intelligence, while more recent work has been concerned with whether or not there is a positive effect. This shift in emphasis is related to the subject populations that were under study. The early work was conducted primarily in the United States with immigrant groups, and the recent work with middle-class populations in Canada and Europe. Although these studies all compare monolinguals with bilinguals, close inspection reveals different motivations behind the studies. The researchers were working under different sociological circumstances. They differed in what moved them to look at the relationship between bilingualism and intelligence in the first place. They chose different methodologies that reflected their motivations. And their motivations markedly influenced their interpretations of their findings.

It is difficult to overstate the importance of the *Zeitgeist* in which the scientist works. The importance of understanding this influence is particularly pressing in the case of the social scientist, whose subject matter is so closely connected to his or her own membership in society. Let us begin, therefore, by going back some eighty years to absorb the social context in which the relationship between bilingualism and intelligence began to be investigated in the United States.

The "Old" and "New" American Immigrants

The first studies of bilingualism and intelligence were not concerned with bilingualism per se. If they considered it at all, they rejected bilingualism (or lack of English ability) as an explanation of intelligence, preferring instead to attribute such differences to racial and ethnic origins.

The motivation for these American studies of the early 1900s was the concern over the changing pattern of immigration from Europe. The Dillingham Commission, set up by Congress in 1907 to investigate the changes, reflected this social trend. It drew a solid distinction between "old" and "new" immigrants, the temporal boundary being set in the early 1880s. The commission lauded the old immigrants from northern Europe, who had dispersed throughout the country and been rapidly assimilated. Its contrasting view of the new immigrants from southern and eastern Europe was characterized by historian Maldwyn Jones (1960) as follows:

This "new" immigration had consisted, [the commission] declared, largely of unskilled male laborers, a large proportion of whom had come to the United States not as permanent settlers but simply as transients. Almost entirely avoiding agriculture, they had flocked to the industrial centers of the East and Middle West, where they had "congregated together in sections apart from native Americans and the older immigrants to such an extent that assimilation [had] been slow." (P. 178)

What the commission failed to take into consideration, however, was the differences in the length of time the two groups of immigrants had had to settle in their new country. As Jones makes clear, the characterization of the new immigrants is one that applies equally well to the initial wave of both groups. (1960, pp. 177–82).

Coupled with the characterization of the new immigrants as transient and isolated was the view that they were of inferior intelligence. Francis A. Walker (1840–1897), president of M.I.T., wrote,

These immigrants are beaten men from beaten races, representing the worst failures in the struggle for existence. . . . Europe is allowing its slums and its most stagnant reservoirs of degraded peasantry to be drained off upon our soil. (Quoted in Ayres 1909, p. 103)

This characterization of the new immigrants fueled the public outcry for the restriction of immigration of southern and eastern Europeans. The caricature of the new immigrants became an accepted stereotype of these ethnic groups.

The creation of an instrument to measure intelligence went hand in hand with the movement to restrict the flow of the new immigration (Gould 1981; Kamin 1974) though there is debate over the degree to which the testing results were actually employed in the formulation of policy (Samelson 1975; Snyderman and Herrnstein 1983). Following Francis Galton (1890), a number of psychologists in the late nineteenth century were searching for objectively administered measures of intelligence to reflect this most complex of human traits. It would be convenient, they thought, if people could be classified along a single dimension, if "intelligence," like height, were a simple measurement. Then if some measure of this variable called intelligence could be constructed, the measure would be an indicator of a person's worth, and social decisions could be made (and justified) on this basis (Laosa 1984). As Galton, father of the eugenics movement, once wrote,

One of the most important objects of measurement . . . is to obtain a general knowledge of the capabilities of a man by sinking shafts, as it were, at a few critical points. In order to ascertain the best points for the purpose, the sets of measures should be compared with an independent estimate of the man's powers. (1890, p. 380)

The earliest attempts to find measurable capacities linked to intelligence were made in the area of physical characteristics, such as grip strength, lung capacity, and acuity of hearing, which not surprisingly proved unrelated to mental capacity. The critical contribution was made by Alfred Binet, professor of psychology at the Sorbonne, whom the French government appointed in 1904 to devise a method of identifying children who would not benefit from instruction in regular classes and should be segregated for special instruction.

Binet devised a test that included items of some complexity and of varying levels of difficulty. One of Binet's greatest insights was that test items could be arranged with respect to the average age at which children passed them, so that simple observation of a child's performance on these items would permit a general assessment of mental age. The items tapped performance on a variety of skills, including counting coins, repeating sentences, naming the months of the year, noticing pictures with missing parts, and arranging a series of weights.

Binet himself, primarily interested in the assessment and remedial aspects of his work, was quite atheoretical in his approach to intelligence. He was vehemently opposed to the idea that what his test measured was some fixed entity, unmodifiable through experience. As Leon Kamin (1974) remarks, "It is perhaps as well that Binet died in 1911, before witnessing the uses to which his test was speedily put in the United States" (p. 5).

In 1910, H. H. Goddard, who was director of the Vineland School for Feeble-Minded Girls and Boys in New Jersey, translated the Binet test into English for use in the United States and made it available for use in assessing the intelligence of immigrants. In one study, Goddard (1917) took the English-language version of the Binet test to Ellis Island, the point of entry for newly arrived immigrants. In testing thirty adult Jews through an interpreter, he assessed twenty-five of them as "feebleminded." Regarding their performance on a word-fluency section of the test, Goddard wrote:

What shall we say of the fact that only 45 per cent can give sixty words in three minutes, when normal children of eleven years sometimes give 200 words in that time! It is hard to find an explanation except lack of intelligence or lack of vocabulary and such a lack of vocabulary in an adult would probably mean lack of intelligence. How could a person live even fifteen years in any environment without learning hundreds of names of which he could certainly think of 60 in three minutes? (P. 251)

The fact that his test found over three-quarters of this group feeble-minded did not raise doubts in Goddard's mind about the validity of the test, even though he had administered it under circumstances that were unfamiliar to and most likely traumatic for the new arrivals. Rather, Goddard took these assessments to be true measures of his subjects' intelligence and concluded that "we are getting now the poorest of each race. This makes them a highly selected group at the start" (p. 266). Goddard's recommendation, based on this research, was that "if the American public wishes feeble-minded aliens excluded, it must demand that Congress provide the necessary facilities at the ports of entry" (p. 271).

19

Following Goddard's lead, there was an almost immediate explosion of new tests and research. (By the 1930s, a bibliographic listing of research studies on testing in America was 251 pages long, and a "bibliography of bibliographies" itself took a full six pages [Goodenough 1946]). Lewis Terman, a professor of psychology at Stanford University, was perhaps the strongest advocate of the tests. He extended the Binet test to include older children and adults and refined the method for determining the intelligence quotient (IQ). His version of the test, for example, included the now-familiar multiple choice format, such as "Napoleon was defeated at: Leipzig / Paris / Verdun / Waterloo." Also included were sentences containing absurdities to be noticed and explained, such as "Yesterday the police found the body of a girl cut into 18 pieces. They believe that she killed herself" (Terman 1916, 1926). His revisions of the Binet test (the Stanford-Binet) came to be the prototype IQ test, an industry standard against which all new tests had to be compared.

The outbreak of World War I made possible testing on a large scale. Professor Robert Yerkes, of Harvard University, in collaboration with Terman and Goddard, persuaded the United States Army to test some two million draftees, purportedly to aid in classifying the new recruits. They constructed two group tests, one intended for those who could read and write English (Alpha) and one for illiterates and "foreigners" (Beta), who were given instructions in pantomime. Since the soldiers represented a variety of foreign nationalities, it became possible to make group comparisons by racial origin.

Famous among the popularizers of these data was Carl C. Brigham, who analyzed them in a book titled *A Study of American Intelligence* (1923). Of prime interest for Brigham was the pattern in test performance among the new immigrant groups. While the "foreign born white drafts" who had been in the United States for over twenty years were comparable to "native born white drafts," those with shorter years of residence in the

United States fared much more poorly, a fact that Brigham interpreted in the following way:

Migrations of the Alpine and Mediterranean races have increased to such an extent in the last thirty or forty years that this blood now constitutes 70 percent or 75 percent of the total immigration. The representatives of the Alpine and Mediterranean races in our immigration are intellectually inferior to the representatives of the Nordic race which formerly made up about 50 percent of our immigration. (P. 197)

Statistical problems in this analysis aside (see Gould 1981), a major alternative explanation stood in the way of this conclusion. The number of years of residence in the United States is obviously related to the knowledge of English and the level of acculturation to American society. It is thus directly related to the ability to answer correctly such questions as "Why should a married man have his life insured?" (Alpha Test 3, Item 13).

Brigham's response to this problem can be seen as the origin of the so-called "language handicap of bilinguals" issue. Brigham was an uncompromising hereditarian, who believed in the unmodifiability of native intelligence. Intelligence tests measured native intelligence, and nothing, not even unfamiliarity with the language, attenuated their results. The issue of language handicap, then, as it was originally raised, had to do with a measurement issue, of whether persons who happened to be bilingual were hindered by their lack of control of the language of the test.

In arguing that bilinguals did not suffer from a language handicap in taking intelligence tests, Brigham separated the new immigrant groups into those who had taken the Alpha (for literates) and those who had taken the Beta (for illiterates and foreigners). He showed that the pattern of decreasing scores with recency of immigration held not just for those who took the Alpha test, which might be expected if there were a language handicap, but also for those who took the Beta test, which presumably did not depend on knowledge of English (p. 102).

Brigham had little sympathy for the possibility that attitudes toward testing and other cultural factors might have significantly influenced the results.

It is sometimes stated that the examining methods stressed too much the hurry-up attitude frequently called typically American. The adjustment to test conditions is a part of the intelligence test. We have, of course, no other measure of adjustment aside from the total score on the examinations given. If the tests used included some mysterious type of situation that was "typically American," we are indeed fortunate, for this is America, and the purpose of our inquiry is that of obtaining a measure of the character of our immigration. (P. 96)

Apparently, Brigham assumed that test-taking ability is part of native intelligence.

Perhaps the most telling evidence of Brigham's hereditarian attitude is his attempt to rule out the language handicap by dividing the Nordic immigrants into those from English-speaking countries and those from non-English-speaking countries. When these groups are compared, a clear difference emerges in favor of the English-speaking Nordics. The analysis showing the language handicap is as clear-cut as any of those in Brigham's book. But rather than dwell on this obvious contribution of experience to the test scores, Brigham chose to dismiss it by saying, "There are, of course, cogent historical and sociological reasons accounting for the inferiority of the non-English-speaking Nordic group" (p. 171). He then compared the non-English-speaking Nordic group with the Mediterranean group and found a difference in favor of the Nordics, "a fact which clearly indicates that the underlying cause of the nativity differences we have shown is race, and not language" (p. 174).

Bilingualism and the Nature-Nurture Issue

In contrast to the hereditarian view of bilingualism that emphasized the genetic quality of groups who happened to be bilingual, psychologists of the experiential orientation stressed the role of the environment of the bilinguals. This tension over "nature versus nurture," a controversy that can be found running through much of academic psychology, is to a large extent a matter of emphasis. Very few hereditarians deny any contribution of the environment, and few experiential psychologists deny the relevance of a person's genetic endowment. Rather, the difference lies in their beliefs about the extent to which traits such as "intelligence" can be modified through experience.

During the early part of the twentieth century, the struggle between the two positions was symbolized by the ongoing debate (National Society for the Study of Education 1928, 1940) between psychologists at the Iowa Child Welfare Station at the University of Iowa (George Stoddard and Beth Wellman) and those at the University of Minnesota (Florence Goodenough) and at Stanford University (Lewis Terman). The Iowa emphasis on experience is reflected in a textbook by Stoddard and Wellman (1934), in which they acknowledge that "the great bulk of mental ability as measured by tests comes as a direct inheritance" but emphasize that "the real question concerns the amount of variability which can still be effected by later influence" (p. 170).

The Minnesota/Stanford attitude is best characterized as unforgiving, preferring an explanation based on heredity even when an alternative account based on the environment is possible. An illustration of this attitude can be found in the following argument, provided by Goodenough (1940) to explain the low intelligence of people of an inbred, "backward mountain community" called Colvin Hollow:

23

Given two centuries of social anemia, during which time all the ablest members of the group have been continuously drained away, leaving only the intellectual and volitional weaklings to interbreed and reproduce their kind, *need we seek further for an explanation of the state of educational backwardness and intellectual degeneracy found?* (P. 329, emphasis added)

The question of bilingualism and intelligence must be seen in the context of these conflicting approaches. For hereditarians, bilingualism was irrelevant to the major focus of study. Eager to show that intelligence was based on heredity, they were not the ones to argue that poor performance on intelligence tests could reflect a language handicap. Rather, it was those researchers with the experiential orientation who considered bilingualism—a learned characteristic—to be the cause of low intelligence.

The Hereditarians and the Language Handicap

Arguing for the genetic inferiority of bilinguals therefore required the hereditarians to demonstrate that the bilinguals did not suffer from a language handicap when their intelligence was being tested. Lewis Terman's students played a central role in this debate.

Terman himself began framing the debate in 1918, when he reported that for both monolingual English-speaking children and children of Portuguese and Italian immigrant families, a simple vocabulary test was a good reflection of mental age as measured in an IQ test. Terman reported that after children had been in school three or four years, their vocabulary and mental age scores correlated as well for the foreign children as it did for the Anglo children. He failed to note that the high correlation for both groups might arise from the fact that both measures reflect the degree of knowledge of English.

In 1922, Kimball Young published an influential article in *Scientific Monthly*, summarizing a set of arguments against the language handicap. In one argument, he held that the inferiority of the foreign children persisted even after the children had had a chance to learn English. In support, he cites a Master's Thesis directed by Terman, in which southern European children were followed up over a two-year period; they remained behind American children of northern European stock.

Another form of argument, supported by Young's own dissertation, was that verbal tests (the Army Alpha) are a better predictor of school performance (as judged by children's grade level relative to their age, by teachers' estimates, and by school grades) than nonverbal tests (the Army Beta). From this, Young drew the conclusion that "the asserted language handicap under which the foreign children are supposed to labor does not exist, at least so extensively as imagined" (p. 428). Young apparently was reluctant to consider the possibility that school performance is dependent on English skills, which are better measured by the Alpha. As a contemporary critic of Young wrote, "A teacher's estimate of a child's intelligence will unquestionably be influenced by the child's ability to use the English language, and, of course, all the child's school work is conditioned by his ability to understand and make use of English" (Pintner 1923, p. 292).

Such dissenting opinions, however, represented a minority view. The majority opinion is reflected in the review of Young's dissertation that appeared in *The Journal of Educational Psychology*:

The study sheds a bright light on the question of the part played by the language difficulty in the differences among racial groups, repeatedly found in the intelligence scores. By correlations between the several sorts of data, Mr. Young shows very conclusively that the language factor is by no means as great as is commonly believed, and that the differences in scores [between racial groups] is much more largely one of native intelligence. This constitutes a genuine contribution. (Kelly 1923, p. 256)

Young's article also cites data from Japanese and Chinese immigrant children, who generally tested better than Italians and Portuguese and almost on a par with Americans. Assuming that European languages are more similar to English than are the Oriental languages, he argued that "surely the language handicap is of greater potency in the Oriental than in the European" (p. 430). In retrospect, this was probably one of the better arguments advanced by Young against the language handicap; in fact, it is enjoying a revival among contemporary researchers who argue that it is cultural, not linguistic, differences that matter (Troike 1981).

Young's arguments notwithstanding, the inevitable evidence for an English language handicap soon began to surface. Pintner (1923), for example, constructed a "Non-Language Test," which he administered along with the National Intelligence Test, a group test derived from the Army Alpha, to foreign-born children. He found that the children fell considerably behind national norms on the NIT but at national norms on the Pintner Non-Language Test. Margaret Mead (1927) gave the Otis Group Intelligence Scale to sixth- to tenth-grade Italian immigrant children. She found higher IQ scores both as a function of the amount of English spoken at home and as a function of the length of residence in the United States.

Evidence for the language handicap was soon emerging even in Terman's own backyard. Darsie (1926), his own student, administered the Stanford-Binet to 570 Japanese-American children in California. His results were quite straightforward: "Japanese children as compared with American show a mean retardation of 14.25 months in reading, 12.5 months in language, 1.75 months in arithmetic, and 6.0 months in general information. In spelling they average 2.75 months above American children" (p. 86). The more the skills tapped involved English, the larger the discrepancy between English-speaking and Japanese children (the one exception being spelling, which Darsie dismissed as due to the "acute visual perception and sustained attention" of the Japanese [p. 33]).

On the whole, Darsie was forced to admit that the foregoing analysis . . . conclusively establishes the essentially linguistic character of the Binet scale" (p. 59). In his conclusions, however, are to be found the germs of the hereditarian response to the problem posed by the language handicap. The argument goes full circle: "It must not be overlooked, however, that the existence of a pronounced language handicap may itself be indicative of lack of capacity to master the language adequately" (p. 84). Since children of northern European stock apparently have less difficulty mastering English, Darsie concluded (while admitting to the closer linguistic affinity), they must be of superior intelligence.

This line of argument was perfected by Florence Goodenough (1926), who summarized data on the persistence of the foreign language in the homes of immigrants of different nationalities. She showed a negative relationship between the amount of foreign language used in the home and the median IQ of the groups. The less foreign language they used (and the more English), the higher their IQ. Simple correlations never establish causality (a basic principle of statistical inference, which Goodenough surely knew and probably taught), but Goodenough was willing to rest her case:

> This might be considered evidence that the use of a foreign language in the home is one of the chief factors in producing mental retardation as measured by intelligence tests. A more probable explanation is that those nationality groups whose average intellectual ability is inferior do not readily learn the new language. (P. 393)

Thus was created the party line of the hereditarians: the language handicap of foreign children in intelligence testing is minimal, so what the tests indicate is that these children are from inferior genetic stock. Even if the language handicap does impede performance, that does not belie the validity of the tests, because the language handicap is itself a result, rather than a cause, of inferior intelligence. Such were the dark beginnings of the term *language handicap* in the study of the bilingual.

The Experiential View of Bilingualism

New technologies in an industrial society are shrouded by an aura that often makes them resistant to critical evaluation. There is no question that intelligence tests in the early 1900s were such an enshrouded technology. American psychologists generally considered intelligence tests to be their ticket of admission to the brotherhood of the natural sciences. If one considers the "hard" sciences to be defined by rigorous methodology, careful measurement, and quantification (rather than by the questions one asks), psychometrics certainly provides room for such activities. Because of the respect American psychologists had for intelligence testing, the debate centered almost exclusively on whether differences among individuals and groups on these measures reflected heredity or experience, and not whether the measures themselves were adequate and equivalent for all the individuals tested.

In this context, if you tested bilinguals on a measure of verbal intelligence, and if the bilinguals showed inferior performance, you were bound to one of two conclusions. You could conclude, as the hereditarians did, that the bilinguals were genetically inferior. Or you could conclude that bilingualism caused some kind of mental confusion, resulting in the poor development of verbal skills. The possibility that the tests were limited in their ability to measure intelligence in this population was not considered.

One of the more perversely humorous examples of this underlying faith in the tests comes from the conclusion that A. J. Mitchell (1937) drew from a very well intentioned study comparing Mexican-American children's performance on an English intelligence test and on a Spanish translation of it. He found that there was consistently better performance on the Spanish version, which he regarded as a truer estimate of the children's intelligence. Rather than conclude that the English test was useless, however, Mitchell recommended that "thousands of cases" be tested in both languages for each grade and that a "correction figure" be calculated to adjust scores obtained from testing in English. No matter what their motivations were, the psychological researchers in those days were committed to the idea that these tests really measured intelligence.

Within the psychometric tradition, the earliest work in support of the negative effects of the experience of bilingualism, widely cited in the American literature, can be found in the British journals, especially in relation to Welsh-English bilinguals in Wales. Frank Smith in 1923 reported in the *British Journal of Psychology* a study comparing monolingual and bilingual third- and seventh-graders in the same school. He found that the monolinguals were better in tasks involving dictation, sentence-forming, and composition in English. He also reported a two-year longitudinal follow-up on similar measures, in which he found more improvement over time for the monolinguals than for the bilinguals. Smith concluded that "bilingualism may yet be shown to be no intellectual disadvantage in the young; but the tests described in this paper clearly support the view that under present methods it is a positive disadvantage" (p. 281).

The following year, Saer (1924) reported a more systematic study of Welsh-English bilingual and monolingual children aged seven to fourteen, in which the measures included the Stanford-Binet, a test of "dextrality," and vocabulary and composition tests. Saer divided the subjects into rural and urban samples and found that there were differences between bilinguals and monolinguals from the rural areas but not between those from the urban areas. In a second study, Saer found a similar pattern of differences in a comparison of bilingual and monolingual university students from rural and urban areas.

Of prime interest for our purposes is not the result but the interpretation of the apparent differential effects of bilingualism on children in rural and urban environments. Saer apparently was oriented toward emotional and "psychodynamic" explanations, and he claimed that for the urban bilingual children, "any emotional conflict between the use of Welsh and English that may arise is resolved by the child at an early age" (p. 37). On the other hand, for the rural child, "since the Welsh [language has] for him a high affective tone, and since the cathartic influence of play does not operate, for he uses Welsh in play, a conflict must arise between his self-regarding sentiment or positive self-feeling and his negative self-feeling or his instinct for submission" (p. 37).

Among American researchers, Yoshioka (1929) advanced the interpretation that the experience of bilingualism had negative consequences on intellectual development. He conducted a small study of Japanese-American children, to whom he administered English and Japanese versions of the National Intelligence Test (for which norms were available in English and Japanese). His conclusion was that "bilingualism in young children is a hardship and devoid of apparent advantage, because bilingualism appears to require a certain degree of mental maturation for its successful mastery" (p. 479).

Yoshioka's research was followed up by Madorah Smith (1931, 1939), the most influential proponent of the negative consequences of bilingualism, whose studies were extensively cited in later literature (see, for example, McCarthy 1946; Thompson 1952).

Smith received her doctorate at the Iowa Child Welfare Research Station at the University of Iowa, the center of research oriented toward experiential influences on intelligence. In her dissertation, published in 1926, Smith had pioneered a method of analyzing free speech utterances of young monolingual children. After obtaining her degree, Smith moved to the University of Hawaii and began applying her method to the speech of bilingual children from the wide variety of language backgrounds represented on the islands (Smith 1939). She studied the speech of children between the ages of two and six from Japanese, Chinese, Korean, Filipino, Hawaiian, and Portuguese backgrounds and compared them with the Caucasian norms that she had developed for her dissertation.

We will return to Smith's extensive study in the next chapter, when we contrast this line of work with that of the linguists who focused on the intricacies of language rather than on differences between individuals. For now, suffice it to say that when she compared her bilingual samples with her monolingual sample from Iowa on a variety of measures of language, the bilinguals showed inferior performance. Smith concluded that "an important factor in the retardation in speech found in the preschool population is the attempt to make use of two languages" (p. 253). This conclusion, implicating the bilingual experience rather than the genetic quality of the children who happened to be bilingual, is quite different from the kinds of conclusions the hereditarians would have drawn from the same data.

Smith continued her crusade against early childhood bilingualism in a study (1949) of preschool children of Chinese ancestry in Hawaii, who apparently were English-dominant but spoke some Chinese at home. She translated into Chinese a vocabulary test she had developed in Iowa and administered both versions to these children. She found that the vocabulary scores of these bilingual children in both languages were below the monolingual norms, although when the scores from the two languages were added together, they were comparable. She concluded that "it would seem unwise to start any but children of superior linguistic ability at a second language unnecessarily during the preschool years" (p. 309).

Smith's line of argument was followed up by Anne Anastasi,

professor of psychology at Fordham University, much of whose career has been devoted to arguing the "fallacies of 'culture-free' testing and of attempts to assess innate potential" (Anastasi 1980, p. 27). In one study (Anastasi and Cordova 1953), Puerto Rican children (ages eleven to fifteen) in New York City were given Cattell's Culture Free Test in English and Spanish versions. The test was nonverbal, "all items being perceptual or spatial" (p. 5). Anastasi and Cordova found that the language of test administration made no difference. Their subjects performed below the norms in both languages. Anastasi attributed the poor performance to the fact that these children's bilingualism "appears to be of the bifurcated variety, the children's mastery of either language being restricted and inadequate" (p. 13). It is entirely possible to argue that the data had no bearing on bilingualism, since the test itself was nonverbal in nature. Nevertheless, while acknowledging the importance of other factors, Anastasi maintained that bilingualism was the major villain:

Among the reasons for [the poor test performance] are the very low socio-economic level of the Puerto Rican children, their bilingualism which makes them deficient in both languages, their extreme lack of test sophistication, and their poor emotional adjustment to the school situation. In so far as this maladjustment itself appears to have arisen from the children's severe language handicap during their initial school experiences, a solution of the language problem would seem to be a necessary first step for the effective education of migrant Puerto Rican children. (P. 17)

The early history of research into bilingualism and intelligence in the United States is thus convoluted. The initial research concerned the new immigrants, who performed poorly on tests of intelligence. The hereditarians argued that this poor performance reflected inferior genetic stock, not a language handicap in test-taking. As the evidence mounted that bilinguals were operating under a handicap, the hereditarians interpreted this handicap itself to be the result of innately inferior intelligence. On the other hand, the experientially oriented psychologists took the language handicap in bilinguals to be the result of experience, specifically the experience of being exposed to two languages. In either case, the concept of language handicap, originally construed as a variable related to test-taking factors, came to be a trait of the bilingual individual's mind, whether based on experience or on genetic quality.

A Positive View of Bilingualism

In Canada, a different set of sociological events surrounded the study of bilingualism, particularly in the Montreal area. In the 1960s, it was becoming increasingly clear that with the rise in the political status of the French language (confirmed by the Official Languages Act of 1968–69, which granted equal status to English and French at the level of the federal government), bilingualism was the wave of the future and essential to political power. Parents, especially middle-class parents, were beginning to be concerned with making their children into bilingual citizens. Yet there was also concern, in large part due to the earlier American research, that bilingualism could have harmful effects on children's intellectual development.

It was in this context that Elizabeth Peal and Wallace Lambert conducted their influential study (1962). In their monograph, they reviewed the earlier studies of the language handicap of bilinguals and discredited their validity. These studies, they argued, failed to take into account the fact that the bilingual and monolingual subjects came from different socioeconomic backgrounds. In most cases, bilinguals from poor backgrounds were compared with monolinguals from higher social classes. Moreover, many of the earlier studies did not adequately ensure that their subjects were truly bilingual.

Peal and Lambert's discussion of the early literature was kept at a purely methodological level, steering clear of the issues of hereditarian versus experiential biases that loomed over that research. Their methodological concerns led to a criterion for sample selection that became standard for subsequent research. They drew a distinction between true, "balanced bilinguals," who are proficient in both their first (L1) and second (L2) languages, and "pseudo-bilinguals," who for various reasons have not attained age-appropriate abilities in their second language. As Peal and Lambert wrote, "The pseudo-bilingual knows one language much better than the other, and does not use his second language in communication. The true (or balanced) bilingual masters both at an early age and has facility with both as means of communication" (p. 6). The bilinguals in their sample were all judged to be equally good in their two languages, on the basis of relatively equal performance on language tasks (including a vocabulary test) in both languages, as well as on subjective self-ratings of their ability in the two languages.

Their bilingual and their monolingual subjects were all ten-year-old children from the same French school system in Montreal. The two groups were equivalent in their measures of socioeconomic status, both solidly middle class. They were administered both verbal and nonverbal measures of general intelligence. Contrary to the findings of previous research, the bilingual children performed reliably better than the monolinguals on both the verbal and the nonverbal measures. The bilingual children's superiority in nonverbal tests was more clearly evident in those subtests that required mental manipulation and reorganization of visual patterns, rather than simple perceptual abilities. A statistical analysis of the structure of the relationship between the different measures indicated that the bilinguals were superior to the monolinguals in concept formation and in tasks that required a certain mental or symbolic flexibility. Thus originated the claim that bilinguals enjoy a certain advantage in "cognitive flexibility" over their monolingual counterparts.

Ever since Peal and Lambert's study, researchers in bilingualism and intelligence have been careful to select subjects who fit some criterion of balance between their two languages. A wide variety of tasks have been given to groups of bilingual and monolingual children of various ages. Peal and Lambert's results have generally been replicated with children in western Ontario and other parts of Canada (Liedtke and Nelson 1968; Bain 1974; Cummins and Gulutsan 1974), Switzerland (Balkan 1970), Israel (Ben-Zeev 1977a), South Africa (Ianco-Worrall 1972), and even the United States (Ben-Zeev 1977b; Duncan and De Avila 1979). These studies are based primarily on middle-class populations. Overwhelmingly, they claim that bilingualism has positive effects (see a recent review by Rafael Diaz [1983]).

These recent studies suggest the following conclusion: take any group of bilinguals who are approximately equivalent in their L1 and L2 abilities and match them with a monolingual group for age, socioeconomic level, and whatever other variables you think might confound your results. Now, choose a measure of cognitive flexibility and administer it to both groups. The bilinguals will do better

Some Methodological Problems

What is wrong with the above conclusion? To a rigorous experimental psychologist, such a study has several weaknesses in its method. In order to see what they are, let us indulge in an intellectual exercise and conjure up the ideal experimental design to study the relationship between bilingualism and intelligence.

You begin by taking a random sample of individuals and assigning them randomly to either an experimental group or a control group, thereby controlling for any background "noise" in sampling. You test both groups before their treatment, to ensure that they do not differ on your measures of cognitive flexibility. The experimental group is then placed in an environment that fosters bilingualism, while the control group remains in a monolingual environment. Once the treatment has had time to take effect—that is, once the subjects in the experimental group have become balanced bilinguals—you administer your dependent measures. As a good experimentalist, you make sure that the person who administers the dependent measure does not know whether the subject being tested is in the treatment or the control group, because we know that no matter how well intentioned the experimenter may be, he or she can bias the outcome of the study if this procedure is not followed. And, lo and behold, you find a difference in favor of bilinguals. Under these ideal conditions, you could reasonably conclude that bilingualism causes cognitive flexibility. You could also go on to speculate about why you got this result and set up various other experimental conditions to test your hypotheses.

In what ways do the current studies of bilingualism and intelligence deviate from this ideal? Let me indicate their shortcomings by describing what I consider to be one of the best studies in this area, conducted by Bruce Bain and Agnes Yu (1980).

The researchers attempted to test the effect of raising children in a bilingual home. Specifically, they were interested in the ability of bilingual children to use language to help direct their thoughts and actions. Bain and Yu placed advertisements in school and university community newsletters in Alsace (France), Alberta (Canada), and Hong Kong asking for parents of newborns to volunteer in a study of "unilingual speech acquisition" or of "bilingual speech acquisition." From those who responded to the advertisements, they chose thirty sets of parents who would raise their newborns bilingually and sixty sets of parents who would raise their newborns monolingually. Each bilingual family was paired with two monolingual counterparts, one for each of the two languages. In each family, at least one parent had a university degree "and was either a practising school teacher, graduate student, or university professor" (p. 306). When the study began, all the infants were between six and eight months old.

Bain and Yu visited the homes of the subjects at the beginning of the study and offered instruction on how to raise the infants in the monolingual environments. As Bain and Yu describe their procedure,

It was emphasized that regardless of who initiates an exchange, be it the child or a parent, and regardless of which language or mixture of languages the child initially uses, each parent was to conduct all exchanges with the child in his or her designated language. We demonstrated how the parents should set up specific language zones in their home. (P. 307)

The parents of the monolingual children were given a general tutorial on language and cognitive development.

When the children were twenty-two to twenty-four months old, and again when they were between forty-six and forty-eight months old, they were given a variety of cognitive tests devised by the Russian psychologist Luria (who followed the tradition of Vygotsky, described in chapter 4). For example, in one task the experimenter hides a marble under one of several cups, and the child is told which cup it is under. In another task, the child is to follow such instructions as "When the red eye goes on, say 'squeeze,' and squeeze the ball. Say it and do it." The results showed that at twenty-two to twenty-four months, there were no differences between the groups, but at forty-six to forty-eight months, the bilinguals reliably outperformed the monolinguals. They suggested to Bain and Yu the positive effects of rearing children bilingually.

Bain and Yu's study is a noble attempt to show the effect of bilingualism on cognitive development. They studied the subjects longitudinally, and it is of interest that the two groups did not differ at twenty-two to twenty-four months, suggesting that there were no initial differences between the groups and that the bilingual treatment brought about the difference at forty-six to forty-eight months. They also drew the bilinguals and monolinguals from a similar occupational class. Thus far, they approximate quite well the experimental design of my fantasy.

The fantasy falls apart, however, when we consider that the children were not randomly assigned to the two groups. Of critical importance is the question of who decided whether the subjects would be in the bilingual group or the monolingual group. If Bain and Yu had had the power to do the assigning, then we could rest reasonably assured that the experiences of the bilingual children caused them to perform better on the cognitive tests, because they would have been selected on a random basis. But that was not the case. In the context of this study, the parents who responded to the bilingual advertisement had presumably already decided to raise their children in this manner. The bilingual subjects, then, were raised by a set of parents who were probably interested in the language heritage of their children and were perhaps considerably different from parents who (whether they had the option or not) raised their children as monolinguals.

Having dealt a painful bruise to Bain and Yu's study, let me turn to the rest of the studies, which suffer from additional flaws. The control imposed by Bain and Yu, of testing children both before and after they have had the chance to become bilingual, is an important feature that has been neglected in other studies in this area. Because of the cross-sectional nature of the studies, we are unable to infer the direction of cause and effect. Peal and Lambert themselves acknowledged that "one may ask whether the more intelligent children, as measured by nonverbal intelligence tests, are the ones who become bilingual, or whether bilingualism itself has a favorable effect on nonverbal intelligence" (1962, p. 13). As the teacher in elementary statistics repeats over and over, correlation does not imply causation.

An even more serious problem was raised very early on by John Macnamara (1966). Regarding Peal and Lambert's method of selecting only balanced bilinguals, he wrote, "It is extremely likely that in selecting for the bilingual group native French-speakers who had become balanced bilinguals, the authors selected children who on the whole were highly gifted and had a flair for language learning. So any linguistic comparison between these children and the monoglot was probably biased in favour of the former" (p. 21).

Macnamara's objections, and even more vehement reiterations of these arguments by MacNab (1979), have gone virtually unrecognized, as if the problems do not exist (but see Lambert and Anisfeld [1969] and Cummins [1976] for discussion of this issue). The paradigm had shifted in the science of bilingualism and intelligence, and the *Zeitgeist* allowed for studies showing positive relationships.

One recent attempt at addressing the methodological problems pointed out above can be found in a study that Rafael Diaz and I conducted in New Haven (Hakuta and Diaz 1984; Hakuta 1984b). We decided to try to circumvent the problem of between-group comparison by looking at the effects of bilingualism *within* a group of bilinguals. We reasoned that if bilingualism has a positive effect on measures of cognitive ability, then we should be able to show that those who are more bilingual do better on these measures than those who are less bilingual. Furthermore, we decided to employ a longitudinal design, so that we could look at the effects over time.

Our sample included more than three hundred Puerto Rican elementary school children in the bilingual education program in the New Haven public schools. All the subjects were from extremely poor home backgrounds, and all were considerably more proficient in their Spanish than in their English (the criterion for inclusion in the bilingual program). Their Spanish can be interpreted as their verbal ability in their native language, while their English reflected their degree of bilingualism.

The most important measures of cognitive ability were (1) Raven's Progressive Matrices, a nonverbal test of intelligence used by Peal and Lambert and found to be related to bilingualism, and (2) a measure of "metalinguistic awareness," or the ability to reflect on and evaluate the forms of language (which was administered in Spanish). The critical question was how their abilities in Spanish and English (as measured by a vocabulary test) would bear on these measures.

In brief, it turns out that Raven's is positively related to the degree of bilingualism (ability in English), while the measure of metalinguistic awareness is more strongly related to the native language ability (ability in Spanish). In one sense, it appears that we have support for the notion that bilingualism and nonverbal intelligence are related in a positive way, as found in the more recent studies. It is bothersome, however, that metalinguistic awareness is only weakly related to bilingualism. The difficulty with this pattern of results is that it is not theoretically neat. The most logical route for bilingualism to have an effect on intelligence is through language. One can easily imagine a mechanism in which bilingualism first results in verbal flexibility (reflected in metalinguistic skills), which then generalizes to nonverbal skills. Our results, however, suggest that bilingualism might have an effect on nonverbal intelligence but less of an effect on metalinguistic awareness.

Our current interpretation is that bilingualism in this group bears little relationship to performance on these measures. Rather, we think that English and Raven's are related most strongly because English is the skill that children are concentrating on learning in school, and Raven's is a good measure of overall ability of children to learn in school. There is the distinct possibility, however, that the effects of bilingualism have not had the chance to appear in this population because they are nowhere near being balanced bilinguals. If a certain threshold level of competence in both languages is required for positive effects to show (Cummins 1976), it may be that this population has not yet crossed the threshold.

We do have some indications of what would happen if our subjects were followed up for several more years and if their bilingualism were allowed to develop (this is in practice impossible, because the policy of transitional bilingual education in the United States means that children are mainstreamed into monolingual English classes as soon as their English is sufficient for survival, and their Spanish then becomes unsupported). Our longitudinal analysis shows that with increasing years of exposure to English, the relationship between English and Spanish becomes substantial (by the end of three years, the correlation between abilities in the two languages approaches .70). This means that, as we follow these students, assuming that English remains related to Raven's and Spanish to metalinguistic skills, these two skills will converge. If subjects are sampled when that occurs, it will appear that the ones who are more bilingual will do better on both metalinguistic and nonverbal measures of cognitive ability. What the study reveals, in essence, is that the way in which sampling is conducted and the way in which bilingualism is defined are going to determine much of the pattern of results.

Reconciling Differences

Having shown the limitations of the methodologies of current studies, we must still try to account for what appear to be contradictory conclusions about the effects of bilingualism. The effects, negative or positive, correlate with the methodology used. When bilinguals are unselected and come from lower socioeconomic backgrounds, negative effects are found. When bilinguals are selected for balanced bilingualism and come from middle-class backgrounds, positive effects are found. It is a serious puzzle for anyone seeking consistency in the world. What should be the locus of the resolution?

A scientist is most comfortable staying at the level of the methodology of studies. Peal and Lambert offered a methodological refinement in 1962, in terms of selection of monolingual and bilingual subjects. Through rigorous selection of balanced bilinguals from similar socioeconomic groups, they found positive effects. The implication was that if only the earlier studies had controlled for such factors, they would have found the same positive results.

Jim Cummins (1976) argues along the same lines when he claims that subtractive bilingualism, in which the second language replaces the first language, results in negative effects, while additive bilingualism results in positive effects. He speculates that there must be a "threshold" effect, requiring a certain level of competence in both languages before the positive effects can appear. The earlier studies showing negative effects, by virtue of not selecting for balanced bilinguals, included cases of subtractive bilingualism. My own study just described above, of course, also falls in this camp of attempts at methodological refinement.

Such methodological explanations tend to abstract the bilinguals away from the social conditions in which they live and to focus only on their degree of bilingualism. It so happened that the immigrants with low socioeconomic status were not so bilingual, while the post–Peal and Lambert bilinguals of middle-class background had high degrees of bilingualism.

We must, however, attempt to look beyond our methodological quibbles. It is easy to forget that methodologies are not magical entities that exist independently of researchers. Researchers create and choose their methodologies. I suggest that the choice of methodology—of whether to use unselected bilinguals or balanced bilinguals, for example—reflects both the world view of the researcher and the social status of the researcher relative to the subject population. The researcher sits at the control panel, as it were, and manages the knob of methodology, which in turn determines the pattern of results obtained. This image is a bit too strong, even for my most cynical moments; researchers obviously do not so consciously manipulate their results. Nevertheless, in the long run, a full account of the relationship between bilingualism and intelligence, of why negative effects suddenly turned into positive effects, will have to examine the motivations of the researcher as well as more traditional considerations at the level of methodology and the mental composition of the bilingual individual.

Joshua Fishman (1977) diagnosed the problem accurately when he wrote:

My own socio-historical perspective (bias?) leads me to doubt that answers . . . can be found by better controlled experiments, which in essence, cannot explain shifts in social climate that take place across a decade or more. I would predict that every conceivable relationship between intelligence and bilingualism *could* obtain, and that our task is not so much the determination of *whether* there is a relationship between the two but of *when* (i.e., in which socio-pedagogical contexts) *which kind* of relationship (positive, negative, strong, weak, independent or not) obtains. (P. 38)

To this I might add that in the end, all this research notwithstanding, the question of bilingualism and intelligence, of whether they are linked positively or negatively, will evaporate in the face of deeper issues surrounding both bilingualism and intelligence. The fundamental question is misguided, for it entails two key simplifying assumptions. The first assumption is that the effect of bilingualism—indeed, the human mind—can be reduced to a single dimension (ranging from "good" to "bad"), and that the treatment (bilingualism) moves the individual child's standing up or down the dimension. The second assumption is that choosing whether the child is to be raised

43

bilingually or not is like choosing a brand of diaper, that it is relatively free of the social circumstances surrounding the choice.

"Is it good or bad for children to be bilingual?" As these simplifying assumptions are scrutinized over the course of the remaining chapters of this book, the need to ask such questions should diminish proportionately.

Chapter 3

Childhood Bilingualism

THIS CHAPTER details two classic and contrasting studies of early childhood bilingualism. Its centerpiece is the scholarship of Werner Leopold, a linguist who recorded in unprecedented detail the language development of his bilingual daughter. His work is contrasted with that of psychologist Madorah Smith, who was more interested in differences between children than in their common developmental characteristics. I will use Leopold's and Smith's studies to discuss more recent work on this topic, including the massive shift in research philosophy that occurred in both linguistics and psychology in the 1950s, a trend whose consequences will be apparent through much of the remainder of the book.

Werner Leopold, Linguist

In 1921, while American psychologists were in the heat of the debate over the intelligence of bilinguals, a young German scholar named Werner Leopold was completing his doctoral dissertation in English literature at the University of Göttingen. Leopold's thesis was titled "The Religious Roots of Carlyle's Literary Activity," an unlikely scholarly contribution for someone who would figure prominently in a book about bilingualism written more than half a century later.

In April 1983, I paid a visit to Leopold and his wife, Marguerite, in their pleasant retirement community in Lacey, Washington. In many respects, I was paying homage to my intellectual ancestry, for Leopold is now considered one of the founding fathers of the study of child language and bilingualism. During the course of the day, he told me much about the flow of events that surrounded his lifelong avocation.

After obtaining his degree, the young Leopold was uncertain of his future as a scholar. Germany was still recovering from the First World War, and there was a long waiting period for the privileged university positions. Through a childhood schoolteacher, he obtained the name of a German businessman in Costa Rica who was looking for a tutor. Although the job was far removed from his training, Leopold felt that it would be a useful way to spend time and learn something new, and he signed a three-year contract.

At the end of his stay in Costa Rica, Leopold decided to visit the United States before returning to Germany. It proved to be a fateful decision. Through a Costa Rican friend, he found a job teaching Spanish at Marquette University in Milwaukee (Leopold had picked up Spanish in Costa Rica and had even published some papers on pedagogy while there). In 1927, after two years at Marquette, he was offered a position teaching phonetics at Northwestern University. During the summer sessions at Northwestern, Leopold taught courses in Spanish. One of his students was a schoolteacher from Milwaukee, who reportedly did not learn much Spanish in the course but did become acquainted with the young instructor, and they were soon married.

Within one year after their marriage, Hildegard Rose Leopold was born on July 3, 1930, the offspring of a German linguist father and an American mother of German descent. At home, Leopold spoke only German, both to his wife and to his daughter. Marguerite spoke only English, but she had sufficient command of German to understand what Leopold said. So in family conversations, Leopold spoke German, and Marguerite spoke English. Hildegard was exposed to both languages and learned to use both.

Leopold took an immediate interest in the sounds that his daughter began to make. As a phonetician, he had a well-trained ear and the objectivity necessary to make detailed observations. He took it upon himself to make a complete record of Hildegard's speech. Although several psychologists and other nonspecialists in linguistics had previously made diary studies of children's language acquisition, Leopold was aware that child language was considered to be outside the linguist's professional concerns (one exception being a study by Ronjat [1913]). As he later observed:

We [linguists] have studied language and languages of every conceivable type, standard languages, dialects, languages not written, languages of special groups, with ever varying methods, throwing light into every nook and cranny of the speaking activity. Why should just child language, which is incontestably a province of language, be outside the pale of linguistic inquiry? (1948, p. 9)

Beginning when Hildegard was eight weeks old, Leopold took vast numbers of notes, recording her vocalizations on slips of paper that he always carried in his pocket. As an older child Hildegard would ask, "What are you writing?" "I am taking notes for my work," Leopold would reply. Over the weekends, Leopold would meticulously log the notes in a diary. This activity continued with a few minor interruptions until Hildegard turned eight, after which Leopold kept track of particular features that struck him as interesting.

The observations were published under the modest title *Speech*

Development of a Bilingual Child: A Linguist's Record in four volumes
between 1939 and 1949. They cover a total of 859 printed pages,
a masterpiece of devotion to detailed description. Although
Leopold offered commentary and generalizations as well, he
saw himself first and foremost as a descriptivist. The work is,
in his own words, "an exact record of one child's language-
learning as a contribution to the collection of materials which
is still needed to reduce the speculative element in theorizing"
(1947, p. 262). Defending himself against a possible criticism of
hyper-accuracy, Leopold quoted the linguist Antoine Grégoire,
who asked, "Scientists study wasps and ants with painstaking
minuteness; why not devote the same attention to small children?" (p. viii). That he did.

One of the strengths of Leopold's diary approach, which
consciously eschewed theorizing, was that his observations
were not limited to a single aspect of language. Linguists typically take a "divide and conquer" approach: they decompose
language into discrete levels that are analyzed more or less
separately. Roughly speaking, analyses can be conducted at the
level of sounds, of words, of sentences, and of meaning. Since
each of these aspects can be looked at independently in studying language development, a particular theoretical orientation
might lead one to concentrate on one of them at the expense of
the others. Leopold did not restrict his study to one area. In his
first volume, he analyzed Hildegard's vocabulary development.
In the second volume, he concentrated on the development of
her sound system (which was Leopold's specialty area). In the
third volume, he looked at how she formed word combinations
and sentences. These first three volumes covered her development through the first two years. In the fourth volume, he
simply reproduced his extensive diary notes for the remainder
of the observation, including those he had made for Hildegard's
younger sister, Karla.

The bulk of Leopold's detailed observations concern Hildegard's development through the end of her second year. During

the first two years, although she was spoken to in different languages by her parents, she did not associate the languages with specific persons, although there began to appear a few primitive signs of differentiation, such as reserving the German *(Gute) Nacht* for her father, rather than her earlier *(Good) night.*

In general, Hildegard did not separate the two languages in her vocabulary. During these years, English and German synonyms appeared to be in competition, occasionally coexisting. Leopold records that from 1;0 until 1;9,* Hildegard consistently used the German *Ball.* At 1;9 she started using the English *ball* (easily distinguished from the German by pronunciation), and the English and German forms coexisted. By the end of the month, the English form had taken over (1949a, p. 178).

Many of Hildegard's early words dropped out of active use. During the first two years, Hildegard used 377 different words. Of these, 36 percent were no longer used by the time she was 1;11. More German words suffered during the second year than did English words, in part because she had picked up many German words during a three-month visit to Germany around the time of her first birthday; upon her return to the United States, English became dominant since her father was her only regular source of German.

It was not until her third year that Hildegard appeared to treat the two languages as separate linguistic systems. She used the two languages differentially to her parents (the Leopolds told me that she complained that her mother's German sounded bad and pleaded for her not to use it, and that she expressed surprise when her father used English). By this time, she was also quite adept at translating between the languages.

Even though Hildegard freely mixed words bilingually in her first two years, she did not confuse the sounds of the two

*The numerals indicate age in years and months. Thus 1;0 means age one year, and 1;9 means age one year and nine months.

languages. Leopold found that deviations from the adult standard were due not to interference between the languages but to more general processes of simplification and substitutions that are systematic and can be found in monolingual children as well.

Leopold came to a similar conclusion about Hildegard's grammar during her first two years. He noted, however, that grammatical features of language such as inflections and auxiliary verbs are not prominent features of language development during these years, so it is not surprising that very little mixing occurred. When Hildegard was older, between 4;11 and 5;6, she went to Germany and used mostly German. Upon her return to the United States, her English regained ground, especially with the influence of school, and English became her strongly dominant language. At these points, there were more indications of interference between the two languages, although much of it consisted of substitution of vocabulary.

In looking at the development of meaning in Hildegard's language, Leopold masterfully described the complex task that the child faces in learning the semantic space occupied by words. He pointed out that Hildegard frequently took a word and extended its use to similar objects. Leopold also emphasized the importance of what he called the "gradual intellectualization of speech" in development. He pointed to the use of one term for logical opposites, such as "up" for both "up" and "down," from which developed the use of the contrasting term indicating its opposite (1949a, 144).

Regarding the general role of bilingualism on Hildegard's language development, Leopold offered the speculation that, contrary to many critics of childhood bilingualism (he had in mind the countless studies of bilinguals made by his psychologist contemporaries), bilingualism could have some distinct advantages for the child. He suggested that Hildegard, being forced to use two languages, to have two words for a given referent, precociously came to separate the word from the referent. She had an early understanding that words are only arbitrarily assigned to meanings, a fact that monolingual children do not appreciate until much later in their development.

The richness of Leopold's description of Hildegard's development, however, cannot be conveyed in a simple summary of the sort offered above. The quality of the detail that is characteristic of Leopold's diaries must be sampled to be appreciated. In the course of quoting the diaries, I have omitted some technical details, while at the same time I have tried to preserve the spirit of respect for detail to which Leopold adhered.

The first volume gives an exhaustive list of Hildegard's vocabulary in the first two years, with commentary on the use of each word. The first word to achieve active use was "pretty":

pretty 0;10. She learned to say the word in Milwaukee 0;10, taught by the relatives, usually whispered, sometimes with full voice; each sound was slowly and distinctly articulated, the [r] being a briefly rolled tongue-tip [r], which had never occurred before. Of her early words, this was the first permanent one. At 0;10, "pretty" was one of her two active words (the other one was *there*) in the form [prĪtĪ], usually without voice, always articulated with striking distinctness, often used with the same demonstrative gesture of the right hand as "there." The usage was identical 0;11 in Hamburg; the form [had many variants]; [p] and [t] were constant, but the sound between them [varied]. [prĪtĪ], regularly whispered, remained in full activity in Germany, where she heard practically only German; she never tried "schön," which she often heard, even to 2;0. At the end of the sojourn in Germany 1;1, "pretty" became rare. On the boat 1;2 she understood very little English, even when it came from her mother, but she continued to say "pretty"; the word showed a remarkable vitality. At 1;4 [pwĪtĪ] was still voiceless and remained so steadily until 1;8. Two days later the form was [pəti], 1;4 [pyĪtĪ], with rising diphthong, still used for pictures, which continued to interest her. Once, half asleep on the arm of her mother, she felt her necklace without seeing it and said "pretty"; that was probably not a direct reaction to the tactile sensation, but to the visual impression which was evoked associatively by it. At 1;5 the word had become rare, whispered words disappearing at that stage. But at 1;6 it was heard again as [pyĪtĪ] with rising diphthong, this word and *tick-tock* surviving in whispered articulation. At 1;8 it was more frequent again, most commonly used for pictures of flowers, but also for clothes; it was still whispered, but not nearly so common as before when it had to take the place of specific nouns. Later 1;9 [pwIti bi], *pretty please* with reference to candy which she could not reach; the expression corresponded only accidentally to the conventional "pretty please" of children; the "pretty" was not an intensive to reinforce "please," but an expression of interest in the object, the desire being now isolated from it by the addition of the more specific "please." In the conventional expression, the semantic accent is on "please," in hers, on "pretty." During 1;10 there is no record of it. During 1;11 it became more frequent again, but now usually as an attributive adjective: *pretty dress,* etc. (1939, pp. 119–20)

Leopold also noted Hildegard's use of bilingual synonyms:

"Hot" became active one month before "heiss," at 1;4. At 1;5 "heiss" became more frequent. At 1;8 "hot" was more common and continued so until the end of the second year. But it did not displace the German equivalent entirely, and the latter had better phonetic form. It had the final consonant from 1;7, tentatively even since 1;5, whereas "hot" did not acquire it until 1;11. There was no functional distinction between the two synonyms. (1939, p. 178)

Because the father was the only source of German, German words tended to be replaced by their English synonyms.

Regarding the development of word meaning, Leopold provided detailed accounts of how meanings were gradually extended:

Hildegard used *tick-tock* from 0;11, first with reference to my wrist-watch, soon also for a wall-clock. At 1;0 she applied it to four or five watches and clocks which differed considerably in appearance, location, etc. At 1;0 I showed her a gas meter, naming it in German, "Gasuhr." She said *tick-tock.* It is not easy to decide whether this was a purely linguistic reaction to the word "Uhr" or an association with time-pieces by the shape of the instrument. . . . The round shape must have become characteristic of a *tick-tock* at some time, perhaps because some of the time-pieces, although angular in frame, had a round dial.

At 1;2, on the ocean boat, she was greatly interested in a fire hose wound on a red spool, which she greeted again and again enthusiastically as *tick-tock*. . . . At 1;3 she called a bathroom scale *tick-tock,* again on account of its round dial. . . . Roundness was not the only criterion, however. By 1;4 she identified clocks in the street, whether round or square. She was groping in more than one direction for making her use of the word identical with the baffling extentions and restrictions of the standard language. . . . She continued to attach the word to varying objects upon clues which did not satisfy the adult speakers: at 1;4 to the drawing or photograph of a machine, . . . at 1;9 to a round eraser for typewriter use. (1949a, pp. 126–27)

He noticed subtleties that only observant and expert parents might observe, including the differential use of the German "bitte" and its English equivalent, "please":

At 1;10 it was observed that *bitte* was used for spontaneous wishes, *please* only as a conventional addition to requests upon demand. The latter was said in compliance with social training, whereas the former, older and better established, had been found to be a useful concomitant of wishes, which augured well for their fulfillment. In fact, *bitte* went back to the one-word stage 1,5, during which it was the exclusive linguistic expression of a wish, to which the content of the wish had later been added by a second word. The younger *please* 1;9, on the other hand, was nearly always a functionally less important addition to another word, at first even to *bitte* itself. (1949a, p. 151)

By age 2;2, Hildegard was actively conscious of her two languages:

She now asks the eternal *what-*question apparently in the expectation of bilingual answers. She first asks her mother, then her father for the name of the same object. When others are present she asks them too. A young lady, a former student of mine and now a friend of ours, engaged Hildegard in a conversation and claims to have received the information that she (Hildegard) did not speak German, but Papa did. There is no doubt that she is now conscious of facing two languages. What astonishes me is that she knows the names of the languages. (1949b, p. 14)

But this awareness of two languages was not always present, as recorded when Hildegard was 2;9:

Her mother often tells her the story of the three bears. Some time ago I told her the same story in German. She exclaimed enthusiastically: *Papa knows it too, Mama!* She did not comment on the linguistic form. Bilingualism may well be a gain, because it induces concentration on the subject matter instead of the words. (1949b, p. 35)

Leopold was constantly on the lookout for the influence of the two languages on each other:

The distinction between "in" and "to" in English expressions of place is difficult for her. Her mother asked her: "Does Ruthie know you are going to Milwaukee?" She turned to the other girl and said: *Ruthie, next week I am going in Milwaukee.* This cannot be due to German influence. German would not use "in" in this example. (1949b, p. 41)

When Hildegard was 4;11, she visited Germany, at which time she became fluent in German. By the time the Leopolds returned to the United States, when Hildegard was 5;6, her language was almost exclusively German. Leopold gives the following account of the return:

The language problem began after the arrival in Evanston. She could get along with my wife's brother George and his family, who called for us at the station in Chicago, because they knew a little German. On the next day, however, she played all day with Mary Alice, who does not know a word of German. Before she went over to call for her friend, she asked to have the English sentence which she was to use said for her, and practiced it in several repetitions. While they were playing we were struck by her unwonted silence. She understood everything, to be sure, but could not express herself in English. During the forenoon she said only brief, awkward sentences. Even on the same day, however, progress was noticeable in the afternoon. (1949b, p. 124)

Six days later, Leopold noted:

The silent stage has passed. She chatted incessantly in English. She has really complete ability to express herself. The individual words were, however, pronounced with unnatural distinctness, even for a child. German words crept in unconsciously. Quite often she halted, obviously because the German word came to mind and had to be translated. Germanisms were more frequent than on other occasions when no extensive conversation in German went before. Samples: *I may not talk English to my papa, I have to talk German. He is funny. And I like to talk English very much. But manchmal I make mistakes, in German and in English.* (We laughed; she did not know why; the German word had intruded quite unnoticed by her.)—*Foolish Kinder have to go back to school* (said to Molly, even repeated when she did not understand).—*Then is here your school.* —*This geh . . .—belongs to this doll* (she was about to say "gehört").—*Too near the Fenst . . .—the window.—We play now this.—Which grade is man in when man nine years old is?* (German *man;* German word-order in the subordinate clause! This is very unusual). (1949b, p. 125)

At age 7;1, Hildegard continued to speak German with her father, but the force of the English-speaking environment was taking hold, although she continued to take pride in her bilingualism:

Hildegard continues to speak German to me, but her German is halting and studded with Anglicisms and English words. Occasionally she starts in German and switches to English when she does not succeed. . . . She is proud of her bilingualism and is always quite willing to speak German to me. It works much better when she is alone with me for some length of time. She usually speaks German to me even when others are present and I speak English myself. (1949b, p. 144)

By the time Hildegard turned fourteen, her use of German, unsupported at school, was flagging. Near the end of the diary is this rather touching account:

Yesterday we went to Peninsula State Park for a picnic and walked over some of the trails. At times I was alone with Hildegard and felt reminded of our long hike eight years ago. She was still a good hiker, but linguistically the situation had changed. Whereas then she had chattered cheerfully in German, she now made her few laconic remarks nearly always in English. A few times I made her repeat her statements in German. She did not object and expressed herself well enough. The next time, however, she would say something in English again. I have always studiously avoided making German a matter of annoyance to her. I do not insist pedantically on the principle, hoping that she will herself someday have the wish to resume the practice more energetically. There is danger that much of what has been built up laboriously over the years will be lost. But there are things in the life of a family which are even more important than the preservation of a linguistic skill, and the stage is critical. (1949b, p. 153)

As a descriptivist, Leopold offered in Hildegard's diary an intricate picture of the complexity of bilingualism.* He was fascinated by every twist and turn in his daughter's language development. He documented the ebb and flow of her two languages and related them to changes in the linguistic environment in which Hildegard was developing. He pointed to ways in which Hildegard mixed the two languages into single utterances and offered speculations on how language choice was determined.

One question that Leopold has been asked with great frequency is the effect that bilingualism had on Hildegard's development. Leopold has been reluctant to offer generalizations. He was always aware of the fact that his was a case study. With a sample size of one, how could he say what Hildegard's development would have been like if she had been raised with just one language? He did, however, offer the following speculations about the effects of bilingualism:

*To anyone who doubts the accuracy of Leopold's observations, made without benefit of a tape recorder, I offer the following anecdote. In the spring of 1983, when I visited the Leopolds, Professor Leopold was approaching ninety. During our visit he gave me a bibliography published by the Modern Language Association that he felt would be useful to me. In writing a transcript of our interview, I casually mentioned this fact. A draft of the transcript was sent to Professor Leopold, who wrote two pages of corrections to it. Among the corrections, he insisted that I note that it was not just a Modern Language Association bibliography he had given me, but that it was "Volume 3, Linguistics." The value that Leopold placed on accuracy and detail, not to mention the feat of memory (particularly considering, with all due respect, his age), left me suitably impressed.

Thus, apart from the accomplishment of understanding and using two languages, which nearly everyone would rate as a gain, I see in early bilingualism the advantage that it trains the child to think instead of merely speaking half mechanically. Of course, I see the other side. A monolingual develops, through the compelling influence of his single language, a simpler and therefore more forceful view of the world. I do not overlook the difficulties inherent in growth nourished from a split root instead of a single strong tap root. It will lead to conflicts, which can wreck a weak personality, but will improve the mettle of a strong one, who can overcome the difficulties. The difference is the same as between a highly educated and an uneducated person. Ignorance and superstition make the decisions of life simple. Education does not make life easier, but better and richer. Few would condemn education for this reason. Bilingualism should be seen in the same light. (1949a, p. 188)

Leopold was not necessarily committed to showing whether bilingualism is a handicap or an advantage. Bilingualism is a phenomenon that comes about as the result of different social and familial circumstances, and as a scientist, he chose to describe one particular case. What he saw was an intricate picture, one that he believed could be adequately understood only after more careful observations like his study of Hildegard.

Leopold's Legacy

It would be fair to say that Leopold's primary interest was the analysis of language. He studied the general development of the child only to the extent that it related to the development of language. His daughter Hildegard was a vehicle who happened to be the carrier of language. The picture that Leopold saw as the ultimate goal of his activity was the embodiment of language in different mediums, Hildegard being one. Leopold was interested in observing the changes in Hildegard's language and seeing how they compared with changes in language in other mediums. He wanted eventually to see child language (a term that he coined) compared with historical changes that come about in language over time (an activity that Slobin [1977], among others, has pursued).

Studying child language, Leopold believed, would reveal much about general principles of language and language change: "Every pattern of grammar, every process of language shows up in child language in a nascent state, in coarser, more tangible shapes, compressed into a much shorter time and therefore more accessible to observation" (1948, p. 9). He wanted to see parallels between language contact, such as the contact at borders between two communities that speak different languages, and the influence that the two languages within Hildegard were having on each other.

Leopold's long-range goals have in many ways been fulfilled. The study of child language is now a legitimate concern of linguistics, in large part due to the respect that his study of Hildegard had attracted. Yet as we talked in 1983, proud as he was of his accomplishment, it was evident that he did not feel fully appreciated by contemporary scholars. The reasons for this will become evident at the end of the chapter, when I discuss the paradigm change in linguistics precipitated by Noam Chomsky, who shifted emphasis from the kinds of data, exemplified by Hildegard's speech records, to which Leopold so strictly adhered. In a letter, Leopold remarked, "Sometimes I get the impression that child language research has by-passed my contribution." I am convinced, however, that, his own reservations notwithstanding, Leopold's work will always remain the paragon of case-study research in language development.

Madorah Smith, Psychologist

One cannot truly appreciate the depth of Leopold's work without contrasting it with the work of the psychologists who were his contemporaries. If I could have one wish as a historian of bilingualism, it would be to arrange for a meeting between Werner Leopold and Madorah Smith. I would love to hear them argue their opinions about what bilingualism means and how to research it. Smith, the psychologist, was a contemporary of Leopold's (born in 1887, a few years before Leopold). She figured prominently in the story of bilingualism and intelligence testing, as we saw in chapter 2. Smith conducted a study of bilingual children in Hawaii and arrived at a conclusion on the effects of bilingualism that was markedly different from Leopold's views. For Smith, bilingualism caused a retardation in language development "so marked that, on most criteria, at the time of school entrance they are at about the level of three year-old children from a less polyglot environment" (Smith 1939, p. 271).

Smith's work differed from Leopold's in more than the conclusions that she drew. Her study of bilingualism in Hawaii, contrasted with Leopold's study, stands as an instructive example of the trade-offs that must be made between research emphasizing qualitative detail and research emphasizing quantitative rigor. Quantitative she was: one thousand children participated in her study. Because of her large sample size, Smith, unlike Leopold, was in good position to make statements about how individual children differed from each other. She could quantitatively evaluate the various claims about the effects of bilingualism.

Her monograph titled "Some Light on the Problem of Bilingualism as Found from a Study of the Progress in Mastery of English Among Pre-School Children of Non-American Ancestry in Hawaii" is a monument to quantification. In the 162-page report, there are forty-nine tables and six figures, all painstakingly compiled without benefit of a computer. They are the quantitative analog of Leopold's diary notes.

Smith's primary data consist of fifty consecutive sentences taken from each child while the child was at home and at play with another child, usually a sibling. The children, between two and six years old, came from homes where Chinese, Japanese, Korean, Hawaiian, Portuguese, and Filipino were spoken. The observers who recorded the sentences were usually speakers of the respective home languages.

Smith created many quantitative indices of the children's language, but she paid particular attention to the number of errors made by the child, where errors were defined as deviations from standard usage. The charge that bilingualism retards language development is based principally on analyses using this measure. Smith compared the data obtained from the children in Hawaii with those of monolingual children she had previously studied in Iowa and found that the bilingual sample made more errors than the monolingual Iowa sample.

Within her sample from Hawaii, Smith divided the children into those whose sentences were mostly English and those whose sentences contained a substantial mixture of the non-English language. She showed that the group whose sentences were mostly English made fewer errors than the more bilingual group. She also divided the children according to their home language environment. One group was rated as those from homes where "correct English only was used," another from homes where "good English and another language were spoken" (p. 136). She found that the group that heard two languages at home made more errors than the group hearing only "correct English."

With the benefit of hindsight, it is easy to criticize these findings. In particular, the index of error rate is so flawed that the vast amount of quantitative information is uninterpretable. For example, Smith included among her errors instances when the child mixed languages. When a Japanese boy said "Oka San [sic], this kind," it was considered an erroneous utterance because he used the Japanese word for "mother." But is this really an error? It is certainly appropriate for bilinguals to mix languages, as long as all parties involved in the conversation understand the two languages. In fact, such language can serve stylistic and social purposes, as we will see in chapter 7.

Any idiomatic expressions that were not part of the standard English dialect were also counted as errors, even those that Smith acknowledged were characteristic of the English spoken in Hawaii. From the standpoint of the child growing up in the complex linguistic environment of Hawaii, one can hardly call sentences containing such expressions "errors."

The reason I dwell on the flaws of Smith's analyses is not that I think they need to be corrected. They do not. Contemporary researchers, should they choose to repeat Smith's study, would most likely avoid these technical flaws. They would not expect every child learning English to speak like children in Iowa. Then why flog a horse that has been dead for over a quarter of a century?

The most important reason for examining Smith's study is that it tells us about the particular view of language and of bilingualism she held. Whenever flaws that seem obvious today were overlooked by previous researchers, one should suspect that it was not because the researchers were ignorant, devious, or stupid. More likely it was because their world view of the phenomenon was radically different from ours. And Smith's view should be regarded as that shared with other nonlinguists of her day.

Smith believed that the task of the researcher was to document as rigorously as possible the verbalizations of the child. By so doing, she was documenting all that was necessary to account for the child's language development. Deep mental structures representing language were of no concern to the psychologist. What mattered was overt behavior. If you took this belief and tangled it with the fact that the children she studied were mixing their two languages, you would have to conclude that the children were confusing the two languages. Observing the fact that many of the older children used English in over 95 percent of their sentences, Smith concluded that "they have learned to distinguish reasonably well between the languages" (p. 165). On the other hand, if they mixed the two languages, the languages were being confused.

I have scoured Smith's monograph, to no avail, for any mention of the possibility that perhaps the children mixed languages because when they were observed they were with other children who understood both languages. Smith notes only that it is "a peculiarly unfortunate error, as it becomes impossible for anyone not knowing both languages to understand the speaker" (p. 176). One can only conclude that, for Smith, mixing languages was not something done by choice among bilinguals but instead a reflection of the mental state of the child. In her world of explanations, she left little room for situational constraints that might influence whether the child mixed or did not mix languages.

Interestingly, the effect of situational constraints can be seen even in Smith's own data (one consolation of her compulsive reporting is that new interpretations of the data can be made). Smith's pet theory, inherited from her training at Iowa, was the importance of kindergarten in the child's development. One subsample of her study included data collected at a kindergarten where only English was spoken. Smith compared the language from these children with the data obtained from a similar group of children observed at home, who did not attend kindergarten. She showed that there was a substantial difference between these children in favor of those attending kindergarten. This difference was attributed to the fact that the children attended kindergarten. These groups differed on another crucial characteristic, however: the situation where the data were obtained. The kindergarten group was observed in kindergarten, where English was expected, and the nonkindergarten group was observed at home, where the non-English language was acceptable.

What would happen if children who attended kindergarten were observed at home, rather than at kindergarten? Smith in fact conducted such an analysis, although with a different group of children. She compared a group of kindergarten attenders with nonattenders, both observed at home. These groups showed no differences (although Smith, through a stretch of imagination, concluded that the results "favor the group that attends kindergarten" (p. 239). Thus, even in Smith's own data, it seems to be the case that what affects language mixing is the situation where the language is observed.

Just as I have no doubt about the correctness of my interpretation, I also believe that this interpretation of the data never crossed Smith's mind, even though the two sets of results are presented side by side. For Smith, language, like intelligence, may be the product of the environment, but it is something that is expressed consistently in behavior, across different situations. The difficulty in accepting the possibility that language may differ by situation is that it then ceases to be something that is carried around in the head of the child and easily quantified.

A similar need for simplicity arises in the case of the language environment of the child. Smith reduced the language of the home to a five-point rating scheme:

If correct English only was used in the home, the rating was five; if good English and another language were spoken, four; if, besides a foreign language, both correct and pidgin English were heard by the child, as in the case where one parent only spoke correctly, the rating was three; if only pidgin English, two; if only a foreign language, one. (P. 136)

She reported that the average language rating was 2.5 for the Chinese, 2.0 for the Japanese, 3.0 for the Portuguese, and so forth.

How should these be interpreted? When you average numbers, you are making the assumption that the numbers bear a specific relationship with one another. A score of "4" is twice the size of a score of "2," and a score of "3" falls smack in between these two. Were this not the case, the average would be meaningless; you might as well average the uniform numbers of Jim Rice (14) and Carl Yazstremski (9) and say that 11.5 represents their average. Smith could only have used the average if she saw the home language environment as falling along a single linear continuum, extending from a poor environment (score 1), where only a foreign language is spoken, to a good environment (score 5), where only correct English is spoken.

Smith thus tried to simplify language in a number of ways. First, she simplified the problem of definition of bilingualism by making it equivalent to the observed behavior of the child. The use of just English was interpreted as the successful separation of the two languages. Mixing of the two languages was seen as a sign of mental confusion. Second, she assumed that the situation in which language is used has little effect on what is observed. She could therefore interpret the relative mixture of the two languages as a function of the child, carried around in the child's head across all linguistic situations. And third, she saw the linguistic environment as a single continuous dimension, with a progression from foreign language to gradual incremental mixtures of English.

Why did Smith want to reduce the marvelously complex phenomenon of bilingualism, so delicately described by Leopold, into a few quantitative indices? Doubtless it partly had to do with the high value that psychologists place on quantification as an end to itself. What else would explain the many compulsive tables in the monograph? (My favorite one is Table 5, which reports, by age, race, and sex, the average time that it took to record the fifty consecutive utterances. The inclusion of these data might be understandable if any subsequent analyses depended on this table, but not so. They are reported because they are numbers, and numbers are sacred.)

A more important reason for the simplification is that, as a psychologist, Smith approached the study of bilingualism from the perspective of individual differences. A psychologist typically looks for individual characteristics that would predict differential performance on the phenomenon of interest, such as language. That was why she compared bilinguals with monolinguals, boys with girls, and the various racial groups with one another. Smith also looked for differences among children from different home language backgrounds. If language were seen as a complex phenomenon that expresses itself differently in any given individual, depending on the situation in which it is used (say, between home and kindergarten), then the problem of individual differences would increase in magnitude to such an extent that it would be very difficult to investigate. One who is interested in individual differences, therefore, is better off not believing this to be the case.

Smith the psychologist thus stands in contrast to Leopold the linguist. Given her interest in the mass of variation between different children, she saw language as one of many variables on which individual children could vary, and she could tolerate a simplified index of language. Leopold's unit of analysis was language. In his world, the child was just one of many potential vehicles in which language could be observed, and for him the individual characteristics of any given child were of secondary importance.

More Recent Studies

At least twenty-three other case studies have reported in considerable depth the simultaneous language development in bilingual children. They have confirmed and added to Leopold's initial discoveries about infant bilingualism.

One insight that can be gained from these studies is that there are many ways in which children can learn two languages simultaneously. Hildegard grew up in a "one parent–one language" home—that is, each of her parents used a different language; however, she lived mainly in the United States, where only English was widely spoken. By contrast, the children of linguist Marilyn Vihman, Raivo and Virve, heard mostly Estonian at home, but from the age of fourteen months went to a day-care center where only English was heard (Vihman 1982a,b). Other children have heard varying amounts of mixed usage of two languages at home. In the cases studied, the children all succeeded in becoming bilingual, but with varying degrees of mixed usage of the two languages. At present, there are perhaps not enough cases to make statements about the effects of particular configurations of language input, but McLaughlin (1984) has proposed that the one parent–one language method seems to yield the least amount of mixing.

In general, the initial stage of bilingual acquisition is characterized by a lack of differentiation between the two languages. The child considers the two languages of his or her environment to be a single language. The fact that children do not discriminate in their use of languages depending on the person with whom they are talking, even in cases where the parents speak different languages, attests to the generality of what they are learning when they acquire language. Obviously, they are not learning specific words to be used with specific people.

This period of undifferentiation is generally reported to continue until somewhere between the second and third birthdays.

During this period, words and sounds can be mixed. Vihman reports, for example, that Raivo used the American [r] in his Estonian for two months (Vihman and McLaughlin, 1982). Occasionally, inflections and even entire sentence structures are mixed. Volterra and Taeschner (1978), for example, report that after their Italian-German bilingual subject distinguished between the vocabularies of the two languages, she still applied the same rules of word combination to both languages. Such examples suggest that during the first two or three years, the major task facing children simultaneously exposed to two languages is to differentiate the sounds, vocabulary, and grammar of the languages.

The case studies do not tell us how this differentiation takes place, but they amply record the fact that it may occur at a relatively young age. In most children by the age of three to four, languages are rarely mixed (although intentional mixing of languages for stylistic purposes can be common). At this point, children can begin to show the ability to translate. In addition, many children are reported to express conscious awareness of their use of two languages. For example, as early as age two, Raivo Vihman expressed embarrassment when he became aware that he had spoken to his English monolingual cousin in Estonian. At age 3; 11, he showed his full awareness of different languages by interjecting "But not in Estonian, of course!" whenever his mother recounted conversations that she had had with speakers of English.

Many of the case studies report, as did Leopold, that bilingualism seems to foster an early awareness of language (Jill and Peter de Villiers [1978] heard a four-year-old say, "I can speak Hebrew and English," to which his five-year-old American friend said, "What's English?" [p. 151]). Unfortunately, case studies will not tell us whether this is really the case, whether this awareness is only more evident because the bilingual child is in a situation where it can be expressed more easily, or whether the child being observed simply happens to be precocious. We also cannot discount the fact that many of the case studies were conducted by linguists on their own children, and it is not entirely unlikely that linguists have the kinds of conversations in their homes that would encourage the development of awareness of language. Statements about the effect of bilingualism on metalinguistic awareness should be treated with as much vigilance as earlier statements about bilingualism and intelligence from the previous chapter.

The Challenge to the Empiricism of Werner Leopold and Madorah Smith

Although Leopold and Smith differed in the focus of their empirical energies, Leopold describing language and Smith describing individual differences, they shared a common assumption in their conduct of research. I have already argued that Smith chose to define the children's knowledge of the two languages in terms of their behavior. Leopold was also working within a linguistic tradition that ascribed great weight to the actual utterances of the child.

In a paper presented to the Linguistic Society of America in 1948, Leopold appealed to linguists to make detailed observations of such children, "to add sorely needed case histories of infant bilingualism and infant language to the available material, as indispensable spade work for the higher purposes of linguistics" (p. 11). His plea was received with much sympathy.

To understand what Leopold envisioned for linguistics, it is important to understand what he meant by the "higher purposes of linguistics." In calling for the rigorous collection of data from children's language, Leopold was echoing the predominant view of American linguistics in his day, known as structural linguistics. Structural linguistics drew its life from the dominant intellectual force in the United States, empiricism, which was also the inspiration for psychology. Empiricist philosophers, at least in a simplified version, claimed that all knowledge is derived from experience alone. The implication of empiricist philosophy for science was that it must be conducted in such a way as to reflect observation directly.

In the case of structural linguistics, this meant that the scientific analysis of language should begin with a corpus of utterances, which should be rigorously described (taxonomy). As Zellig Harris put it, "The over-all purpose of work in descriptive linguistics is to obtain a compact one-one representation of the stock of utterances in the corpus" (quoted in Newmeyer 1980, p. 5). Because of the direct relation between observation and knowledge, the rigorous recording of utterances would naturally lead to better knowledge about language. Structural linguistics had no place for frivolous activities such as attempting to explain broad general characteristics of human language. The prevalent attitude was to keep your head down and describe what you saw in the corpus. Martin Joos was quite stern: "Children want explanations, and there is a child in each of us; descriptivism makes a virtue of not pampering that child" (quoted in Newmeyer 1980, p. 5).

What Leopold had succeeded in doing was to make child language a legitimate domain of inquiry for the structural linguist. It now appeared that linguists could without embarrassment obtain a corpus of the child's utterances and apply to it the same discovery procedures used by structural linguists for describing other languages. Leading linguists, such as Hockett, drew parallels between the similarities of the tasks facing the linguist and those facing the child. The future seemed bright for the study of child language by linguists, in the descriptivist manner exemplified by Leopold. At that point, however, the mainstreams of linguistics and psychology took a radical turn, an event that would have an impact on conceptions of the bilingual mind as well as on second language acquisition, topics of the next three chapters. Essentially, the new dogma—variously called generative grammar, mentalism, and cognitivism—dictated that psychological and linguistic inquiry be directed toward the postulation of abstract mental structures and processes, away from empiricist descriptivism.

The coup was led by Noam Chomsky (1957, 1965), whose vast influence on the study of language development will become abundantly clear in the chapters to follow. He attacked structural linguistics in many places where it hurt, but where his attack hurt most was in the adequacy of the "discovery procedures" operating on a corpus of utterances. Chomsky showed that there were many characteristics of language that could not be described adequately by the traditional procedures. He demonstrated that a far more abstract description of language was needed to account for our knowledge about language. His famous example is the following pair of sentences:

(1a) John is easy to please.
(1b) John is eager to please.

Traditional methods would provide similar analyses of these two sentences. However, Chomsky argued that the same operation performed on these sentences yields results that are not equally acceptable:

(2a) It is easy to please John.
(2b) *It is eager to please John.

(The asterisk is a linguistics convention, indicating ungrammaticality of a sentence.) In order to differentiate between the two sentences, Chomsky argued for the necessity of an abstract underlying structure that would paraphrase as something like "For someone to please John is easy" and "John is eager to please someone." If one accepted Chomsky's analysis as correct, there was no way that one could get there from the surface appearance of the original pair of sentences. Chomsky had exposed the dead end of structural linguistics. The deep aspects of language cannot be distilled by the methods of induction, of distilling the corpus of utterances.

With such brilliant arguments, Chomsky changed the thrust of mainstream linguistics. It went from descriptive structuralism, nose buried in the data of utterances, to what is called "generative grammar." The new goal of linguistics became to identify a grammar (equivalent to a scientific hypothesis) that defines a finite set of rules that would generate all (and only) the grammatically acceptable sentences of the language. Whether a particular sentence appeared in a corpus or not, it required explanation if it was grammatically acceptable in the language.

The agenda for mainstream linguistics thus modified, Leopold's descriptive approach toward language development was no longer seen as adequate for the same reasons that the methods of structural linguistics were inadequate. For example, Hildegard's diaries, no matter how detailed, could not unveil the abstract underlying structure of her knowledge of German and English. The new approach to language development, topics for chapters 5 and 6, attempted to address this question of abstract knowledge, even though the methodology of detailed observation perfected by Leopold continued to be the major source of data in this new paradigm.

A similar fate awaited empiricist psychology. Like Smith, most psychologists until the late 1950s were adamant in making observable behavior the domain of their inquiry. Language was defined as verbal behavior, and there was no need to talk about abstract mental structures. As far as the mainstream empiricist psychologist was concerned, talk about the structure of the mind (mentalism) enjoyed the same status as talk about ghosts. Although there were some early signs of discomfort with the pure empiricist approach (for example, Lashley 1951; Miller,

Galanter, and Pribram 1960), Chomsky's role in the decline of empiricist psychology cannot be denied. By 1962, the influential psychologist George Miller was saying, "I now believe that mind is something more than a four-letter, Anglo-Saxon word —human minds exist and it is our job as psychologists to study them" (p. 761). In the following chapter, the effects of the new mentalism inspired by Noam Chomsky will be readily evident in my description of the complex efforts to construct a map of the bilingual mind.

Chapter 4

The Bilingual Mind

A MAJOR WEAKNESS in the traditional study of bilingualism and intelligence, as we saw in chapter 2, has been its preoccupation with individual differences in intelligence, as measured by performance on an IQ test. Few scholars have been willing to address the mechanisms of the mind that produce the observed results.

In this chapter, we seek a mental topography of the bilingual individual, a map to reveal the inner workings of the bilingual mind. Three questions will guide the effort. First, how should we conceptualize the relationship between language and thought? Second, how are the two languages of the bilingual related to each other? And third, do different kinds of bilingual experiences produce different kinds of bilinguals? In the final section, I will speculate about the wisdom of conceptualizing bilingualism at the level of mental topography.

Language and Thought

The search for the bilingual mind must begin with an understanding of general theories about the relationship of language and thought in the human mind. Some of these theories, such as those of Benjamin Lee Whorf and Lev S. Vygotsky, lead us to expect bilingualism to have a profound impact on thought; others, such as the theories of Noam Chomsky and Jean Piaget, would point toward minimal influences of bilingualism. What, then, are these theories that would predict such different results? Can we draw any conclusions from their collective wisdom, despite their differences?

WHORF'S THEORY OF MIND

Linguists are in the business of building implicit theories of the mind. There is no way they can avoid doing so, because language is so central to our conception of our mental system. Benjamin Lee Whorf (1897–1941) was a linguist (and a full-time fire insurance agent in Hartford), who worked in the anthropological tradition of Franz Boas (1858–1942). Boas, undoubtedly the most influential figure in American anthropology at the beginning of this century, emphasized the diversity of cultures and languages, rather than their common core. With the encouragement of Boas's student Edward Sapir, Whorf popularized the notion that different languages divide up reality in different ways. For example, the Hopi Indians have just one word for the English referents "airplane," "dragonfly," and "aviator." On the other hand, Hopi distinguishes between water in an open space and water in a container. In another popular example, Whorf noted that the Eskimos have many different words for snow, depending on such features as crustiness and when it fell, while English only has one. Most bilinguals can cite a number of examples of divergent categories in the languages they know. Counting in Japanese involves adding a word at the end of the number to indicate the shape of the object being counted. There are different words for long cylindrical objects, flat objects, animals, and people. By contrast, counting in English is unremarkable. One can also come up with examples from grammar. Whorf found that Hopi has verb endings that indicate whether the statement being asserted is a specific historical fact or a general truth (Whorf 1956, p. 114). The list can go on and on. Such facts could be seen as instances of *linguistic relativism,* the idea that languages differ in how they carve out segments of reality.

Linguistic relativism is not a terribly controversial position. It is simply an interesting empirical observation. However, Whorf did not stop there. Sometime quite early in his career, Whorf scribbled a note expressing dissatisfaction with the field of psychology, since "it throws little or no light on problems of the normal human mind or soul" (Carroll 1956, p. 40). He was particularly upset with the lack of explanations for the origins of meaning, and in a preamble to what he would propose in stronger form he wrote: "Language is the great symbolism from which other symbolisms take their cue" (p. 42). Later, more elegantly, Whorf wrote:

We dissect nature along lines laid down by our native languages The categories and types that we isolate from the world of phenomena we do not find there because they stare every observer in the face, on the contrary, the world is presented in a kaleidoscopic flux of impressions which has to be organized by our minds—and this means largely by the linguistic systems in our minds. We cut nature up, organize it into concepts, and ascribe significances as we do, largely because we are parties to an agreement to organize it in this way—an agreement that holds throughout our speech community and is codified in the patterns of our language. The agreement is, of course, an implicit and unstated one, BUT ITS TERMS ARE ABSOLUTELY OBLIGATORY; we cannot talk at all except by subscribing to the organization and classification of data which the agreement decrees. (1956, pp. 213–14)

In this, his most famous passage, Whorf clearly states his controversial hypothesis of *linguistic determinism,* that language determines the shape of thought. Combined with linguistic relativism, the Whorfian hypothesis, as it came to be known, claimed that speakers of different languages had different patterns of thought.

Dan Slobin (1979, pp. 174–85) has suggested that much confusion in evaluating the Whorfian hypothesis has resulted from Whorf's lack of specification concerning three of its aspects. The first involves the kind of linguistic facts that are being referred to. As we saw above, language has both lexical levels and grammatical levels, and Whorf himself, perhaps in his enthusiasm to convey the core of his hypothesis, conflated the two. The second concerns the kind of "other" mental phenomena with which language is being connected. That is, should language be seen as related to sensation and perception, such as our division of the color continuum, or should it be more closely connected to "higher level" processes such as memory or even to a global "world view"? And third, there is the nature of the connection. Should it be viewed as deterministic and absolute (a "strong" Whorfian position), or should it be seen as a predisposition (a "weak" Whorfian position)?

The evidence for the strong position at both the lexical and the grammatical levels is at best equivocal. For some domains, such as color perception, the evidence is overwhelmingly against the Whorfian hypothesis and rather in favor of the notion that there are universals in our color perception regardless of language. Still, there is suggestive evidence that would keep the hopes of the Whorfian alive. In one study (Carroll and Casagrande 1958), children speaking Navaho, a language whose grammar marks the shapes of objects being referred to, were found to be sensitive to the dimension of shape in sorting objects at an earlier age than are children speaking English. More recently, Bloom (1981) reported differences in the ways Chinese and English speakers respond to questions depending on the nature of their native language structures.

I tend to agree with Slobin that there is little support for a strong form of the Whorfian hypothesis, that the linguistic boundaries rigidly determine our limits of thought. In the case of bilinguals, as John Macnamara wryly remarked, the bilingual in the world of the strong Whorfian hypothesis is doomed:

He might when using L1 or L2 always function cognitively in the manner appropriate to L1; he would then have great difficulty in understanding speakers of L2 or in being understood by them. Alternatively, he might always function cognitively in a manner appropriate to neither language and run the risk of understanding or being understood by nobody. Or he might have two cognitive systems, one for each language. He could then communicate with speakers of either language but he would have great difficulty "communicating" with himself. (1970, pp. 26–27)

The weak form of the hypothesis, however, is more difficult to reject. As applied to one's memory and world view, the weak Whorfian position suggests a tendency to operate along the lines defined by language. This tendency has more to do with guiding our choice of alternatives than with rigid determination. For example, the Japanese speaker might be more likely to pay attention to the shapes of objects when counting than a speaker of English would. Or an Eskimo may be able to remember the precise kind of snow that was falling on the day his mother died because he has specific words available for types of snow. In this weak sense, the Whorfian hypothesis has some intriguing implications for bilingualism and thought. It is possible that a bilingual person, depending on the language in which his or her thinking is guided, might take different paths. Whether there are real differences to be found at the level of memory and other cognitive processes, depending on the language, is an open question.

One can stretch this weak Whorfian view a bit further and suggest that the bilingual is a happy thinker. Any given problem can be handled through two linguistic systems, and the languages can be alternated in search of the one that would more efficiently guide thinking. Such a suggestion has even been made to account for differences in the superior problem-solving ability of bilingual children (Kessler and Quinn 1980, pp. 297–98). To support such a position, however, one would have to conduct research directed toward specific differences between languages.

If the Whorfian view of the relationship between language and thought is true, it would have great bearing on the way we conceptualize the mental topography of the bilingual. The strong version of the hypothesis equates language with thought, and since languages differ in the aspects of reality to which they refer, the implication is that the bilingual would have two systems of thought. In addition, the Whorfian view is closely tied to the empiricist tradition of behaviorist psychology, which emphasizes the role of experience. An early view, advocated by John Watson, went so far as to argue that "what the psychologists have hitherto called thought is . . . nothing but talking to ourselves" (1930, p. 238). In general, to the extent that one's linguistic experience is seen as central in shaping thought, we can legitimately expect the experiences of the bilingual to result in a richer view of reality.

VYGOTSKY'S VIEW OF THE MIND

Another theory that emphasizes the relationship between language and thought as well as the role of experience is that of the Russian psychologist Lev S. Vygotsky (1896–1934). As a principal architect of Marxist psychology in the post-revolutionary period, Vygotsky emphasized the role of society and technology in shaping the nature of the human psyche. He considered language to be an important tool through which society transmits its knowledge and values to the child. The analysis of the interaction of language and thought, he believed, would reveal the mechanisms of the ways in which society magnifies the individual qualities.

One behavior that particularly drew Vygotsky's attention was the speech of young children. Specifically, he was interested in the speech they seemingly direct at themselves, often when they are solving problems. This speech, which Vygotsky called "egocentric speech," can be distinguished from "social speech," which is used in communicating ideas with other children and with adults. The relationship between these two kinds of speech illustrates the role of language in the socialization of the child as a thinking member of society:

The first significant illustration of the link between these two language functions occurs when children find that they are unable to solve a problem by themselves. They then turn to an adult, and verbally describe the method that they cannot carry out by themselves. The greatest change in children's capacity to use language as a problem-solving tool takes place somewhat later in their development, when socialized speech (which has previously been used to address an adult) *is turned inward.* Instead of appealing to the adult, children appeal to themselves; language thus takes on an *intrapersonal function* in addition to its *interpersonal use.* When children develop a method of behavior for guiding themselves that had previously been used in relation to another person, when they organize their own activities according to a social form of behavior, they succeed in applying a social attitude to themselves. The history of the process of *the internalization of social speech* is also the history of the socialization of children's practical intellect. (1978, p. 27)

In short, language provides the medium through which adults socialize children into their way of thinking.

The final product of this socialization is an adult whose thought is guided by inner speech. Vygotsky believed that if socialization did not bring thought and language together, these two capacities would go unrelated. "A word devoid of thought is a dead thing," he wrote, "and a thought unembodied in words remains a shadow" (1962, p. 153).

Given the importance of language in defining the shape of thought, it would be reasonable to suppose that the bilingual would have more flexibility in his or her thought processes. Given the importance of socialization in Vygotsky's system, however, one would also have to consider the circumstances under which the two languages were internalized. If the languages were learned and used for different purposes—if one were used at home and the other at school, for example—then it is unlikely that both languages would be available for any given purpose. On the other hand, if both languages were used for similar purposes—as in a fully bilingual school—then both would presumably be available and would afford the person a wider range of thought. An example of such a possibility is reported by Morrison (cited in Peal and Lambert 1962), who asked an eleven-year-old Gaelic-speaking boy whether he had just solved a problem in Gaelic or in English, to which he replied, "Please, Sir, I tried it in English first, then I tried in the Gaelic to see would it be easier; but it wasn't so I went back to English" (p. 280).

OPPOSING VIEWPOINTS: CHOMSKYAN AND PIAGETIAN MINDS

Let us now consider some positions that offer no reason for bilingualism to affect thought. Noam Chomsky claims that the mind is best thought of as a set of unique faculties, one of them being language. His favorite metaphor is that language is an organ of the mind, much as the stomach is an organ of the digestive system. In the same way that the properties of the stomach are autonomous from those of the liver, language possesses unique properties different from those of other mental faculties such as visual perception. Chomsky demonstrates his point through highly abstract rules of grammar, using arguments of the sort presented in the previous chapter. For example, Chomsky argues that such abstract rules as those specifying the agreement of form between the subject and the verb in the present tense in English *(The girl loves shark,* but *The girls love shark)* are specific to language and are not found in other domains of thought.

In a compartmentalized view of mental capacities such as this, how do "language" and "thought" interact? Fodor, Bever, and Garrett (1974), Chomsky's forceful proponents, offer an admittedly tentative but appealing model based on the computer. They propose that there must be some common language (which they call "mentalese") similar to the internal machine language used by computers for actual computations. Communications with the central processor can be achieved in any number of more "user-friendly" languages, which the computer first translates to machine code. One can think of human natural languages and other compartments of the mind as the user-friendly languages. As Fodor, Bever, and Garrett write,

Linguistic inputs, like sensory inputs, are integrated and interpreted in light of memories and current nonverbal experience. . . . Presumably the computations underlying these integrative processes are typically effected in central code. If this is so, then the production and comprehension of speech involves translating between this central code and a natural language." (P. 378)

In Chomsky's view, then, the acquisition of a language consists of choosing among the alternative and pre-existing languages for feeding information into the basic machinery of thought. The hardware of the machinery is already present at birth, as are the critical characteristics of the target language in the form of language universals. In this view, bilingualism could not have much effect on thought. The two languages would have separate channels into machine code. Furthermore, it is difficult to see, in this view, how the context of the acquisition of the two languages would result in particularly different "types" of bilinguals.

Jean Piaget (1896–1980), the Swiss developmental psychologist renowned for his studies of intellectual development, is the other theorist who would see no special significance to bilingualism in influencing the course of cognitive growth. However, his reasons would be quite different from Chomsky's. Unlike Chomsky, Piaget was a generalist who emphasized the unity of the way in which knowledge develops. Piaget's beliefs about the noncentrality of language stem from his definition of intelligence and its origins (Piaget 1980).

The particular model of mature adult knowledge that Piaget

emphasized was formal logic—for example, the capacity, found in most adolescents, to formulate and test scientific hypotheses in terms of *if . . . then* relationships. In search of the origins of this knowledge, Piaget investigated the development of knowledge in young children. In children around age seven, he found evidence for a less powerful but nevertheless systematic logic. For example, children at this stage are not fooled (as are younger children) into thinking that water poured from a fat beaker into a tall thin beaker has somehow changed in volume. They have developed the knowledge that the operation of pouring water can be reversed, thus going back to the original quantity. Piaget argued that the foundation for this knowledge can in turn be found in the first eighteen months of life, during the period he called the *sensorimotor* stage. At this stage, knowledge exists as concrete actions on the part of infants. He showed, for example, that infants at the end of this stage have developed the knowledge that objects continue to exist even if they are no longer visible. Unlike younger infants who cease to reach for an object once it is hidden from view (as by placing a handkerchief over it), the infant at the end of the sensorimotor period will continue to look for it. Piaget reasoned that this knowledge consists of a motor representation, that objects can be retrieved by removing the obstacle.

Piaget's view of knowledge is a very general one. For example, the ability of the seven-year-old to say that a given quantity of water poured into differently shaped beakers maintains the same volume is a specific manifestation of the more general knowledge about reversibility. In turn, the knowledge about reversibility applies not just to volume of liquids but to solids, gases, and number. Piagetian psychology, then, is founded on the belief that this general form of knowledge is the source of all domains of cognition, including language. Since this knowledge is in turn the product of a developmental process that begins in the sensorimotor actions of the infant, bilingualism could not alter the form of this knowledge.

Piaget and Chomsky, while sharply divergent on fundamental issues about human development (see Piattelli-Palmarini 1980), would share the view that in terms of their cognitive development, bilinguals do not require special treatment. For Piaget, the reason is that language is not an important causal agent in the development of knowledge. For Chomsky, the reason is that language is autonomous from the rest of cognition.

THE UNDERLYING TENSIONS AMONG THEORIES OF MIND

Theories are like people. They cannot be pigeon-holed into neat categories or lined up against a simple yardstick. Looking at the four theories we have discussed, we can see several tensions pulling them into several different alignments with respect to their significance for bilingualism.

One important tension is the extent to which individual functions of the mind have independent structure. Does the structure found in language repeat itself in other components of thought, or does each component have its own unique set of characteristics? Chomsky and Vygotsky both emphasize the independence of functions, while Piaget stresses their common elements. A strong Whorfian view suggests that the structures of language and thought are equivalent, while a weaker view allows for some disjunction. It would appear that the more one tends to emphasize the uniqueness of the functions, the less one can accept the view that bilingualism influences thought.

A second tension is the nature of human development. What is development the development of? Is it best viewed as an active (context-independent) or passive (context-dependent) process? For Whorf, development consists of a process in which external (linguistic) reality stamps categories into the mind—a passive view. For Chomsky, the structures are part of the genetic endowment of humans, requiring little more than minimal stimulation from the environment to mature. Piaget sees development as the gradual structuring of an internal representation of the world, based on the child's active "operation," or experimentation, with external reality. Vygotsky sees development as the synthesis of hitherto separate, specialized functions mediated by society. To the extent that a theoretical position takes a "passive" view—that is, it is dependent on context—the experience of bilingualism would leave its marks on thought.

A third, related tension is the locus of structure. Is it in the internal reality of the mind, or is it in the external world? Chomsky would argue for its location entirely in the mind. Whorf would claim the extreme opposite, that our perception of reality—thought—cannot exist independent of the culture that transmits the linguistic structure.

Piaget and Vygotsky are both midway between these two extremes, but they differ on a fourth tension point: the nature of external reality. For Piaget, the problem of external reality is centered around the physical world, which is more or less universal across cultures. Water poured from one container into another remains constant in quantity, regardless of changes in physical appearance. By interacting with the world, the child constructs a knowledge structure about this sort of physical reality. For Vygotsky, the external reality is first and foremost cultural. Culture is the agent that brings together different internal human capacities that would otherwise exist unrelated. Cultures vary tremendously in the ways they recruit different capacities, so the Vygotskian perspective provides a context in which to study cultural influences on thought, one such influence being bilingualism.

These tensions, woven together, constitute what I consider to be the heart of the theories of language and thought. Theories, like people, do not have to be embraced or rejected wholeheartedly. In general, if one's orientation is toward the view that bilingualism influences thought, one will tend to believe that there are general capacities common to language and thought that are structured and influenced in the course of development, and that development is influenced by external contingencies in the form of culture acting as a midwife. On the other hand, if one believes that language and thought are autonomously structured and that these structures are biologically determined and that they actively (and selectively) absorb environmental factors, then one will find the influence of bilingualism on thought trivial.

The Relationship Between the Two Languages

Bilinguals are commonly asked what language they like to think in and whether the thoughts they think differ according to which language they're thinking in. I suspect that these questions hold fascination because they hint at a duality within the individual: two different patterns of thought in the confines of one head. This possibility is interesting for much the same reason that split-brain patients and multiple personalities seize the popular imagination.

The evidence for a bilingual's having two personae, one for each language, comes from three levels of investigation. The neurological level looks at the physiology of the brain and asks whether the languages are differentially localized in the brain. The information-processing level, in the realm of cognitive psychology, addresses the question through psychological experiments in which mental processes are measured. The educational psychology level looks at groups of students who are being educated bilingually and seeks to ascertain whether they demonstrate learning that is common to both languages.

THE NEUROLOGICAL LEVEL

The most compelling evidence for the organizational characteristics of the two languages might be found in data showing that certain areas of the brain are associated with particular

languages. Much has been learned about the functional localization of speech through the study of monolingual individuals
who have suffered injury to certain parts of the brain (mostly
through strokes and traumatic injury). For example, over 90
percent of the cases of aphasia (loss of language) result from
injury to the left hemisphere (Penfield and Roberts 1959). Specific areas of the left hemisphere have also been identified with
different aspects of language, such as grammar and meaning.

If different aspects of language are stored in different locations in the brain, might not a bilingual who suffers damage at
a given location evidence different kinds of loss for the two
languages? Observation of recovery patterns in bilingual
aphasics reveals that in about half the cases, the different languages recover at the same rate (Paradis 1977; Albert and Obler
1978). In other cases, the first language recovers before the
second language. In still others, the more recently used language
recovers first. In some more eccentric cases, the two languages
fluctuate in their recovery patterns. Witness the variety in these
descriptions provided by Michel Paradis (1977):

When Minkowski's patient began to speak, he could express himself
more easily in French because he could not find his words in Swiss
dialect (his mother tongue and most fluent language before his acci-
dent) or in standard German. This condition lasted for a few weeks,
during which time the patient gradually regained normal use of dialect
and of standard German, while his French regressed at the same rate.
(P. 67).

Chlenov reports on a German who, after having suffered a trauma to
the skull during the Spanish civil war, spoke only English at first. Then,
while his native German improved gradually, his English regressed. (P.
74)

Wald relates the case of a Russian female patient who spoke only
English for several days following an apoplectic stroke. During that
period, she could understand questions put in Russian but would
answer them only in English. Later, her Russian was restored and her
English worsened. (P. 74)

Veryac's patient did not begin to understand her English mother tongue until she could speak French well again, 5 months after insult. (P. 74)

Ovcharova *et al* relate the case of a patient whose spoken Turkish was almost unimpaired but who spoke Bulgarian with a Turkish accent and used Turkish word order and grammatical structures. Moreover, this patient often replaced Bulgarian with Turkish phrases. (P. 77)

The variation in patterns of recovery may be due to what Paradis (1981) has labelled the "dual system hypothesis." It may be that the two languages are represented in overlapping but distinct areas of the brain; whether the damage is differential or not, then, would depend on whether it happens to strike an area where the two languages overlap or an area where only one is represented.

One problem with these studies is that they capitalize on unfortunate accidents such that the researchers are not free to specify nor to determine precise locations of damage. In fact, neurological insults are in most cases quite diffuse. Neurological damage can be described as something like rot in a cabbage, spread out across and through various layers, making assessment of any specific damage very difficult.

In addition, it is often too easy to forget that recovery from aphasia, though describable in neurological and linguistic terms, is also a tragic and dramatic situation in which a person, unexpectedly stripped of language, is struggling to regain composure as a human being. It has been suggested that part of the differential recovery pattern from aphasia may be due to psychological factors associated with this trauma (Grosjean 1982).

The possibility of separate representation receives support from a remarkable study by George Ojemann and Harry Whitaker (1978), in which they mapped the language-relevant region of the cortex of two bilingual patients. This technique involved a mild electrical stimulation that was applied to specific areas of the cortex while the patients, under local anesthesia, were undergoing surgery for treatment of epilepsy. During this stimulation, the patients were asked to provide the names of pictured objects in a specified language. The assumption underlying the procedure was that electrical stimulation inhibits the activity where it is applied, leading to inability to name objects. One subject was a thirty-seven-year-old Hollander who moved to the United States and learned English at the age of twenty-five; the other was a twenty-year-old college student whose primary language was English but who spoke Spanish at home. For both subjects, there was an area where stimulation led to inability to name in both languages, but there were also areas that showed reliable tendencies toward inhibition of one or the other of the languages. There was also the suggestion that the weaker language was represented in a wider area of the cortex than the primary language.

Perhaps of even more popular interest in the search for neuropsychological differences in the organization of two languages is the problem of hemispheric lateralization. It has become almost a cliche that the two hemispheres of the brain have specialized functions, even though experts still disagree considerably on the extent of the differences (Gazzaniga 1983). The left hemisphere is said to be more analytic, the right hemisphere more holistic.

It has been observed that after damage to their right hemisphere, bilinguals are more likely to suffer from aphasia than are their monolingual counterparts (Galloway 1980). If true, this would imply that the bilingual is more dependent on the right hemisphere for language. However, as Vaid (1983) wisely cautions, there is a tendency to report only the unusual and interesting cases.

Studies using visual presentation of stimuli to the left or right hemispheres tend to support the view that bilinguals show greater right-hemisphere involvement in processing linguistic stimuli than do monolinguals (Obler 1979). (One should be careful, however, not to interpret these studies as showing that one language is contained in the left hemisphere, the other in the right. Indeed, it is very rare that one finds right-hemisphere dominance in either of the two languages. Usually the picture is one of less right-hemisphere dominance in one language than in the other, but in most cases, the left hemisphere is the dominant one.)

One variable that Obler suggests in accounting for greater right-hemisphere involvement is the proficiency of the subjects in the second language. She cites a study by Galziel et al (1977) that looked at native Hebrew-speaking children learning English. The research showed that with greater proficiency in English, there was a correspondingly greater left-hemisphere dominance on stimuli presented in English. Taken in conjunction with Ojemann and Whitaker's apparent finding that the primary language is more localized than the weaker language, this finding may suggest that increasing proficiency in a language is accompanied by increasing localization in the left hemisphere.

With regard to the question of the independence versus interdependence of languages in the bilingual mind, what can we conclude? We know that brain damage can result in differential effects on the two languages and that this may in part be due to differential localization of at least parts of the two languages, although the story is undoubtedly a complex maze of psychological and neurological factors. There is some evidence to suggest that the right hemisphere plays a greater role in processing one of the languages, presumably the weaker of the two. In most cases, however, both languages are more left-hemisphere dominant; one is simply more so (or less so) than the other.

THE INFORMATION-PROCESSING LEVEL

Paul Kolers in 1963 placed the issue of the independence versus interdependence of the bilingual's two languages in the context of information-processing approaches to human cognition. This view of the human mind had its immediate origins in theories of information structure and information flow that were being developed by engineers, especially those with an interest in machine pattern recognition and, more generally, computers. Implied in this view is the metaphor of the human mind as a computer. The mind can be modelled like a flow chart for computer programming, with boxes linked by arrows indicating the direction of movement of information. The basic activity of the information-processing psychologist is looking for "critical experiments" that will decide between alternative models of information flow and storage.

Take, for example, a well-known fact about human memory performance called the "lag effect." If I read to you from a list of words, and if some words are repeated further down the list, it is known that if the repetitions are spaced apart adequately, the probability that you will remember those words is approximately twice that of remembering any word read once. In other words, you benefit considerably from the repetition. However, the closer together the repetitions are, the lower the probability becomes, although of course never lower than the probability of a single presentation. Bilinguals have been presented with mixed language lists, where a given word is repeated, but in different languages. If the two languages were interdependent, one would argue that similar effects should be found as in monolingual lists. That is, the longer the lag, the higher the probability of recall. Contrary to this expectation, it has been found that the lag effect does not exist; that is, even with short lags, the probability of recall is additive. Indeed, in this sort of experiment, a given word, repeated in a different language, acts as if the same word were repeated with a longer lag in the same language (Glanzer and Duarte 1971; Paivio and Lambert 1981).

In contrast to this evidence in support of the independence hypothesis, there are numerous studies showing that bilingual sets of words behave very much like monolingual ones, facilitating as well as interfering with recall in ways very similar to monolingual lists (Young and Saegert 1966; Kintsch and Kintsch 1969; Lopez and Young 1974; McCormack 1974, 1977). These studies are taken as an indication that the bilingual stores the two languages together, because the bilingual subjects act as though the particular language in which they hear words and sentences is unimportant and go straight for the meaning. As Kolers and Gonzalez (1980) have remarked, such studies are so numerous that "on the basis of census alone, there is more evidence for the interdependence than for the independence position" (p. 54).

One problem with integrating this area of research is that it is often unclear just what the experiments are tapping. As Kolers and Gonzalez noted, different investigators have used different procedures, and their results cannot always be generalized. In fact, to the outsider, this genre of research in learning and memory appears to consist primarily of arguments over what it is that the different methodologies measure (certainly an issue of primary importance, but frustrating nevertheless to those interested in substantive conclusions).

Perhaps the question of independence versus interdependence was fated for mixed findings from the beginning (Grosjean 1982). It is obvious that at some level we have a common conceptual store for both languages. Otherwise, it would be impossible, for example, for me to tell you in English about my trip to Japan, during which I did not use a word of English. It is equally obvious that the two languages must be independent at some level. We must compliment the bilingual mind for its ability to keep the two languages separate, as evidenced by the relative lack of interference between them.

With the benefit of hindsight, a mixed picture becomes less surprising. It would have been more fruitful to define the research agenda differently, as the search for the conditions under which the *form* of the presentation (in this case, the language) is an important variable in performance and the conditions under which the underlying *function* (or meaning) is more important. It would seem that a research program explicitly aimed at getting varying results—some in which form is important and others in which function is important—would illuminate better the ways in which the two languages are related to the conceptual system.

For example, it appears that in tests of recall memory, where the degree of clustering between items can be objectively measured, bilinguals tend to cluster words by conceptual category (such as "drugs") rather than by language. As Kolers and Gonzalez (1980) point out, this probably means that category clustering in this situation is more efficacious for recall than language clustering. They note, however, that organization by language is sometimes preferred. They cite a study in which trilinguals, given the choice of three languages and three categories, organized them by both.

A related and, to me, somewhat remarkable finding is that, in recalling a bilingual mixed list of words or sentences, subjects can easily remember the language of presentation (Kolers 1965; Lambert, Ignatow, and Krauthamer 1968; Rose et al. 1975). A major factor in these experiments is probably their lack of context. Basically, it is like being asked to recall the following list of French and English words: *crab, Pierre, chapeau, student, camion, movie, elephant, oiseau.* It seems to me that language in this case assumes the role of an important contextual support because of the lack of any other context. (Participating in these experiments, as you might guess, is punishingly boring.) It would be interesting to see the conditions under which this ability to remember the language of presentation deteriorates.

I find it difficult to agree with McCormack's assessment in 1977 of the state of the art:

Only thirteen years have elapsed since Kolers (1963) raised the independence-interdependence issue. During that brief period of time, sufficient data have been collected to enable us to conclude that the single-store position makes most sense, both in terms of parsimony and in terms of its predictive and explanatory power. The game, which we call science, rarely reveals such rapid progress. (P. 64)

I am inclined to believe, with Kolers (1978) and others (Paivio and Desrochers 1980; Paradis 1980), that we are far from having settled the issue, that there are remarkable situations where the languages are kept distinct, and indeed that the issue should be redirected into looking for systematic situations that cause a person to behave in a way specific to the language, or in a way that conforms to meanings regardless of the language in which the experience occurs. What I think these experiments have shown is the remarkable flexibility of the human mind.

THE EDUCATIONAL PSYCHOLOGY LEVEL

Various forms of bilingual education programs, which we will discuss in detail in chapter 8, can be seen as field experiments in which the question of independence versus interdependence of skills across languages can be resolved. Ample evidence for transfer can be found in a report by Lambert and Tucker (1972) of a French immersion program for English-speaking children in St. Lambert, a suburb of Montreal. In this innovative program, beginning in kindergarten, classes for monolingual English-speaking children, except for English language arts classes that begin after their second year in school, are conducted exclusively in French.

Since the primary objective of the research was to evaluate the program's overall effectiveness, the details are missing, but suffice it to say that the children in this program were doing as well on measures of English and other skills as control children who were receiving monolingual instruction. Referring to the transfer of skills across languages, Lambert and Tucker wrote:

We refer here to the higher-order skills of reading and calculating, which were developed exclusively through the medium of French and yet seemed to be equally well and almost simultaneously developed in English. In fact, we wonder whether in these cases there actually was a transfer of any sort or whether some more abstract form of learning took place that was quite independent of the language of training. These developments took place so rapidly that we had little time to take notice of them. It seemed to us that all of a sudden the children could read in English and demonstrate their arithmetic achievement in that language. (P. 209)

Lambert and Tucker's conclusions find support, by and large, in other evaluations of bilingual education elsewhere in Canada and in the United States.

Jim Cummins (1980, 1981) has brought together evidence from various studies that have compared language proficiency scores in two languages to argue that there is a cross-lingual dimension to language proficiency. That is, there is some common underlying capacity reflected in both languages. As nearly as I can tell, this capacity is not too different from the notion of general intelligence that was discussed in chapter 2 and that carries with it the dangers of reification of the test results. If empirical support for this cross-lingual dimension continues to build up, we should not stop there but should continue to search for the basic structures that lead to this result. Cummins's notion, by the way, is criticized by Troike (1981) for failing to consider sociolinguistic circumstances and by Edelsky et al. (1983) for adopting a test-based definition of language proficiency and literacy. It is far from a proven fact.

FACTORS THAT DETERMINE INDEPENDENCE AND INTERDEPENDENCE

To repeat, I believe that the question of whether the two languages of the bilingual are independent or interdependent misses the mark. The real question is the identification of the conditions under which the two languages maintain separation and those under which they are apparently merged. I would venture the guess that the language variable would be important in tasks where language occupied a central role. For example, memory experiments in which language was the major category would show the role of language. Other stimuli that would be specifically bound to language should show similar effects. A *haiku* poem in Japanese is different from its translation into English. If haiku poems were used as stimuli in a memory task, there is no doubt in my mind that the language of presentation would be well remembered.

On the other hand, the ready transfer of academic skills in students educated bilingually suggests that general skills are not linguistically based. It is up to future research, however, to determine whether some school skills might transfer more easily than others, depending on the extent to which they are dependent on language.

Can We Build a Typology of Bilinguals?

The question of what individual differences result from what different kinds of experiences holds fascination, particularly among psychologists, and this question has been asked of bilinguals. Do different ways of learning the two languages result in qualitatively different kinds of bilinguals?

One distinction that has been drawn, and that is related to the independence versus interdependence debate, is the distinction between *compound* and *coordinate* bilinguals (Weinreich 1953; Ervin and Osgood 1954). According to this distinction, compound bilinguals are products of a learning environment where the two languages are used concurrently. They tend to fuse the two languages such that, in their mental system, concepts have verbal labels from both languages attached to them. The compound bilingual, in other words, is one whose languages are interdependent. By contrast, coordinate bilinguals learn the two languages in separate environments, most commonly when they are educated in a language different from their home language. Coordinate bilinguals maintain different conceptual systems for the two languages, much like the kind of bilingual mind advocated by the independence position discussed earlier.

Like the independence-interdependence debate, the compound-coordinate distinction and other candidates for types of bilinguals have been studied from the points of view of neurology, information-processing, and educational psychology. Unfortunately, as will soon become evident, this area of research is very messy. The primary purpose of this section is therefore to indicate future directions for salvaging the interesting idea of a typology of bilinguals.

THE NEUROLOGICAL LEVEL

Lambert and Fillenbaum (1959) reported an intriguing pilot study comparing compound and coordinate bilinguals who had suffered brain damage and become aphasic. The compound bilinguals they studied were fourteen aphasics from Montreal. Case reports from these patients were compared with those of coordinate bilingual aphasics from Europe. The study concluded that the coordinate bilinguals tended to show damage that was more localized with respect to either language, while the disturbance in compound bilinguals was more generalized across the two languages. Such evidence would indeed provide strong support for the view that different bilingual experiences result in distinct neurological organizations of the two languages.

The initial enthusiasm for this promising finding (Diebold 1968) has eroded as more cases have been examined and as the cases, including Lambert and Fillenbaum's original group, have been scrutinized with renewed vigor. The major problem is the extremely idiosyncratic ways in which individual cases are reported by the doctors examining the patients. Paradis (1977) conducted a case-by-case study of the literature and wrote the following account in sheer frustration:

It is seldom possible to obtain a correct appraisal of the kind or even the degree of bilingualism of a patient prior to insult. The relatives are usually of very little help, for their assessment of a patient's bilingualism is generally quite subjective and lacks differentiation as to the various aspects of the patient's language. . . . Evaluations are mostly given in global terms of greater or lesser overall fluency. Sometimes even this information cannot be elicited from the patient nor from anyone else. . . . No two authors will give the same details about a case history: Items range from remarks on whether a patient masturbated a great deal as a youth to detailed descriptions of aphasic symptoms in each of a patient's languages. . . . From the information actually available it is not possible to correlate type of bilingualism with a particular pattern of restitution. (Pp. 99–100)

The data, in short, are unreliable, in terms of both the patients' history and the nature of the linguistic damage that resulted. Clearly, better and more systematic data will have to be collected before any conclusions can be reached.

Related to the compound-coordinate distinction is the age of becoming bilingual. Presumably, those who become bilingual at a younger age are more likely to have learned the two languages in similar settings (compound) than are those who learn the second language when they are older (coordinate.)

Fred Genesee and his colleagues (1978) reported a study of bilinguals who could be classified as "early" and "late" bilinguals, in which he monitored their levels of electrical activity in the two hemispheres of the brain with an electroencephalograph (EEG). While their EEG patterns were being monitored, the subjects listened to a mixed list of English and French words and were asked to identify the language in which each presentation was made by pressing a button. The results, though complicated, suggested to the authors that the subjects who had become bilingual in adolescence showed patterns distinct from those who had become bilingual early. In particular, they suggested that the early bilinguals showed greater use of their left hemisphere, while late bilinguals evidenced greater right-hemisphere involvement.

Using different methods, however, other researchers have failed to find evidence of right-hemisphere bias in adolescent bilinguals (for example, Soares and Grosjean 1981). It is possible, as Obler (1979) has speculated, that there were differences in proficiency in the second language between the early and late bilinguals in the Genesee study that might account for his finding of greater right-hemisphere involvement. In general, the neurological evidence for the existence of different kinds of bilinguals is sparse. A haunting problem, and one that will crop up as we consider the evidence from the information-processing approach as well, is that of accurately classifying research subjects in terms of their bilingual experiences.

THE INFORMATION-PROCESSING APPROACH

Studies comparing compound and coordinate bilinguals on information-processing tasks have yielded such a confusing set of findings that my better judgment is to avoid the area altogether. These two types of bilinguals have been compared on a broad range of tasks. For example, they have been asked to rate individual words in terms of their connotations on a variety of dimensions of meaning (a measure called the *semantic differential*). Other studies have measured the amount of fusion between color words and the colors themselves, using the Stroop Color Word Test (stimuli in such tests involve color words printed in a color different from that denoted by the word itself). Studies along this line include those by Lambert (1969), Lambert, Havelka, and Crosby (1958), and Newby (1976).

Karl Diller (1970), in reviewing this research, points to two problems. First, the relationship between these different tasks and the original compound-coordinate distinction is poorly specified. The distinction is meant to be one at the level of what is called *denotative meaning,* that is, what the words of the two languages refer to. Yet many of the studies comparing compound and coordinate bilinguals use measures that seem to tap the *connotative* meanings of words. And second, as in the neurological studies, clear-cut definitions of compound and coordinate bilinguals are hard to make, so that it is difficult to ascertain that different studies using these labels are actually referring to the same things. As a result, many cognitive psychologists believe that the compound-coordinate distinction should be buried and forgotten. I will argue against a premature funeral at the end of this section.

THE EDUCATIONAL PSYCHOLOGY APPROACH

In chapter 2, in discussing the relationship between bilingualism and intelligence, I alluded to Cummins's proposals that the type of bilingualism may mediate the positive and negative effects of bilingualism. Essentially, Cummins (1981) argues that there are three types of bilingualism: limited, partial, and proficient. Limited bilingualism is characterized by low proficiency in both languages, partial bilingualism by a native-like level in one of the languages, and proficient bilingualism by native-like levels in both languages. Cummins suggests that limited bilingualism results in negative cognitive consequences, while proficient bilingualism can have positive consequences.

At present, what few data exist to support the hypothesis are primarily based on psychometric tests that admittedly assess intelligence and achievement only superficially. Support for the negative effects of limited bilingualism comes from Swedish research with Finnish immigrant children (Skutnabb-Kangas and Toukomaa 1976). The researchers found that Finnish children who were enrolled in Swedish-only programs and reportedly developed proficiency in neither Finnish nor Swedish performed considerably more poorly on measures of achievement

in comparison to both Finnish and Swedish monolingual counterparts. In a recent review of the Swedish literature for the
Swedish National Board of Education, however, Christina Bratt
Paulston (1982) concluded that "there is *no* empirical evidence
to support the existence of such a language development
hiatus" (p. 42). In addition, Skutnabb-Kangas and Toukomaa
themselves have cautioned against generalizing their findings to
other sociolinguistic situations.

Results from this area of research are immensely difficult to
interpret, as Paulston (1980) points out, because the type of
educational program is determined by sociological and political
forces that have little to do with language per se. Whether the
degree of bilingual proficiency achieved can, by itself, influence
the cognitive structure of the individual child is a question of
immense importance, but at this point a question to which the
answer must await future research.

A PERSPECTIVE ON THE TYPOLOGY OF BILINGUALS

The compound-coordinate distinction has been debated for
almost thirty years, with no conclusive results. To understand
this stalemate, one must go back briefly to the history of the
idea. Discussion of the compound versus coordinate differences
in bilingual organization began in the linguist Uriel Weinreich's
(1953) classic treatise on bilingualism. Weinreich discussed the
different kinds of relationships that could hold between words
and their referents, and introduced the idea of compound and
coordinate organization. A careful reading of Weinreich's discussion (particularly pages 9–11) suggests that his primary concern was with the way in which different relationships between
words and referents could occur *within* any given bilingual, with
a secondary emphasis on the possibility that this analysis would
yield a typology of bilingual individuals (Haugen 1970). Psychologists Susan Ervin and Charles Osgood (1954) quickly translated Weinreich's distinction in terms of individual differences,

and it is this aspect that has stayed with us through the empirical studies of compound and coordinate bilingualism that we have reviewed.

Much of the confusion could have been avoided if the charge of the researchers had been to look for concepts that are organized in either a coordinate or a compound fashion *within* bilingual minds. This was the spirit of Weinreich's proposal. If individual differences appear in this analysis, fine. But the starting point should have been (and still could be) variations within the individual.

I do not claim (as a strict Chomskyan or a Piagetian would) that there is no such thing as a useful typology of bilinguals based on their learning history. It would be exciting if different cognitive structures could be shown to result from different kinds of bilingual environments. But the evidence at this point is thin, and I am skeptical of the eagerness to jump to conclusions about individual differences at the expense of seeking out characteristics within the individual mind.

Reflections on the Bilingual Mind

Three tools of social science have been used to illuminate the problems of this chapter—the approaches of neurology, information-processing, and educational psychology. The relationship between neurological structures and behavior is obviously not simple. Between bilingual behavior and the complex network of interconnecting neurons in the brain there must be multiple levels of organization. Answers to questions that are trivial by comparison, such as how simple learning is represented in the brain of the rat, have thus far eluded scientists. Our deprived state of knowledge about the organization of the bilingual brain is not surprising, then; it would not have been more than a happy coincidence if neat results had emerged from such crude research procedures as have been employed to date.

It is important to consider the possibility—indeed, the likelihood—that there is no simple, one-to-one correspondence between psychological variables and neurological organization. As Paradis (1981) has pointed out, it should be considered a hypothesis, not a given, that types of bilingualism are reflected in different neurological organizations. I agree and would add that we should assume there is no simple correspondence until shown otherwise; that is, the burden of proof should be on the side arguing for the correspondence.

Consider the example of how our psychological state of hunger is represented at the physiological level (Gleitman 1981). It had been discovered that a variety of physical states, including blood-sugar level, stomach cramps, and temperature of the hypothalamus (a part of the brain) can independently signal the psychological condition that we experience as hunger. A useful way to think of psychological variables is that they recruit from a variety of structures into their own unique organization, and that the organization of psychological variables can proceed at a level removed in a complex way from the physiological organization. There is no logical reason why psychological organization should necessarily correspond to neurological organization. One should avoid the temptation to believe, as many do, that the neurological evidence is somehow a truer reflection of reality than the psychological level. The studies of bilingual information processing raise concerns that I have long felt about research reports in which it is assumed that for any given area of research, there is *one single model* that must be true and that the purpose of experiments is to prove which model (of many alternatives) is the true one. I suspect that it is misleadingly simplistic to look for the "one true way," and I have often wondered how malleable the results of these experiments might be. In other words, if the goals of the research were to be changed from the search for the true model to the search for the kinds of things that would have to be done to obtain different results, what would I find?

Malleability of results is directly related to the problem of individual differences. To the extent that results are malleable, observed differences between individuals can be seen as choices they are making between alternatives, for various reasons (which may include trivial ones, such as how they were feeling that day, or their attitude toward the experimental procedures). On the other hand, to the extent that results are unmalleable, individual differences reflect differences that are stable and difficult to change.

At this point, bilingual experiments have not demonstrated the unmalleability of performance, or put more strongly, there is reason to suspect that the kind of procedure involved influences whether the subject behaves as though the two languages are interdependent or independent and whether there are coordinate or compound systems. We still do not know the conditions that determine the different outcomes, but it is an encouraging start, from the perspective of individual differences, that it is more a matter of choice than of rigid determinism. It would be well for cognitive approaches to bilingualism to keep in mind the mental flexibility of human beings.

The educational setting provides perhaps the most interesting context in which to explore both of the issues addressed in this chapter. The context is relevant, and experimental manipulations can be made in teaching curricula to test for specific theories about interdependence and about typologies of bilinguals. Unfortunately, the measures used in this area tend to be gross overall measures of aptitude and achievement that do not attempt to illuminate the specific processes involved in school learning. The best of all possible worlds could be achieved by conducting information-processing experiments in the context of bilingual schooling.

There are many gaping holes in the general subject that this chapter has addressed, the topography of the bilingual mind.

The mind is a complex thing, and we have restricted it to an account of knowledge, omitting other domains such as emotions and feelings. The reason is simple. Few studies of "the other kind" exist.

Susan Ervin-Tripp (Ervin 1964; Ervin-Tripp 1967), one of the most creative researchers in our field, has, however, made a contribution with a study of "the other kind." She used the Thematic Apperception Test (TAT), a projective test commonly used for psychological assessment. The test consists of a series of relatively innocuous pictures of people, whose expressed emotions are ambiguous. Ervin-Tripp gave this test to Japanese-English and French-English bilingual adults in both of their languages and found that their responses differed depending on the language of the session. For example, in Japanese sessions with her Japanese-English bilinguals, she found more emotional expressions and themes related to family relationships and close personal ties. In contrast, the English stories by the same people were abstract and cold and more about formal relationships. She also found different kinds of responses among her French-English bilinguals. Consider the following responses given to a picture of a couple by a twenty-seven-year-old French woman who spoke English with her husband and child:

[French, first session] She seems to beg him, to plead with him. I don't know if he wants to leave her for another woman or what, or if it's her who has . . . but she seems to press against him. I think he wants to leave her because he's found another woman he loves more, and that he really wants to go, or maybe it's because she . . . she's deceived him with another woman. I don't know whose fault it is but they certainly seem angry. Unless it's in his work, and he wants to go see someone and he wants to get in a fight with someone, and she holds him back and doesn't like him to get angry. I don't know, it could be many things. . . .

[English, second session] Oh, that one. In the past, well I think it was a married couple, average, and he got out of the Army and got himself a job or something like that or has decided he would go to college. He's decided to get a good education and maybe after he would have a better job and be able to support his wife much better, and everything would come out for the best. He keeps on working and going to college at night some of the time. Now, let me see. He finally decided that was too much. He found he was too tired, he was discouraged and something went wrong with his work. The boss told him that, well, his production had decreased or something like that, that he didn't get enough sleep or something like that, that he couldn't carry on studies and working at the same time. He'd have to give something up, and he's very discouraged and his wife tries to cheer him up. Now, let me see. And eventually he'll probably keep on working his way through and finally get his diploma and get a better job and they will be much happier and . . . well, his wife will have helped him along too and as he was discouraged and all and was willing to give up everything, she boosted him up. That's all. (Ervin 1964, p. 504)

Ervin-Tripp offers the interpretation that "In French the picture elicited a variety of themes of aggression and striving for autonomy. In English the heroine supports the husband in his achievement strivings" (p. 504).

There are, of course, many difficulties with this kind of research, which Ervin-Tripp herself acknowledges, but the results are provocative and instructive. As scientists, we are easily entrapped by narrow definitions and implications of theories. A fascinating idea such as Whorf's—that the world is full of diverse views that go hand in hand with cultural and linguistic diversity—is cooked down to nothing more than a few experiments on color perception and word meanings (see Fishman 1982). In thinking through the problem of bilingualism and thought, particularly as we think about studies showing no effects of bilingualism, we should remain suspicious that we are becoming the victims of our own tunnel vision.

Chapter 5

How Children Learn a Second Language

MOST OF US hold it as an article of faith that children are magically equipped to learn a second language. Traveling abroad, we observe adults struggling along with their phrase books and stock greetings, while children seemingly absorb the local language to the point of fluency, often interpreting for their parents. In this chapter, I will describe one such child, a five-year-old Japanese girl who learned English with remarkable speed, without formal instruction. That will set the framework for a general discussion of second language acquisition in children.

A Japanese Child Learns English

In the early 1970s when I was an undergraduate, I met a visiting scholar from Japan. Mr. Tanaka (not his real name) invited me home to dinner to meet his family. The Tanakas had just moved into the first floor of a typical multifamily unit in a working-class, English-speaking neighborhood in Somerville, Massachusetts. Mr. Tanaka's spoken English was what might be described as "halting" (he was more comfortable with written English); his wife had studied English in college and was quite fluent. The family member who most interested me, however, was their five-year-old daughter. We will call her Uguisu ("nightingale" in Japanese).

When I first met Uguisu, she had just been enrolled in a neighborhood public kindergarten and had begun to make friends with children on her street. Since she was receiving no formal instruction in English at school, Uguisu made for a nice comparison with children who acquire English as their native language. That first evening, I tried unsuccessfully to get Uguisu to speak English. Apparently, her one English phrase was *not in particular,* which she had picked up from her mother.

The next few months were difficult ones for Uguisu. Her parents reported that she complained of headaches and was generally cranky, which they attributed to the pains of being in a new environment and coping with an unfamiliar language. She played well, sharing toys with her friends, and she occasionally used a few English phrases—usually imitations of what her friends had just said. For example, she learned to say *I'm the leader,* which her friends used to yell out as they stormed around the house, and she used it frequently in a variety of contexts, such as when she wanted to show her friends how to play with toys. When asked in Japanese what she thought that meant, she translated it as "I am the big sister," that is, a show of authority. It was not until almost seven months after her initial exposure to English that Uguisu's English really blossomed. Her parents felt that this flowering was triggered by a lengthy automobile trip that the family had taken. On the trip, they were accompanied by an American adult, with whom Uguisu got along well, and this may have given her the needed confidence to use the "data" that she had stored up over the months.

From that point on, her rate of development was awesome; a nightingale had been turned loose. During the next six months, English became her predominant language. She even started talking to her parents in English, which they did not actively discourage, although they usually responded in Japanese. And she used it when playing on her own, such as in the bathtub with her toys. I suspect that within eighteen months after her initial exposure to English, only a trained ear would have been able to distinguish her from a native speaker (see Hakuta [1974, 1976] for full reports on her development). At the end of two years, the family returned home to Japan.

During my two-year acquaintance with the Tanakas, we became close friends. Every two weeks or so, I would visit their home with a tape recorder and record Uguisu's conversations. I transcribed the recordings, which ran roughly two hours apiece, into protocols written in traditional orthography, with notes on the context. The transcription process was laborious, but it was the only way I could really grasp the details of Uguisu's second-language development.

How dependent was her English development on the crutch of her native language, Japanese? How different was her development in English from that of children learning English as their native language? How typical was Uguisu as a second-language learner? These questions can only be answered with respect to particular—and changing—views of language development, views of what it is that actually develops. Let us start with a brief account of trends in the study of first-language acquisition, from which much of the research activity in second-language acquisition has stemmed.

The Research: A Changing Focus

One traditional and popularly held view about how children learn language is that they do it by imitating their parents and by receiving feedback from the parents, who correct their erroneous speech. Language is passed back and forth between the child and the parent, as a ball of clay is passed from one hand to the other, with each pass producing a smoother product. This view is consonant with empiricist philosophy (the philosophical basis of the work of Werner Leopold and Madorah Smith) and its psychological disciple of behaviorism, whose goal is to provide a description of the concrete and measurable conditions under which observable behaviors occur. The successive molding of language can be thought of as the building of chains of behavior (called "habits") that are externally observable (both to the parent and to the scientists) and thus subject to modification.

We saw in chapter 3 that the empiricist approaches to both linguistics and psychology have come under heavy fire from Noam Chomsky, who argues for the inadequacy of attempts to derive linguistic knowledge from externally observable (hence "experiencable") data. The empiricist account of language acquisition, the molding of clay, could not be the right one in the Chomskyan world, because for him language is an abstract entity that simply cannot be molded by parent, teacher, or any other external source. It must be derived from knowledge that is already resident in the child.

Before Chomsky, with the exception of a few notable scholars such as Leopold, very few researchers conducted systematic studies of language development. The paucity of studies can be attributed to the assumption of the empiricists that "verbal behavior" was not significantly different from other types of behavior; in fact, the laws of behavior were assumed to extend across types of behaviors and across species. When Chomsky raised a serious challenge to psychologists by pointing to the inadequacies of their accounts of human language, there arose a need to document carefully the development of language in children.

Among those who began collecting systematic data in the early 1960s were Roger Brown, Susan Ervin, and Martin Braine. These researchers independently recorded the language development of small numbers of children. In their data, they found striking regularities that appeared to be governed not by parental molding but rather by the child's internally driven search for the structures of language. One popular example was the child's use of the English past tense ending *-ed.* It was observed that when children learned this form, they extended it to irregular verbs, with resultant "errors" such as *goed* and *eated.* These children were credited with creatively ironing out the idiosyncracies of the language, since they presumably had not heard these forms from their adult models.

A somewhat more elaborate example comes from Ursula Bellugi (1967), who focused her study on the development of English negation. She reported three stages of development, where the first two stages consisted of forms not found in adult speech. *No I like that,* the child would say rather than the adult's *I don't like that.* Observations of such systematic development that appeared almost autonomous and child-generated (rather than being imperfect imitations of adult speech) lent credence to Chomsky's views. Reflective of the trend was the metaphor used by Brown and Bellugi (1964) in characterizing language development as "more reminiscent of the biological development of an embryo than it is of the acquisition of a conditioned reflex" (p. 151).

It would be fair to say that during this period, the major focus of development was on the aspects of language that Chomsky emphasized. This primarily meant interest centered on grammar. It should be noted that Chomsky's argument for the innateness of grammar was a logical one that did not really require convergence with data from child language. It was sufficient to show that abstract aspects of language could not be learned, in principle, from external data of any kind. However, most of the studies were seen to have a bearing on Chomsky's views, because they showed that development had systematic properties and that, like the adult's language system, child language was characterized by linguistic rules. From the beginning, however, Chomsky and his colleagues were critical of the kind of research conducted by developmental psycholinguists, who analyzed actual observed utterances from children, while the Chomskyan position claimed that you cannot derive knowledge simply from observable utterances. This is not to say that Chomsky ignored the supportive findings of the developmental psycholinguists; it is only human to accept results that are consonant with one's beliefs.

Developmental psycholinguists, for their part, found grammatical models to be useful devices through which to view child language. Their excitement was heightened when they found evidence for the "psychological reality" of grammatical variables. For example, Brown (1968) noted a similarity between the grammatical derivation of questions (for example, *What are you reading?*) and questions found in the speech of young children. Specifically, the grammatical derivation called for a source structure upon which a series of operations is performed. One of the operations involved transforming *What you are reading?* to *What are you reading?* In his data from children, Brown found that they produced utterances of the form *What you are reading?*, suggesting evidence for an "intermediate stage" that further bolstered the plausibility of the derivation process itself.

A major source of frustration for developmental psycholinguists who pursued this type of activity was the willingness of linguists to change their grammars, often overnight. Since the data of linguists were primarily intuitions, it was not difficult for them to rearrange their theories on short notice. Although the mapping of grammar with developmental data did not lose its respectability as an activity, frustrations from having constant new regimes in this brand of linguistics led psychologists to look more broadly at child language, to consider aspects of language beyond grammar.

At the same time, there was concern that the intense interest in grammar had detracted attention from the child's development as a whole. For example, although Piaget's theory of cognitive development (chapter 4) had found a comfortable niche in American developmental psychology, it existed independently of the studies of grammatical development. In the spirit of Chomsky, grammatical development was considered an autonomous entity, and therefore it could be studied without reference to context. In contrast to this view, in which uniquely linguistic aspects of development generated curiosity and excitement, the new contextualism, as it might be called, called for the identification of overlaps between language development and other aspects of the child's development.

Particularly notable was the finding that early language development is restricted in the kinds of meanings expressed (Bloom 1970). The restriction turns out to be a function of the level of cognitive development of the child. For example, when children begin combining words at about eighteen months of age, they express simple meanings such as AGENT + ACTION *(Mommy push)* and POSSESSOR + POSSESSED *(Mommy book)*. They do not express complex meanings beyond their level of cognitive development, such as notions of time, collectivity, and conditionals. This finding may appear obvious, but considering the prior emphasis on grammatical form removed from meaning, it was a remarkable phenomenon.

The overlap between meaning and grammar naturally led to interest in communication, especially the underlying function of utterances. It was observed that early language is very much attached to specific contexts. (My favorite example is Linda Ferrier's, whose infant learned to say *phew!* as a greeting in the morning. That's what her mother would say when she came into the room and caught the smell of a diaper needing changing.) This view held that a contextual envelope is created in the course of the development of the parent-child interaction, and early utterances are slotted into this interactional structure. At the same time, the emphasis on parent-child communication brought to the attention of researchers the kind of language mothers used with their children—*motherese,* as it came to be called. Patterns of correlations between motherese and child language seemed to suggest, although debatably, that much of language development could be explained by the interactional and functional qualities of the parent-child situation (see Gleitman and Wanner 1982).

The shifts just described—originating in the view of language as habits and moving from interest in grammar to meaning to communication—perhaps more nearly resemble changes in fashion than scientific progress. For example, the shift from grammar to meaning did not occur because grammar failed as a theory of language acquisition but because researchers were interested in charting new territory.

In general, these studies suggest that the earliest stages of language development are most insightfully described through the communicative approach; that at the stage when words start getting combined, child language is best described in terms of meaning; and that the later stages of language development are interesting because of the sophisticated forms of grammar that emerge. One should not be fooled, however, by the developmental order in which these characterizations of language emerge, from communication to meaning to grammar. It would be rash to conclude that there is a progression, with grammar developing out of meaning and communication. Grammar, meaning, and communication are distinct levels of language and cannot be interchanged. Each has its own course of development, and it is still unclear how they are related to each other.

The Influence of the Native Language

A natural question to ask about second-language acquisition is the extent to which it is influenced by the native language of the learner. It seems logical that learning would be easiest in aspects of language in which the native and target languages share similarities. In fact, the emphasis on the role of native-language transfer has varied greatly over the years. Like the problem of "language handicap" that was bounced around as an academic football between the hereditarians and the environmentalists in chapter 2, language transfer has been an active part of the debate among differing views of language acquisition.

Uguisu's development in English contained some intriguing examples of transfer from Japanese. Her use of the English word *mistake* is an example. In English, the word is most frequently used as a noun, as in *You made a mistake.* In Japanese, the word is most frequently used as a verb, *machigau.* Uguisu's initial use of *mistake* was as a verb, the way she used the concept in Japanese. She used utterances such as *Oh no, I mistake, Don't give me more because you're mistaking, Because I just mistake it,* gradually changing to the more native-like use, such as *I made a mistake.*

Uguisu was making an inference about the "verbness" of the concept of "mistake," based on her knowledge about Japanese grammar. To get a taste of what this kind of knowledge about language consists of even within a single language, consider the following. Suppose that you run across an unfamiliar word in a sentence: *Molly tergiversated until I was literally going up the wall.* You might guess, regardless of whether you can identify the meaning of the unknown word, that the following words are possible: *tergiversation, tergiversator, tergiversatory, tergiversating.* You are able to do so because you have some knowledge about grammatical classes, that is, about the kinds of grammatical contexts in which verbs appear (and so you were able to identify it as a verb), and you can predict what would be allowable variants on the verb. In Uguisu's case, she was able to take the knowledge from Japanese that the concept of "mistake" is expressed as a verb and to extend this relationship to her knowledge about English verbs.

Another striking instance of transfer from Japanese was in her use of the English reflexive. In Japanese, there is an invariant reflexive form, *jibun,* and where English uses the preposition *by,* Japanese uses the instrumental preposition *-de,* equivalent in meaning to the English *with.* When Uguisu first began using the reflexive, she simply used the word *self,* with no prepositional marking, as in *You have to do self, because remember I do self?, I can do it self.* I have noticed native English learners using this simplified form. The next stage was for Uguisu to attach pronouns to *self,* resulting in such uses as *He did it he-self.* At just about the same time, however, Uguisu also began using the instrumental preposition *with,* in cases where *by* would be obligatory in English. For example, *They have to do it with their-self, Make it with your-self over there,* and *You can drive with your-self, couldn't you?* This five-year-old linguist had a representation in Japanese that associated the reflexive with instrumental meaning. She then picked up the English preposition that reflected the instrumental and used it productively to accompany the reflexive.

Another example of language transfer from Japanese could be found in her relatively late mastery of aspects of English grammar that (perversely) indicate subtle meanings that are not made in Japanese. One of them is the plural/singular distinction, as indicated by the *-s* added to the end of most nouns to indicate plurality *(cow, cows).* Japanese makes no such distinction (although the concept of number certainly exists). Another distinction is that between definite and indefinite reference, as marked in the English article system (*Go and read the book* carries a distinctly different meaning from *Go and read a book*). Japanese, like many other languages, does not mark this distinction.

STUDIES IN LANGUAGE TRANSFER

Such instances of native-language transfer could be interpreted in any number of ways, but it is important to note that, historically, transfer came to be associated with the behaviorist's view of language acquisition as habit. Since first-language acquisition was seen as the building up of habits, second-language acquisition was seen as the process of overcoming those first-language habits where the two languages differed and retaining and making good use of the old habits where they were similar (see Rivers 1964 for a superb review). In the early 1960s, there was a strong alliance between behaviorists and linguists who pursued an activity called contrastive analysis, in which grammatical structures of languages were studied for their similarities and differences. The major focus of this alliance was on the detailed contrastive analyses of different languages, in the hope of predicting sources of difficulty in second-language acquisition. One position of this behaviorist–contrastive linguistics alliance was that second-language acquisition must be different from first-language acquisition. As Robert Lado (1964) wrote in his important book *Language Teaching: a Scientific Approach,*

With the first language the child's mind can be thought of as a *tabula rasa* where the patterns become impressed, whereas with a second language the habit patterns of the first language are already there, and the second language is perceived through the habit channels of the native tongue. (P. 6)

Charles Ferguson, then Director of the Center for Applied Linguistics, headed an ambitious project contrasting the phonological and grammatical structures of English with a number of other major languages. In introducing this series, Ferguson wrote:

The Center for Applied Linguistics . . . has acted on the conviction held by many linguists and specialists in language teaching that one of the major problems in the learning of a second language is the interference caused by the structural differences between the native language of the learner and the second language. A natural consequence of this conviction is the belief that a careful contrastive analysis of the two languages offers an excellent basis for the preparation of instructional materials, the planning of courses, and the development of actual classroom techniques. (1965, p. v)

Despite its usefulness, with the behaviorist account of language acquisition coming under criticism, contrastive analysis and the related notion of language transfer were put on trial. The viability of contrastive analysis would probably have come under question even in the absence of habit theory, but with the habit controversy in the background, the attack on contrastive analysis was stronger than it might otherwise have been. Serious doubts surfaced about the adequacy of contrastive analysis in accounting for data from second-language acquisition. Specifically, it both failed to predict all errors that in fact occurred and falsely predicted errors that simply did not occur (Wardaugh 1974).

Like most scientific theories past their prime, contrastive analysis was not given an entirely fair trial. For example, Dulay and Burt (1972, 1973), in a classic study, pitted this view of second-language acquisition against what they called the "L1 = L2" hypothesis. This hypothesis was derived from the contemporary research on first-language acquisition that argued against the habit view and pictured the child as an active agent on the constant lookout for grammatical rules based on innate mechanisms. As implied in the name, the L1=L2 hypothesis claimed that the process of second-language acquisition was the same as that of first-language acquisition.

Dulay and Burt examined errors made by Spanish-speaking children learning English in search of support for either the contrastive analysis position or the L1=L2 position. They considered transfer errors that were "unambiguously" due to native-language transfer as evidence for the contrastive analysis position. On the other hand, developmental errors that were similar to errors normally found in first-language learners were considered to be evidence for the L1=L2 position. (There were a few other categories, but they will not concern us here.) Their dramatic result was that only 5 percent of the errors were attributable to native-language transfer, while a whopping 87 percent supported the L1=L2 position.

The unfairness of this test (and of the consequent overwhelming rejection of the contrastive analysis hypothesis) can be seen by considering what the numbers mean. These percentages are significant only if the units being counted are considered equivalent. In our case, this means that all errors, transfer or developmental, should equally well reflect the second-language acquisition process and that their opportunities for occurrence should be comparable. For every opportunity for a developmental error to occur, there should be an opportunity for a transfer error to occur. Otherwise, a tabulation of the frequencies of each would be meaningless (like noting that there are more outfielders than pitchers on a baseball team and concluding that outfielders are a more important part of the game of baseball).

The cards were heavily stacked against contrastive analysis. A casual look at what kinds of errors were counted as "developmental" shows that they have a high frequency of opportunities for occurrence. For example, Dulay and Burt noted all omission of "functors" (such as the plural -s or articles) as developmental errors, since first-language learners make such errors. Function words are notably frequent in language, and therefore there are frequent opportunities for error in this category. If I say "Two book on table," I have already made three developmental errors.

With respect to the original question that Dulay and Burt asked, about whether second-language learning is better thought of as habit learning or as similar to first-language acquisition in the Chomskyan view, the criticism above is devastating and makes the results uninterpretable. Yet the willingness to put contrastive analysis on such hastily and poorly executed trial indicated that times had changed, that the habit view was out. In any event, the actual numbers aside, Dulay and Burt did successfully show that second-language learners look very much like first-language learners with respect to the kinds of errors they make.

THE MORPHEME SAGA

A microcosm of the interaction between first- and second-language acquisition research can be found in a genre of research nicknamed the "morpheme studies." It is worth describing in some detail, for it exemplifies the ways in which questions regarding native-language transfer were asked using knowledge from research in first-language acquisition.

The word "morpheme" is a technical linguistic term referring to any meaningful word or part of a word that cannot be further dismembered; for example, *mis-understand-ing* consists of three morphemes. In this research, however, its use is limited to a motley set of English noun and verb inflections (such as plural *-s,* possessive *'s,* past tense *-ed,* and progressive *-ing*), the definite and indefinite articles *(a* and *the),* the verb *to be,* and a few others that happened to be studied by Roger Brown (1973) in his influential book on first-language acquisition. From the viewpoint of the range of phenomena that can be found in the grammar of a language, these items are not particularly remarkable. They are, for example, informationally redundant. The sentence "Mommy holding two apple" is missing precisely these items; their addition, to make it "Mommy is holding two apples," adds little information. Brown devoted half his book to the development of this aspect of language, which he called "grammatical morphemes."

Brown was interested in accounting for the order in which these morphemes appear in first-language learners, which is remarkably consistent across different children. He noted, for example, that the order is not explained by the frequency of use of the morphemes in adult speech. The best fit to the data involved complexity of the morphemes in terms of both their grammar and their meanings.

For researchers in second-language acquisition, Brown's study sparked what might be regarded as a minor fad. The reason for the popularity of studying grammatical morphemes was simple. Aside from their intrinsic interest as a perhaps unremarkable yet undebatable aspect of language, grammatical morphemes carried with them a feature that always seems to charm researchers: their suitability as measurement devices (IQ tests in research on immigrants to America became popular in part because they were useful measurement devices). For example, the fact that grammatical morphemes appear with high frequency in ordinary speech meant that enough instances of them could be found in speech samples to allow for measurement. Furthermore, researchers could easily identify contexts in utterances where they should have been used, but were not. Such measurement features, on top of an already existing body of studies from first-language development, produced a considerable number of morpheme studies with second-language learners.

Two questions were of primary interest. First, do second-language learners resemble first-language learners? And second, do second-language learners of different native-language backgrounds go through the same process? Three generalizations can be made. First, the order of appearance of morphemes in second-language learners does not come anywhere near resembling the order found in native learners of English. This finding does not mean that the processes of first- and second-language acquisition are different, however, since the two types of learners are different in respects other than their level of language development. It may be that general cognitive development influences the order found in first-language children. For example, the past tense form may be acquired late because its mastery requires a developed concept of time.

A second finding is that the order of acquiring English morphemes tends to be remarkably similar across children with different native-language backgrounds. Dulay and Burt (1974) compared groups of Chinese- and Spanish-speaking children learning English and found their orders to be practically identical and similar to those obtained from case studies of a Spanish-speaking girl (Hakuta and Cancino 1977) and an Icelandic boy (Mulford, personal communication, 1976).

The explanation for these similarities across different native-language backgrounds has received remarkably little attention in the literature. The general conclusion has gone no further than the claim that there must be common strategies for second-language acquisition that are independent of the native language; it therefore argues against the (now almost strawman) habit theory account. The only notable explanation for the common order is that of Larsen-Freeman (1976), who noticed that the order closely resembled the frequency of these morphemes in adult conversation—the very explanation that was ruled out by Brown as a possibility for his first-language learners. It is ironic that a frequency explanation, which is most consonant with a habit account of language acquisition, is the best account available for evidence that has been put forth as contradicting the habit account of second-language acquisition.

A third generalization is that this common order of English grammatical morpheme acquisition is modified for some of the morphemes by native-language transfer. Uguisu, for example, did not acquire articles and plurals until relatively late. Similarly, Ann Fathman (1975) found in comparing Spanish and Korean children that they differed markedly on just one morpheme—articles, which Spanish has and Korean does not. Annette Zehler (1982) showed in a well-controlled experiment that patterns of acquisition of the English plural were explained not only on the basis of whether their native language marked it, but by the way in which it was marked. Thus, the evidence for native-language transfer continues to appear, particularly in well-controlled studies such as Zehler's.

The morpheme studies are instructive of the way in which first-language research came to be used in the study of second-language acquisition. First a given pattern was found in first-language children that was motivated by concerns relevant to first-language acquisition. The method that yielded the pattern in first-language acquisition research was then applied to second-language learners, but it was usually removed from the question that motivated the first-language analysis. While the researchers in first-language acquisition were looking for explanations of their analysis, the emphasis of the researchers in second-language acquisition was on the method of analysis. The results of this analysis were used to test the question of whether or not there was native-language transfer. If the pattern in second-language learners either resembled that found in first-language learners or, failing that, if the pattern in second-language learners was similar across those from different language backgrounds, that was considered evidence against the contrastive view of second-language acquisition.

The morpheme studies, along with a number of studies on other grammatical structures such as negation and interrogatives, generally suggested the same conclusions as the studies of error types. That is, considerable evidence was brought forth to suggest that second-language learners showed similarities regardless of their native language, yet it proved impossible to do away completely with evidence for native-language transfer.

WHITHER TRANSFER?

Through the research activities we have described, the role of the native language in second-language acquisition was put through a rigorous empirical test. The identification of language transfer with the habit formation of language acquisition, combined with the unpopularity of the latter theory in first-language acquisition, caused researchers to regard language transfer with suspicion. In general, this sentiment led researchers to accept, though with some uneasiness, the results that de-emphasized transfer.

One fact about language transfer must be remembered, however: it is not in fact wedded to habit theory. I would guess that it is compatible with any theory of second-language acquisition, except for some radical ones. A theory that would deny any role of prior experience in the acquisition of new knowledge, for example, would find language transfer incompatible, and a version of radical nativism might claim that humans innately possess the structures of all human languages, so that exposure to a second language merely actualizes the pre-existing structure. But aside from such unlikely possibilities, language transfer could be readily accounted for, and might even be expected, by a non-habit account.

Who, when faced with an unfamiliar language, would not make the most of an already familiar language? By using knowledge of the native language, second-language learners would be following a principle of human development eloquently stated by Werner and Kaplan (1963):

Wherever functional shifts occur during development, the novel function is first executed through old, available forms; sooner or later, of course, there is a pressure towards the development of new forms which are of a more functional-specific character, i.e., that will serve the new function better than the old forms. (Quoted in Slobin 1973, p. 60).

The point here is that transfer need not be seen in habit theory terms. It is perfectly compatible with a mainstream statement of cognitive development.

At present, the most important task facing research is the identification of the conditions under which transfer occurs and the conditions under which it does not. Some of these conditions will be linguistic in nature. For example, Uguisu had difficulty with English articles, but she did not have much trouble with English word order, even though English differs from Japanese in both of these characteristics. A typology of transfer errors based on a careful tracking of those that can be observed would be helpful.

Other conditions for language transfer might have to do with characteristics of the individual learner. For example, I am not sure (in fact, I doubt) whether Uguisu's errors in using the word *mistake* and in using the preposition *with* with reflexives would be found in all other Japanese children learning English. The errors were motivated by her knowledge of the Japanese language, but their occurrence might have been the result of Uguisu's individual "insight" into the relationship between the two languages. My analogy for this possibly idiosyncratic occurrence is that of several Chomskyan linguists sitting around exchanging intuitions about the English language. They all have knowledge of English. Yet even if they were working on the same problem (say, the appropriate description of the sentence), different linguists would come up with different analyses and arguments. Their descriptions would all be derived from the same source of knowledge, English, and they would even share the same form of linguistic argumentation, but what part of it they chose to act upon would be determined by various characteristics of their individual makeup. In a similar way, we would expect that even though there may be a potential for language transfer to occur in second-language acquisition, the points at which it actually occurs may be subject to individual variation.

Another important condition upon which language transfer might depend is the social context of second-language acquisition. Selinker, Swain, and Dumas (1975) conducted an investigation of native English–speaking seven-year-old children in a French immersion program in Toronto. They found a substantial number of transfer errors, such as the following, all attributable to English structure (and certain to mortify the French teacher):

Elle marche les chats. (She's walking the cats.)
Il est trois ans. (He's three years old.)
Il regarde comme six. (He looks like six years old.)
Je vais manger des pour souper. (I'm gonna eat some for supper.)
Le chien a mangé les. (The dog ate them.)
Je juste veux un. (I only want one.)
Le sac a un trou dans le. (The bag has a hole in it.) (Pp. 143–47 passim)

In a classroom where their peers were all native speakers of English, the children were in a unique sociolinguistic situation where transfer errors from English were perhaps more acceptable than they would be in situations with native French speakers.

All these considerations about the conditions for language transfer are reminiscent of the discussion in chapter 4 about the autonomy of the two languages in the bilingual. There we discussed neurological and cognitive psychological evidence concerning whether the bilingual keeps languages in the same store or in separate stores. A major conclusion was that there are conditions under which bilinguals behave as though the two languages are independent, and other conditions under which they appear interdependent. We suggested therefore that the object of inquiry should be the identification of these conditions. Similarly, the most revealing findings about language transfer will be those that tell us the sociolinguistic conditions under which it occurs and those under which it does not occur.

A final remark about language transfer, difficult to resist since

I have not seen it mentioned elsewhere, is that transfer might be seen in the framework of linguistic relativism, in the spirit of Benjamin Lee Whorf. For at the level of grammatical concepts, every bit of transfer demonstrated in second-language learners is a bit of evidence for the notion that the nature of the native language influences the hypothesis, the world view, about language. The ubiquitous *a*'s and *the*'s found before nouns in English may sound like a bunch of nonsense to the Japanese or Korean or Chinese native speaker; to the German or French or Spanish speaker, they are readily known. If second-language acquisition is thought of as a problem-solving task, one might well say that the native language can influence the way in which the problem is solved.

The Role of "Prefabricated" Language

A reasonable caricature of the researcher conducting the genre of studies described thus far would be that of an obsessed grammarian. The child is seen as the discoverer of linguistic structures, whose goal is the acquisition of a logical and fully "generative" language that resembles a Chomskyan grammar. While this may be fine and good as an ideal, the shift in the interest of language acquisition researchers from grammar to meaning and communication signalled a new way of characterizing second-language acquisition.

If it were possible to ask Uguisu to reflect on the process of her second-language acquisition, she would probably tell you that grammar was not the most important thing on her mind. What she did was to learn whole expressions that proved useful in her interactions with friends, utterances like *Don't do that!, Do like this, This is mine, That's not yours, Do you want this one?,* and *I know how to do it* (Hakuta 1974). They were utterances that, as you might imagine in the interactions of five-year-olds, would get things done. Uguisu did not learn these utterances by analyzing their internal grammatical characteristics. She learned them in their whole, prefabricated form. *Don't do that* was not AUXILIARY VERB + NEGATION (CONTRACTED) + MAIN VERB + DEMONSTRATIVE PRONOUN. Rather, it represented the charge to stop doing whatever you were doing. Such prefabricated utterances, though considered uninteresting from the viewpoint of grammatical structure, are of great interest from the perspective of communication. When Uguisu first started using English, well over half her utterances were of this prefabricated variety. Anyone interested in the totality of her language development, then, must in some way account for them.

Uguisu is no exception in her heavy use of prefabricated forms in the early stages of second-language acquisition. Huang and Hatch (1978) report that the first English utterance of a five-year-old Taiwanese boy learning English was *Get out of here,* which he found quite useful. Lily Wong Fillmore conducted a study of five Mexican children between the ages of five and seven who were learning English. A major emphasis of her study was on the numerous prefabricated forms (which she called "formulaic speech") that she observed. Among my favorites of her many examples are *Liar, Panzon fire, Shaddup your mouth,* and *Knock it off* (1979, p. 211).

Over time, prefabricated utterances begin showing evidence of an internal structure. In some way, the child analyzes the components of the whole and begins using the parts in a productive way. One dramatic example from Uguisu should suffice. By her third month in the United States, Uguisu had in her repertoire as a prefabricated form *I know how to* plus a verb phrase. She produced utterances such as the following: *I know how to do it, I know how to make,* and *I know how to draw it cat.* Over time, however, these utterances started showing a subtle but important change. There were utterances such as *I know how do you spell 'Vino'* and *I know how do you write this.* This subtle change occurred gradually over the course of several months. It is a curious progression, because we would expect that if she were relying solely on external models she would stay with what she had. There should have been no particularly strong external pressure for her to change from a "correct" to a deviant form. It is possible to show that what she indeed was doing was constructing an internal grammar that sought consistency among a variety of questions containing *how, what,* and *where* (Hakuta 1974).

The natural question that arises, as the role of socially motivated prefabricated utterances comes to the forefront, is their function in language development in general. Fillmore believes that they command an important role in maintaining the motivational level of the learner. Prefabricated language, because it is embedded in social interaction, is highly memorable. Furthermore, socially embedded language enables the learner to receive feedback from native speakers. As she puts it, "If the learner is not trying out his newly acquired language, he is not in a position to distinguish right guesses from wrong ones and thus discover what he needs to learn" (pp. 211–12). So for Fillmore, prefabricated utterances provide the necessary motivation and feedback for acquiring language.

There seems to be no reasonable doubt that prefabricated language, by virtue of its communicative potential, motivates language acquisition (both first and second). But such a statement is rather like saying that hunger motivates cooking and eating. Communication provides the general raison d'être of language, but it can hardly explain all the characteristics of grammatical structure, any more than hunger can explain the nature of the art of cooking (and the consumption of the results).

Some linguists, however, have suggested that the analysis of communication can be the source of grammatical structures. A general form of the proposition was stated by Evelyn Hatch (1978a): "One learns how to do conversation, one learns how to interact verbally, and out of this interaction syntactic structures are developed" (p. 404). Hatch's speculation, shared by many, was that somehow, in the context of the give-and-take of conversation, linguistic structures could be found. This is quite a different claim from the view that the social interactional nature of language motivates second-language acquisition. Rather, it is a claim for some formal equivalence or specifiable relationship between social interaction and linguistic structure. It is difficult to demonstrate, however, how the specific rules of grammar might be derived from conversational analysis. For example, number agreement between subject and verb in English *(Peter runs; Jill and Peter run)* is difficult to explain in conversational terms.

Ultimately, whether one takes an interest in the extensive use of prefabrications by language learners depends on the definition of language. As I noted in the beginning of this chapter, the study of language acquisition can be looked at from the perspectives of grammar, meaning, and communication, which should be seen as distinct levels of analysis. The levels should not be mixed, because analytically they cannot be (or at least have not been) shown to be equivalent.

A linguist interested in the capacity for acquiring mature linguistic structure, in the Chomskyan definition, would not find prefabricated utterances to be terribly interesting. Such a linguist would want to determine what the learner needs to know in order to analyze linguistic structure. The question of *how* the learner goes about analyzing prefabrications would be of interest, but precisely this information is missing in these studies. So from the grammatical perspective, prefabrications might be only minimally interesting, providing some easily available raw materials for analysis.

Many linguists are not satisfied with such a partial account of language, however. Language clearly serves functions other than being the analytic linguist's tinkertoys. It is the researchers concerned with the generalized functions of language for whom the existence of prefabrications is of interest. Dwight Bolinger (1976) makes the point forcefully:

Our language does not expect us to build everything starting with lumber, nails, and blueprint, but provides us with an incredibly large number of prefabs, which have the magical property of persisting even when we knock some of them apart and put them together in unpredictable ways. (P. 1)

Why do speakers of American English say *a lifetime ago* but not *an extended time ago,* or *somewhere else* but not *sometime else?* We could attempt to build formal rules that will generate the allowable expressions, but Bolinger's interpretation seems persuasive: "We have not heard it done. We have no memory of it" (p. 4).

Studies of the grammatical aspects of language and studies of the broader communicative functions of language are best seen as complementary activities, despite arguments that crop up between advocates of either camp. We all would like to see language whittled down to the bare bones of grammar, while at the same time we appreciate the multiple functions in which it participates. Whether grammar can be derived from communicative functions is an issue that must be settled on theoretical grounds. I personally doubt that it is possible. It would be like trying to explain the engineering structure of the hardware of a computer on the basis of the ways in which society uses the machines.

Are First and Second Languages Acquired in the Same Way?

Whether second-language acquisition is similar to first-language acquisition is an interesting question, but one that has no simple answer. It depends on what aspects of language acquisition you consider to be important. Susan Ervin-Tripp (1974) has remarked that transfer, when seen as an activity in which the learner uses past experience to structure new experience, does not imply that the two processes are different. In both first- and second-language acquisition, learners take the language they hear and use it selectively by building on what they already know. For second-language learners, some of what they already know happens to be the structure of their native language.

From a more linguistic orientation, John Macnamara (1976) noted that "when an infant, a ten-year-old child, and an adult learn Russian, the most remarkable outcome is Russian" (p. 175). Macnamara is more interested in the end product of the language acquisition process. From this perspective, regardless of whether one is learning language the first or second time around, abstract structures must be learned, and for this to happen, the learner must possess certain expectations about language: for example, that it has different parts of speech, rules of grammar, and rules of discourse.

Theorists who emphasize the importance of nonlinguistic, cognitive principles in the acquisition of language, however, would focus on the differences, for second-language learners are generally more cognitively developed than first-language learners. One might characterize first-language acquisition as an interactive process, where the development of cognitive notions triggers a search for linguistic expressions of that notion, and the existence of specific and salient linguistic features stimulates the development of the cognitive notions that they express (Slobin 1973). If the pattern of cognitive development is a critical element in the language acquisition process, then the two processes are best seen as different.

Observed differences between first- and second-language learners are unsurprising, because the latter are, both cognitively and socially, more mature beings. Thus, we are not struck by the fact that second-language learners apparently use more socially embedded prefabricated utterances. Most likely, it is because, along with a more developed memory span, they already possess knowledge about the functional uses of language. As the philosopher J. L. Austin (1975) has put it, they know "how to do things with words."

Second-language learners are also relatively unrestricted in the kinds of meanings they express. Earlier, I mentioned that in the initial stages of first-language acquisition, children express a very limited set of meanings, corresponding to their cognitive developmental achievements. Patsy Lightbown (1977) conducted a semantic analysis of the language of two six-year-old English speakers learning French. She found that from the very beginning, these children expressed a large variety of semantic relations such as manner, intensifiers, and conjunctions. There was not the kind of orderly progression (orderly presumably because of cognitive developmental constraints) found with first-language learners.

Uguisu was similarly eager to learn to express semantically complex ideas from the very beginning. As soon as she was able to produce whole utterances in the form of prefabrications, she was using conjunctions to coordinate them. During the first month, she used *and* and *because;* by the fourth month, she was also using *but* and *so,* and in the next month, she was making *if . . . then* statements. These are not the sorts of constructions that are found in first-language learners until much later stages of development.

All of these differences between first- and second-language learners are not surprising, considering obvious differences in general maturity. They certainly do not suggest that second-language acquisition is qualitatively different from first-language development. First- and second-language acquisition are similar in that they are both examples of the entity called language undergoing change in the context of different mediums. First- and second-language learners represent two such contexts, different in what they bring to the learning situation but similar in their capacity to acquire language and similar in what they end up with through the acquisition process.

How Children Learn a Second Language

Individual Differences Among Children

Uguisu was a very successful second-language learner. So are many other learners who have been reported on in the literature. The studies paint a picture of glowing optimism for children's capacity to learn a second language, but how representative are these children?

There is quite likely a sampling bias, attributable in large part to researchers' intense interest in linguistic structures. One wonders how many children's attempts at second-language learning may have gone unreported because they were unsuccessful or slow, hence uninteresting to the researcher looking for the acquisition of grammatical structures.

Evelyn Hatch, who has supervised a large number of master's theses in second-language acquisition, lets us glimpse a more representative sampling. In the introduction to her book of readings, she mentions a thesis by Denise Young, who started observing three Spanish-speaking children attending an American school. One of them, Alma, learned only minimal amounts of English in eight months. As Hatch writes,

Initially, Young was tempted to drop (Alma) from the study. Then she decided that Alma might be a "late bloomer". . . . Her hypothesis was that once Alma began speaking English, her production would be quite advanced or that she would move much more rapidly through syntactic development stages. This did not happen. When Alma did begin speaking English after eight months, it was the same kind of data that we find in sessions with most learners during the first month of observation. (1978b, p. 12)

Hatch adds that Alma was apparently of normal intelligence, outgoing and aggressive at home. But she was very withdrawn at school. Hatch further observes that in many studies of second-language acquisition, "there is mention of experiences in which the child shows the same frustration, withdrawal, and 'paranoia' as adult language learners" (p. 13).

133

What might be the source of such individual differences? Lily Wong Fillmore made some insightful observations of the personality characteristics of the five Mexican children she studied and tried to relate them to their differential rates of second-language acquisition. She characterized Nora, a highly successful five-year-old, as gregarious and motivated to make friends with the English-speaking children in her classroom. In fact, her friends were exclusively English speakers. Much of her play activity centered around verbal exchange, such as role-playing mothers, babies, and doctors. This was in sharp contrast to Jesus, Juan, and Alej, who were more inhibited and cautious about their English. In addition, Nora engaged in syntactic play that appeared creative:

She said me that it wa' not too raining by she house.
She said it wa' not too raining by she house.
She said she not raining by she house. (P. 225)

Unlike Jesus:

Somebody dance, somebody dance, somebody da, da, da!
Somebody dance, dumbody dance, dumbody da, da, da! (P. 225)

She felt that these differences in activity were related to the children's general personality characteristics, such as Nora's "disposition to figure out how toys, games, and gadgets were put together, and how they worked" (1979, p. 225).

One difficulty with such observations is their subjectivity. I, for one, think that Fillmore is a first-rate observer whose intuitions are better than the finest objective instruments. But we must push the requirement for objectivity to the limit. Unfortunately, the measures of personality characteristics available for use with children are unreliable and difficult to interpret for the majority of the population of children learning a second language. For now, we must be left with these anecdotal impressions of personality differences as a source of individual differences. We will explore this question further in the next chapter, extending the discussion to adult second-language learners.

Another dimension in which individual differences in second-language acquisition have been noted relates to the use of language for different purposes. Language can be used for a variety of functions, from everyday gossip to discussions about bilingualism. In recent years, there has been an awakening of interest in language used for different purposes in different circumstances. One aspect of language use that has attracted particular attention is that of contextualized versus decontextualized use (Olson 1977; Snow 1977; Cummins 1980; Snow 1984). Contextualized language skill refers to the ability "to control the skills associated with face to face conversation, which requires one to monitor one's partner in order to respond effectively and which allows for little advance planning," while decontextualized language skill refers to the ability "to provide a coherent, comprehensible, informationally adequate account without signals from an interlocutor" (Snow, in press). If one were to characterize prior research in second-language acquisition in these terms, it would fall heavily on the side of contextualized use. Fillmore's characterization of individual differences described above, for example, was a characterization of differences in the contextualized use of language in play with other children.

An important question is whether children who are good at contextualized language use are also good at decontextualized language use. It is important not just theoretically but practically, because the language used in academic learning in schools is considered to be predominantly of the decontextualized variety. If it turns out that contextualized and decontextualized language use represent different dimensions of individual differences, then one would have to take a serious look at tests used in assessing language proficiency to see what dimensions of language use they are measuring.

The evidence, though limited, suggests that these two functions of language develop relatively independently. Catherine Snow reports that, in her study of some quite accomplished second-language learners in the United Nations International School in New York, there are low correlations between tasks of contextualized and decontextualized language use, suggesting their independence. That is to say, a skilled conversationalist in a contextualized language task is not necessarily good at decontextualized language use, and vice versa. A second finding of interest was that relative ability in these tasks transferred across languages. Children who were good at decontextualized tasks in English were also good in the same tasks in French, and likewise for the contextualized tasks. These findings have implications for bilingual education and will resurface in our discussion in chapter 8.

Chapter 6

How Adults Learn a Second Language

PETER MARLER (1970), a prominent student of animal behavior, has noted interesting parallels between the development of birdsong and that of human speech. Studying the male white crowned sparrow of California, Marler has found that the song itself is not innately "wired in." In fact, the male must be exposed to the song sometime between the tenth and fifteenth days of his life; apparently even brief exposure to a tape-recorded version of the song will suffice. Biologists call this kind of interaction between maturational readiness and environmental exposure a "critical period." If a male is deprived of a model at the crucial time—for example, if he is raised in isolation—he will develop an abnormal song. This is unfortunate for the bird, since a normal song is essential for maintaining his territory and for attracting a mate.

Like humans, birds have two-sided brains. The left hemisphere is specialized with respect to song. Research with chaffinches shows that if the nerve connections from the left hemisphere in an adult bird are severed, the bird's song is permanently lost or deformed. This does not happen when the same operation is performed on the right hemisphere. The neurological system of the young chaffinch, however, is apparently much more malleable than that of the adult. When the same experiment is conducted with the young, they still develop normal song, regardless of which side is severed.

There have been speculations that human language is similarly constrained neurologically (Penfield and Roberts 1959; Lenneberg 1967). Lenneberg summarized studies of recovery from aphasia (loss of language due to traumatic damage to the brain, usually from head injury or strokes) that supported the notion of a critical period for language acquisition. He argued that the critical period lasted through puberty and that it was related to changes in the cerebral lateralization of function with age. That is, until puberty the human brain is not specialized, at least with respect to language. With the onset of puberty, language functions come to be solidly housed in the left hemisphere of the brain (save for a small portion of left-handed people, who apparently have language in their right hemisphere). In aphasics, loss of language before puberty resulted in recovery, but loss after the critical period, even with large amounts of exposure, was permanent. This picture resembles the situation described by Marler for birds.

Lenneberg also made observations about second-language acquisition, remarking that "the incidence of 'language-learning-blocks' rapidly increases after puberty" and that "automatic acquisition from mere exposure to a given language seems to disappear after this age, and foreign languages have to be taught and learned through a conscious and labored effort. Foreign accents cannot be overcome easily after puberty" (p. 176). Lenneberg's account, in the 1960s, fit well with the initial phases of Chomsky-influenced language acquisition research. In first-language acquisition, it reinforced the belief that the process is to a large extent biologically determined. In second-language acquisition, it went hand-in-hand with Dulay and

Burt's (1972, 1973) claim, described in the previous chapter, that for children, second-language acquisition is identical to first-language acquisition.

If second-language acquisition is so natural and automatic for children because of biological predispositions, the prognosis for adults looks bleak. In this chapter, I evaluate the claim that adults are inferior second-language learners. First, I ask whether adult second-language acquisition is qualitatively different from child second-language acquisition. The conclusion is that there are many similarities. Second, I examine the "difference" question quantitatively. The evidence suggests that older learners show more rapid initial gains in acquisition, but that given sufficient time for learners of different ages to attain their full potential, child second-language learners have the edge. Third, I suggest the limitations of a simple comparison of adults and children, arguing that a large amount of variation exists even among adults and that this variation can be accounted for by a number of individual and social factors.

A Man Named Alberto

In 1973, Herlinda Cancino, Ellen Rosansky, and John Schumann began a detailed study of linguistic characteristics in children and adults (Cancino, Rosansky, and Schumann 1978). Their method was the same as that used in the study of Uguisu (chapter 5). They studied six subjects: two adults, two adolescents, and two children. All six were native speakers of Spanish who were acquiring English without formal instruction.

The analysis focused mainly on grammar. Particularly for negation (*no, not,* and so forth used with verbs), the researchers were able to build a convincing case that all six subjects followed a common sequence of development. Their initial forms reflected Spanish structure and consisted of the morpheme *no* placed in front of the verb. This was gradually replaced by *don't*. Then came a small set of auxiliaries, such as *can't* and *isn't*. The final stage was essentially the native English speaker's system, characterized by the various forms of *"do*-support" such as *doesn't* and *didn't*. The two children and two adolescents seemed to go through these stages relatively quickly and smoothly. For example, by the end of the ten-month observation period none of the four young subjects was using the NO + VERB forms. Neither was Dolores, an outgoing twenty-five-year-old native of Peru with a university degree in public relations. Alberto, a thirty-three-year-old man from Costa Rica, was the exception.

Alberto's negation, in contrast to that of the other subjects, showed no change over time. He kept on using NO + VERB and DON'T + VERB interchangeably. Schumann (1978) showed that Alberto's "fossilization" of development in negation was quite representative of other aspects of his grammar. For example, Alberto rarely produced questions with the auxiliary verb at the beginning of the sentence, and he infrequently used grammatical morphemes (such as past tense -*ed* on verbs). Alberto's marginal acquisition of English, in contrast to that of Uguisu and of the other subjects studied by Schumann, vividly illustrates variation in second-language acquisition.

It is pure conjecture whether Alberto's pattern should be attributed to his age, his personality, or his life circumstances. We will follow up on these possible sources of variations in second-language acquisition later in the chapter.

Do Children and Adults Acquire a Second Language in the Same Way?

Alberto's development, it seems, was qualitatively similar to that of the adolescents and children in the study. The stage at which Alberto's grammar had fossilized, as Selinker (1972) put it, was one through which the other learners had moved in their course of development. To say that child and adult second-language acquisition is qualitatively similar is merely to say that development takes the same route in both; it does not say how *far* along the route any particular learner might go. That is the quantitative issue.

The evidence for the qualitative similarities and differences between child and adult second-language acquisition can be divided into direct and indirect comparisons. Direct comparisons contrast children with adults, while indirect comparisons show that adults, like children, demonstrate systematic, rule-governed linguistic behaviors, though the exact patterns of development may not be directly comparable.

THE DIRECT EVIDENCE

Direct comparisons of the qualitative aspects of child and adult second-language acquisition are rare, but the results (such as those in the study including Alberto) suggest overall similarities. In a study by Bailey, Madden, and Krashen (1974; Krashen 1981), the order of acquisition of English grammatical morphemes (discussed in chapter 5) obtained from adults of different native languages was compared with that of children; they were very similar.

Also relevant are analyses of errors made by children and adults. In general, children and adults make similar kinds of errors. Simplification and overgeneralization of grammatical

141

rules have been reported in child and adult second-language learners (see, for example, Duskova 1969; Richards 1973). These errors are also found in first-language acquisition, as we saw in the previous chapter.

Other studies that compare adult second-language learners with child first-language learners also support the conclusion about qualitative similarities between children and adults. Alison d'Anglejan and Richard Tucker (1975) found that adult French-speaking military personnel attending English language classes at a base school made the same kinds of errors in comprehension that first-language children make. For example, they both misinterpret a sentence such as "Jim promised Peter to read his letter," concluding that Peter is doing the reading.

INDIRECT EVIDENCE

In an ideal world for investigating a developing grammatical system, there would be correspondence, visible to the researcher's naked eye, between different aspects of grammar. Take, for example, two aspects that we have already encountered: negation *(Plato doesn't like fish)* and questions *(Does Aristotle like octopus?)*. There is a common grammatical rule that appears in both of these aspects, called "number agreement," that governs the relationship between the number of the subject (singular or plural) and the auxiliary verb, *does* or *do*. It is the rule that accounts for the changes found from the examples above to these: *Aristotle and Plato don't like fish* and *Don't Plato and Aristotle like octopus?*

In this ideal world, the language learner would show evidence of commonality between these two aspects of grammar with respect to the number agreement rule. When this hypothetical individual learned the number agreement rule, it would appear in both negation and auxiliaries in a predictable way. Such an event would be strong evidence that the learner is developing in a systematic, nonrandom manner, consistent with predictions from grammatical theory. At present, this is not the case.

What has been shown in a number of studies, however, is that an overall index of grammatical development can predict development in different aspects of grammar. Just as in economics, in which an overall index of vitality—the Gross National Product—is shown to correlate with a number of more detailed assessments of sectors of the economy, one can infer from such evidence that the different sectors are interrelated, for if they were not, they would not correlate with the overall index.

Herlinda Cancino and I (Cancino and Hakuta 1981) studied adult Puerto Rican second-language learners of English in the greater Boston area. The subjects had varying amounts of education and of formal instruction in English, mostly grammar taught in Puerto Rican schools. We conducted standard analyses of their grammatical structures, and we also created various experimental tasks for them, such as imitating sentences and repeating stories.

For these subjects, we constructed an overall index of grammatical development that was based on their English vocabulary and a number of subjective ratings of their fluency. We were able to show that this global index very accurately predicted the extent of development of various grammatical structures, including the now familiar negations, questions, and grammatical morphemes.

Similar results have been obtained, using quite different procedures and subjects, by John Schumann and his colleagues at UCLA (Hinofotis et al., unpublished paper). They found that an interview procedure developed by the Foreign Service Institute for assessing global oral language skills was effective in predicting development in a subset of grammatical morphemes.

Evidence for systematization was also demonstrated in a study of Italian and Spanish "foreign workers" in Heidelberg, West Germany (Klein and Dittmar 1979). A careful analysis of minute grammatical details of sentences, summed up in an overall index of development, turned out to "accord well with our intuitions about the syntactic elaborateness of our informants" (p. 124).

All these studies suggest that adult second-language acquisition is systematic (Corder 1971; Nemser 1971; Selinker 1972). Someone who is proficient in a second language will perform better in all aspects of grammar than someone less proficient. Granted, we still lack a coherent account of how the language system ties together the many structural features of language, but the results of the studies so far are encouraging.

QUALITATIVE SIMILARITIES CONSIDERED

The suggestion that child and adult second-language acquisition are qualitatively similar requires some qualifications. First, the nature of the evidence is highly tentative. The patterns may be similar for trivial reasons, such as an artifact of the researcher's analytic procedure. Terms such as those I and other researchers throw around—"stages of negation" and the like— are fancy terms that refer to idealizations whose fit with the data are far from perfect.

Second, all this research is based on the *product* of second-language acquisition. There is no way to observe the actual *process* of acquisition. Even if we were to find similarities in the products of development, the processes that produced them may not be the same. It could well be that language as a formal system is so powerful that any route toward its mastery, no matter what the procedure, would result in similar patterns of development. To draw an analogy, there are probably many different ways to learn to ride a bicycle. Different people may approach the task in different ways, and sources of errors in the process may be quite different, but the scrapes and bruises that result from the learning process (or failure thereof) can be extremely similar because of characteristics inherent in the task.

Quantitative Differences Between Children and Adults

In attempting to account for why Alberto's English fossilized at an early stage, Schumann appealed to social psychological factors. He claimed that in terms of basic intelligence, "Alberto was normal and that he had no gross cognitive deficits that would prevent him from acquiring a second language" (1978, p. 68). Rather, Schumann argued that Alberto maintained a social and psychological distance from the English-speaking community. He worked in a factory where the majority of his co-workers were non-English speakers, mostly Greeks. In general,

he made very little effort to get to know English-speaking people. . . . He stuck quite close to a group of Spanish-speaking friends. He did not own a television, and expressed disinterest in it because he could not understand English. On the other hand, he purchased an expensive stereo set and tape deck on which he played mostly Spanish music. Also, he chose to work at night as well as in the day, rather than attend English classes which were available. (P. 97)

Whether this explanation is the whole story we do not know, nor do we know how social psychological factors apply more generally.

In the remainder of the chapter, we will make the assumption that the development of individual learners can be characterized by simple indices of selected aspects of their language. This simplifying assumption enables us to ask whether there are differences between children and adults in the overall *extent* to which they learn the language.

THE EVIDENCE FOR AGE-RELATED CHANGES

Roberto Bachi (1956) analyzed census data from 15,600 foreign-born males who had immigrated to Israel and were living in Tel Aviv in 1949. (I thank Martin Braine for providing me with this somewhat obscure reference.) Bachi was able to summarize the extent to which these men reportedly used Hebrew (their second language).

The data are crude, because the extent to which one reports using Hebrew is only loosely related to one's ability in the language. Nevertheless, the cast of thousands in this study affords some advantages over the cast of one in Schumann's study. We can look, for example, at the effects of the backgrounds of individuals, including age and length of residence in Israel, on reported use of Hebrew.

Bachi found that, by and large, all age groups showed an annual increase in their use of the second language until about their fifth year of residence in Israel. Beyond this period, none of the groups showed further gains in second-language use.

Bachi further found that the level at which the second-language use reached a plateau was lower in the older than in the younger age groups. This might appear to support the notion of a critical period for second-language acquisition, at least as measured by the extent of use of the second language. However, as Braine (personal communication, 1982) has pointed out, the subjects in their twenties resembled the adolescent age groups more closely than they did the subjects in their thirties and forties. This is certainly not very compatible with the idea of a critical threshold at puberty. Rather, there appears to be gradual but steady decline with increasing age.

Crude as these census data are, they are remarkably similar to the data from other studies that have been conducted with more refined measurement techniques. Susan Oyama (1976, 1978), for example, conducted a well-controlled study with professional-class Italians who had immigrated to the United States at various ages. Oyama measured both pronunciation and sentence comprehension in global terms. For pronunciation, she played tape recordings of her subjects' narratives to native English-speaking judges and had them rate the degree of accent. Sentence comprehension was measured by playing recordings of sentences with interference noise and testing for the subjects' ability to repeat back the sentences. From the viewpoint of scientific objectivity, these measures are several steps above the self-reports of the Israeli census.

Oyama looked for the effect of length of exposure. She found none, probably because all of her subjects had been in the United States at least five years. In Bachi's Israeli study, once the men had been in Israel five years, the length of their residence made no difference on their use of Hebrew. In other words, it may be that once a person has been exposed to the new language for a considerable period of time—somewhere around five years on average—length of exposure is no longer an influential factor.

Oyama did find strong effects for age of exposure in both pronunciation and sentence comprehension. Regardless of length of exposure, the younger age groups were more nativelike. Those who had arrived in the United States when they were between six and ten years old were more fluent than the eleven-to-fifteen group, who in turn were more fluent than the sixteen-to twenty-five group.

The influence of exposure time was studied more specifically by Lee Williams (1974). The study represents the strategic use of a single phonetic feature of language in research and bears some detailed description. In both English and Spanish, the sounds /ba/ and /pa/ are distinguished by a physical parameter called the Voice Onset Time (VOT). If you make these sounds and pay attention to the time lag between the initial burst of air from your lips and the vibration of your vocal cords, you will notice that they are different. For /ba/, the lag is almost nonexistent, while for /pa/, it is considerable. Through a voice synthesizer, it is possible to create sounds that differ only with respect to VOT and to ask subjects if a given sound is a /ba/ or a /pa/. It turns out that native speakers of English consider a VOT of twenty-five milliseconds to be an important boundary. If VOT is less than twenty-five milliseconds, they hear

147

/ba/; if it is longer, they hear /pa/. Furthermore, they have difficulty distinguishing between two sounds that differ in VOT if their difference does not span the twenty-five-millisecond boundary.

Native Spanish speakers, when played the same set of sounds and given the same task of labelling them as /pa/ and /ba/ in Spanish, place their boundary at a VOT of zero milliseconds, compared to twenty-five milliseconds for English speakers. The question can therefore be asked where second-language learners place their boundary and whether this boundary location depends on the background characteristics of the learners.

Williams's subjects were native speakers of Spanish in the United States who varied in two background characteristics: their length of exposure to English (zero to three and one-half years) and the age at which they were initially exposed to English (eight to sixteen years old). She found evidence for the role of both factors. The subjects who had been exposed to English longer more closely approximated the English twenty-five-millisecond boundary, and younger subjects more closely approximated the English boundary than did the older ones.

Williams's finding that varying length of exposure makes a difference does not contradict Oyama's findings. The upper limit of Williams's range of exposure was three and a half years, while Oyama's lower limit was five years. After the initial years, the major variable becomes the age of the learner. Studies that look at subjects whose length of exposure extends beyond five years (a time period that is necessarily arbitrary and whose value will depend on conditions of exposure) might be called *ultimate level* studies, because the effects of exposure have by and large levelled off. Williams's study, on the other hand, looked at short periods of exposure. Such studies might be called *initial gains* studies; what they show are the effects of the initial progress made by learners of different ages.

In general, ultimate level studies suggest that those who learn a second language in childhood (before puberty) are more successful than those who acquire it as adults. This is true not just for accent (Asher and Garcia 1969) but for grammar as well (Patkowski 1980).

The initial gains studies, on the other hand, suggest an advantage for the older learner. For example, Catherine Snow and Marian Hoefnagel-Hohle (1978) looked at American children and adults living in Holland and learning Dutch during their first two to three years of exposure. Subjects were tested on the same set of tasks, tapping pronunciation, auditory discrimination, vocabulary, morphology, and a variety of other aspects of their second-language ability. All subjects were tested at four- to five-month intervals, and all showed quite consistent gains in these measures over time, but the twelve- to fifteen-year-old children performed better overall than younger children on most of their measures. The one exception was in phonology, where there were no differences between the groups.

EVALUATING THE EVIDENCE

The conclusions drawn from the studies require some rigorous examination and qualification. Let us start with the initial gains studies, which suggest, to put it crudely, that getting older means getting smarter, and the smarter you are, the better you should be at learning most things, second language included. This proposition sounds true, but I do not find the studies themselves terribly convincing. Initial gains studies by definition involve subjects with short exposure to the second language, where the important variable is age of initial exposure.

Bear in mind that in the studies of ultimate level, all subjects are adults when they are tested, because of the long time lag between their initial exposure and the time of testing. That is not the case with initial exposure studies, where even at the time of testing some of the subjects are still children. It is simple arithmetic. A child who arrived in Sweden at age five and is tested after three years of exposure to Swedish is still only eight years old. By comparison, a subject who arrived at age fifteen would be eighteen years old. Initial gains studies assume that their tests are comparable when administered to an eight- and an eighteen-year-old.

Snow and Hoefnagel-Hohle did make some effort to adapt their tests for the youngest age groups, but the older child has clear advantages regardless of the test. I have in mind such things as attention span, memory capacity, ability to decipher the experimenter's intentions, and test-taking experience. These considerations make it difficult to know whether the older children and adults outperform the younger ones because they have indeed learned more language or because they are simply better test-takers. Both factors are probably responsible.

A similar consideration comes up in evaluating the results of the phonological aspects. Williams's study is spared because of the highly objective nature of her data, but studies involving raters are shaky. In Asher and Garcia's study, high school students rated the degree of accent in children and adults. The raters agreed well with each other, so that is no problem. However, a six-year-old's voice is clearly different from a twenty-five-year-old's. The raters heard the speech of all the subjects across all ages in random order. The researchers felt that in this manner the ratings of the younger children could be compared with the ratings of the older children and adults, on an absolute scale. When you think about it, however, most people rate a child's performance relative to the child's peer group. For example, when I think that a six-year-old boy tells good jokes, I am comparing him with other six-year-olds I know. I cannot imagine how I could reasonably compare him with, say, my neighbor across the street. Asher and Garcia claim that the youngest children were rated on the average as having a "slight accent," while the oldest were rated as having a "definite accent." I do not understand how these are directly comparable since we do not know whether the raters applied the same objective standards for all age groups. Such are the difficulties that plague cross-age comparisons.

The studies of ultimate level are also not without problems. These studies indicate that with increasing age there is a steady decline in the extent to which a second language is acquired. It should be emphasized, however, that none of the studies are longitudinal; that is, they do not follow the same group over a period of years. The Bachi study, for example, is a single, cross-sectional sample. We have learned from studies of life span development that there can be considerable cohort effects, where there are differences between different age groups due to such historical facts as the amount of public education available to different generations (Schaie and Strother 1968; Schaie and Geiwitz 1982).

Caution is therefore warranted as to the generality of these findings. Can the conclusions be generalized to groups beyond those who have been studied—beyond, for example, the professional-class Italian Americans of the late twentieth century studied by Oyama? Very little attention has been paid to such variables as the social class of the subjects and the sociolinguistic circumstances under which they were exposed to the second language.

A second caution concerns whether the language learner is rigidly constrained by internal characteristics or whether (and to what extent) the environment and social context play a role. It is ultimately an empirical question, but it is one worth raising because of the seductive invitation to conclude that nothing can be done about natural patterns of events. The research findings suggest that, under the conditions observed, older learners on the average have lower ultimate attainment. The malleability of the individual thus becomes a critical issue in considering where one goes from here. At stake is whether this pattern is observed because of dispositions in the learner or because the learner is responding to external pressures of the environment. In other words, is the locus of responsibility for this pattern in the individual, who for some biological or developmental reason has become stubbornly resistant to a new language? Or is it to be found in the environment, the social circumstances that influence "social psychological variables" such as attitudes and intergroup dynamics, which in turn condition second-language acquisition? The former view of the individual I will label as *hardened,* the latter as *malleable.*

I believe that the weight of the evidence moves us away from attributing the pattern of lower attainment to the hardened individual. A biological explanation, at least one formulated in terms of a critical period like that found in Marler's birds, is simply not compatible with the data. The idea that second-language acquisition is limited by a critical period for language acquisition would suggest a sudden decline at around puberty. None of the presently available evidence supports this prediction. In fact, the existence of a developmental timetable for the neurological basis upon which Lenneberg originally proposed the idea of the critical period for language (the onset of lateralization of language in the left hemisphere) has been seriously questioned (Krashen 1973; Kinsbourne 1975).

If it is not something like a critical period that differentiates between children and adults, then what is it? As I argued in chapter 4 in discussing (and criticizing) the attempt to typologize bilinguals into "early" and "late" bilinguals, the notion of age has little explanatory power. For a developmental psychologist, it is something to get away from as quickly as possible. How can that be accomplished?

Factors Determining Individual Variation

One way to get a handle on the issue of age is to disregard it and to look instead for individual differences within age groups. Consider a study by Patkowski (1980), briefly noted earlier, in which he compared the proficiency of adults who had learned English as a second language, either as children or as adults. What he found was that on average, those who learned English as children were more proficient than those who learned it as adults. He also found, however, that there was wide variation within each of the groups, particularly among those who had learned English as adults. In fact, the best adult learners were no different from the child learners. If we could understand the causes of variation within each of these groups, then it might be possible to apply these findings in understanding the overall differences between child and adult learners. For example, it may turn out that good adult learners have more open attitudes toward foreigners. From this, we might speculate that the differences between children and adults have to do with the more open attitudes that children generally hold toward unfamiliar people.

We are nowhere near such a happy situation, but a whole array of variables has been put forward to explain individual differences among adults (who are broadly defined to include adolescents). The explanations range from "internal" qualities to "external" situational factors.

INTELLIGENCE AND LANGUAGE APTITUDE

Basic intelligence is a commonly cited explanation. In the study of second-language acquisition, intelligence is frequently referred to as "language aptitude." We owe the term to John Carroll, a psychologist who created a test called the Modern Language Aptitude Test (MLAT) that was designed specifically to predict performance of students in foreign language courses (Carroll and Sapon 1958). The test measures abilities that are considered important for learning language, including the ability to code the sounds of language, the ability to recognize grammatical structures, and rote memory.

Language aptitude generally is a better predictor of performance than are tests of general intelligence, but the overlap is considerable, so they are often used interchangeably. An extreme position in this area is expressed by John Oller and Kyle Perkins (1980), who write that "many of the bits and pieces of skill and knowledge posited as separate components of language proficiency, intelligence, reading ability, and other aptitudes may be so thoroughly rooted in a single intelligence base that they are indistinguishable from it" (p. 2).

The success of language aptitude tests in predicting the grades of high school students in a foreign language course is undeniable. Estimates vary, but it is safe to say they predict about one third of the variance in foreign language grades* (Jakobovits 1970). Robert Gardner and Wallace Lambert (1972), who have conducted research on this subject in Canada but with extensive replications in the Philippines and the United States, support this finding. Basically, students with high aptitude tend to perform well in foreign language courses. Similar results have been obtained with college students (Oller and Perkins 1980).

Less well researched is the question of whether language aptitude plays a role in adult second-language acquisition in less formal settings. Since measures of language aptitude have mainly been created for use with English-speaking learners of foreign languages, they are totally inappropriate with native speakers of non-English languages—the subjects of the majority of studies that have been conducted thus far. We can obtain only crude estimates of something like language aptitude. For example, in Klein and Dittmar's study (1979), the amount of education that the subjects received in their native country was found to be a rough indicator of language aptitude.

---

*The "percent variance accounted for" is an indication of the strength of the relationship between two features. For example, heights and weights of people are related, enabling us to guess that on average, a tall person would tend to be heavy and a short person light. The larger the amount of variance accounted for by a relationship, the stronger it is.

About 9 percent of the variance in their overall syntactic index in German is accounted for by this variable, a sizeable proportion.

In a study in which Hinofotis et al. (1982) report the overall ratings of the oral proficiency of seventeen adults, a similar trend can be noted. And finally, in the Cancino and Hakuta study (1981) of fifty-seven adult Puerto Ricans, the number of years of education accounts for 16 percent of the variance in overall English proficiency when the length of stay in the United States is statistically taken into account. Moreover, in this study a measure of Spanish vocabulary was also administered. This variable accounted for 13 percent additional variance, over and above the contributions of years of stay and amount of education.

Language aptitude, as indicated by crude measures of years of formal education as well as by more refined measures such as vocabulary tests, thus appears to influence adult second-language acquisition even in these informal contexts.

PERSONALITY

Initial impetus for an explanation relating to personality differences came from Alexander Guiora and his associates at the University of Michigan, who have a psychoanalytic orientation (Guiora, Brannon, and Dull 1972). They were interested in constructs such as "empathy" and "permeability of ego boundaries" to account for individual differences in second-language acquisition. In one rather striking experiment that attempted to reduce inhibition, Guiora gave subjects cocktails with varying amounts of alcohol prior to a task in which they were to pronounce Thai words (none of the subjects had studied Thai). Native speakers of Thai found the pronunciation of the groups ingesting medium amounts of alcohol to be the most authentic. Unfortunately, there are many alternative explanations for the results, and further experimentation has yielded mixed results (reviewed by Schumann [1975]).

Neil Naiman and his associates at the Ontario Institute for Studies in Education (Naiman, Frohlich, and Stern 1975) have made the most systematic, albeit exploratory, study of the relationship of personality variables to success in foreign-language acquisition by high school students. Following a thoughtful review of the personality literature, they looked at a variety of personality variables, such as outgoingness (introversion-extroversion), the ability to perceive figures independently from their context (field dependence–independence), and tolerance for ambiguous situations. They found some systematic relationships. For example, field dependence–independence and tolerance for ambiguity were both related to success as a student. To date, these research findings have not been replicated, but interest in personality variables is likely to continue because of their intuitive appeal.

Although his work is not specifically related to any particular personality theory, Stephen Krashen (1981) proposes that second-language learners vary in the extent to which they consciously monitor their utterances. Krashen claims that individuals subject their verbalizations to varying amounts of editing.

For example, Krashen and Pon (1975) report the case of P, a middle-aged native speaker of Chinese who had begun learning English some time in her twenties and had studied it in college. They asked her son, a native speaker of English, to watch errors in her everyday English. Whenever an error occurred, the son would present the error to her. The authors report:

We were quite surprised to note . . . that our subject was able to correct nearly every error in the corpus (about 95%) when the errors were presented to her after their commission. In addition, in nearly every case she was able to describe the grammatical principle involved and violated. (Quoted in Krashen 1981, p. 13)

Despite her conscious knowledge of the rules (the product of learning, in Krashen's terminology), P hardly used it to monitor her utterances.

Krashen cites the contrasting case of a student in an English as a Second Language class who compulsively monitored his speech:

> In a segment of conversation that lasted slightly less than fifteen minutes, there is not a single lengthy utterance that is not filled with pauses, false starts, repetitions, and other speech repairs. . . . There are over 69 . . . instances of repair (not counting pauses). . . . [His written compositions—] produced in a situation where extreme monitoring is possible—are among the best in his section (Birnbaum 1976, cited in Krashen 1981, p. 15)

A consequence of the approaches that emphasize personal dispositions of individuals—be they empathy, field dependence, or use of self-monitoring—is that their orientation tends to be deterministic. In other words, to the extent that personality variables are important in setting the degree of second-language acquisition, there is little one can do for the unsuccessful language learner.

A somewhat more resilient view of the individual can be found in social psychological and sociolinguistic approaches, which are further down the continuum toward situational emphases. According to these views, the learner is increasingly seen to be embedded in the social situation that, in a sense, has a life of its own. Differences in second-language acquisition are seen as a function of where the individual fits into this matrix of social variables.

ATTITUDES

The main focus of research in attitudes and second-language acquisition has been on the orientation of the learner toward the speakers of the target language. Gardner and Lambert

(1972) were the pioneers in this area, working primarily with native English-speaking high school students learning French in Canada.

The direct way to measure this kind of attitude, which has been coined "integrative orientation," is simply to ask the learners whether they endorse statements about why they want to learn the second language, such as "It will help me to understand better the French people and their way of life" or "It should enable me to begin to think and behave as the French do." The indirect method, developed by the same researchers, is called the "matched guise" procedure. In this task, subjects are asked to listen to a series of tape recordings of the voices of native French and English speakers and to rate them with respect to various personality traits that would indicate whether the subjects liked them or not—for example, whether they are dependable or not, intelligent or stupid, and so forth. Unbeknownst to the subject, the voices come from fluent bilinguals, so that what is heard is a French and an English version of the same person, thus avoiding the possibility that subjects are rating the speakers on the basis of voice quality. This procedure provides a measure of how the subject feels toward French speakers.

Gardner and Lambert found that the direct and indirect methods of measuring attitude yield similar results. More importantly, they found that students with higher integrative orientation—those who are positively disposed toward the French-speaking people and culture—perform better in French, as assessed through various tests. The importance of a positive attitude toward the target language has been shown in a variety of foreign-language learning contexts in Canada and the United States. Reviewing twenty-nine studies from Canada tested with a refined Attitude Motivation Index, Gardner (1980) found that attitudes account for a median 14 percent of the variance in French grades.

Attitude, as measured in these contexts, appears to be independent of language aptitude. For example, Gardner reported that only a median 1.4 percent shared variance between his language aptitude measure and the attitude measure in the twenty-nine samples. Thus there appears to be a solid finding, at least for foreign-language students in much of North America, that aptitude and attitude contribute independently to the degree of second-language learning.

How do we know that positive attitudes result in more second-language learning, rather than that more second-language learning results in more positive attitudes? Longitudinal studies might provide some answers, but they are costly and have not been carried out. Rather, the argument has so far been indirect, based on the fact that the families of the subjects share their attitudes. For English-speaking families, Gardner and Lambert summarize:

Students with an integrative disposition to learn French had parents who also were integrative in outlook and sympathetic to the French community. The students' orientations were not, however, simply a reflection of their parents' skill (or lack or it) in French or of the number of French acquaintances the parents had. That is, the integrative motive is not simply the result of having more experience with French at home. Rather it seems to depend on the family's attitudinal disposition. (1972, p. 5)

Other attitudinal orientations besides an integrative one can apparently lead to successful second-language acquisition. Gardner and Lambert have identified an attitudinal component that they call "instrumental orientation." Although this component has been less well researched, their studies suggest more learning for subjects who report motivation to learn French for reasons such as "I think it will some day be useful in getting a good job" or "One needs a good knowledge of at least one foreign language to merit social recognition" (p. 148).

The labor involved in constructing decent measures of attitudes is immense. Gardner and Lambert have done a heroic job of demonstrating the importance of attitudes and motivation, although longitudinal data are still required to make a solid case for their causal role. (More recently, Gardner [1983] has employed a complex and sophisticated statistical technique called causal modelling to try to infer causation from correlational data, with promising results.) In addition, there is the general problem that studies attempting to show a correspondence between attitudes and behavior often do not find a strong relationship. The more specific the questions in an attitude scale are to the particular behavior in question, the more predictive the scale is; the relationship between very generalized attitudes and specific behaviors is close to nonexistent.

A common criticism of attitudes as a construct is that they do not sufficiently take into account the situational variables, including the situation in which the measurement is being taken. A questionnaire may reflect what the subject perceives to be appropriate responses as well as true attitudes. Nevertheless, a focus on attitudes rather than on personality characteristics emphasizes the malleability and adaptive nature of adult second-language acquisition.

SITUATIONS

The world is complex, and the importance of any given variable, such as attitude, in one societal circumstance is no guarantee that it will be important in another circumstance. Specifying these numerous parameters is an important task for sociolinguistic research. Of critical importance here is the nature of the target language group and where the learner is seen to fit within it. For example, Joshua Fishman and his colleagues (Fishman, Cooper, and Ma 1971) conducted an extensive study of the Puerto Rican community in Jersey City, New Jersey, which can safely be considered a bilingual community. Among their many findings, more of which I shall refer to in the next chapter, was the selective use of Spanish and English depending on social-institutional functions. That is, the choice of Spanish or English systematically varied according to whether the speakers were conversing about intimate topics or about formal institutional ones.

Fishman did not address specifically the problem of the acquisition of a second language, focusing instead on the functional uses of two languages in a community of people who are, to varying extents, already bilingual. It is not hard to imagine, however, how a sociolinguistic view would be important for adult second-language acquisition. Depending on who you associate with, when, and where, the kind of language you hear will be different. Unfortunately, sociolinguistics is a young discipline and has not been applied systematically to the problem of variation in second-language acquisition. A few nibbles at it, however, can be reported.

Klein and Dittmar (1979), in their study of Italian and Spanish guest workers in Germany, found that the best single predictor of their level of German syntax was the amount of leisure-time contact with Germans. Cancino and Hakuta (1981), on the other hand, in the study of adult Puerto Ricans, found that rather than their number of English-speaking friends, the best predictor of their English (other than length of stay, years of education, and Spanish aptitude) was the extent of English used at work. There are many ways of interpreting this pair of results, but I would stress that both of these observations are more or less descriptive of the kind of language situation the learners were exposed to (certainly not rich descriptions by sociolinguistic standards, but better than nothing). It is possible to interpret the contact situations in these cases as reflections of a generally positive attitude toward the target language, but that is not a necessary interpretation, since the emphasis is on description. We will closely examine the problem of sociolinguistic descriptions of bilingualism in the next chapter.

Toward Integration

In concluding this chapter, I should make my own biases clear about where I see the structural aspects of second-language acquisition, described in the first part of the chapter, fitting in with the different factors contributing to individual variation, described in this latter section. Like most researchers in the structural tradition, I consider the qualitative characteristics of a learner's linguistic change over time to be the manifestation of language-specific capacities of the individual. The majority of the different forms that we find in second-language learners are the result of the internal workings of the learners' language acquisition capabilities, in combination with the nature of the language that they hear as their model. For example, the fact that Alberto says *The people no have money* rather than some other variant such as *The people have money no* is primarily due to native language transfer and other, yet unspecified *linguistic,* not social, processes. On the other hand, the quantitative aspects of development, the reason why Alberto's English apparently showed so little change in the direction of the target language, was some combination of the candidate variables mentioned—aptitude, personality, attitude, and situational circumstances. The nature of this combination merits attention.

There is little doubt that the factors are, in principle, separable. That is to say, for example, that knowing a person's verbal aptitude will not necessarily tell you much about the person's personality or attitudes toward the speakers of the target language. Furthermore, each of these factors has been tied to differential success in second-language acquisition under certain conditions of observation, that is, using certain measures of second-language acquisition with certain types of subject populations. The task is to relate the conditions of observation to the background characteristics of learners.

Gardner (1983; LaLonde and Gardner 1984) presents a theory

of second-language acquisition that can be interpreted in this framework. He proposes a fundamental distinction between learning in formal (classroom) and in informal contexts, a distinction that we can speculate to be roughly equivalent to the distinction between contextualized and decontextualized language use (chapter 5). These two contexts can be seen as different conditions of observation. Gardner shows that personality and attitudinal factors are related to second-language use in both informal and formal contexts, but that aptitude is related to language in classroom contexts.

Krashen (1981) suggests that a major difference between informal and formal language situations is the extent to which one is able to monitor one's performance. In face-to-face natural communication, there is little time for monitoring, as there is in formal situations where considerable reflection is possible. Krashen suggests that the monitor is the product of an academic process of conscious learning of grammar and that degree of mastery of grammar is related to language aptitude. Thus, in situations where monitoring is possible, aptitude makes a difference since those with high aptitude will have better monitoring. On the other hand, aptitude fails to make a difference in situations where monitoring cannot occur, in contexts of informal language use.

The relationship between background characteristics and conditions of observation is bound to be a complex one. For example, while Gardner found that aptitude was important only for second-language use in classroom contexts, several other studies have showed a relationship between aptitude and informal learning. Quite obviously, we need a better understanding of the conditions under which aptitude does and does not make a difference in informal language situations.

One should bear in mind that correlations between factors, such as between individual characteristics and language learning, are relativistic concepts. Correlations are always at the mercy of the range of variation in each of the factors. For example, if there were no variation in the extent of second-language acquisition—that is, if everyone in a population learned a second language to some acceptable level—then there obviously would not be any variation to be accounted for. The point is that the importance of factors is expected to change depending on the sociological conditions of second-language acquisition. Thus, in cultures where people are expected to be universally bilingual, one might find that neither aptitude, personality, nor attitude predicts second-language learning. On the other hand, in cultures where a second language is primarily academic in nature (say, the use of French in most parts of the United States), range in French ability may be exclusively dependent on aptitude factors. One can also imagine a situation in which personality is the main variable—a particular teaching method that appealed only to certain kinds of students, for example. In all these settings, one would expect that aptitude, personality, and attitude will show different degrees of importance in predicting different kinds of second-language use. Different bilingual settings, the sociolinguistics of bilingualism, is the subject to which we now turn.

Chapter 7

Bilingualism in Society

ENGLISH was not built into the Constitution of the United States. In fact, John Adams's proposal to set up a national language academy, which would give English the official stamp of approval and prescribe its "proper" usage, was debated by the founding fathers and rejected. The proposal was deemed incompatible with the spirit of freedom in the United States (Heath 1976).

Despite the lack of constitutional protection, English in the United States has come to enjoy a privileged position perhaps unmatched in the annals of human language. Its dominance has been ensured by pressures applied at the institutional level, primarily in the public schools, and by the psychological needs of immigrants to learn English so that they might fully achieve membership in American society. The goal of this chapter is to reveal the institutional and symbolic meanings of language in bilingual societies in general, but I will begin with an explanation of how English has become so dominant in the United States.

Bilingualism in the United States

In its short history, the United States has probably been host to more bilingual people than any other country in the world. One of the most fascinating aspects of bilingualism in the United States is its extreme instability, for it is a transitional stage toward monolingualism in English. Each new wave of immigrants has brought with it its own language and then witnessed the erosion of that language in the face of the implicitly acknowledged public language, English.

The rate of decline of non-English languages in the United States is noteworthy indeed. For example, in 1940, 53 percent of second-generation white Americans reported English as their mother tongue; in their parents' generation, only 25 percent had English as their mother tongue (Lieberson, Dalto, and Johnston 1975). That is a substantial shift in just one generation.

A further indication comes from a comparison of the 1940 and 1960 census figures (Fishman and Hofman 1966). During this period, there was a 16 percent decline in the number of speakers of non-English languages. The number of speakers of Czech, Danish, Finnish, Norwegian, Slovenian, and Swedish, for example, declined by half or more. The only languages to register any increase were Spanish and Ukrainian, reflecting fresh reinforcements from new immigrants in these groups, but even here there have been rapid shifts toward English in recent years (Veltman 1980).

The rate of loss of language diversity in the United States is even more remarkable when compared with that of other nations. Lieberson and his colleagues found an overall decline in language diversity across the thirty-five nations they studied, reflecting the general tendency toward monolingualism, but in no other country did the rate approach the rapidity of the decline in the United States. At the rate of change observed in other nations, it would take 350 years for the average nation to experience the same amount of loss as that witnessed in just one generation in the United States.

There are, of course, reasons aplenty for learning English, many of them economic. Very few people can thrive in this country without a good working knowledge of English. For example, the 1980 census asked people who were not native speakers of English to rate their own ability to speak it. They were asked to say whether they could speak English "very well," "well," "not well," or "not at all." For native speakers of Spanish, the median reported 1979 income among men who claimed to speak English "very well" was $10,938; for "well," $9,592; for "not well," $7,873; for "not at all," $6,083. The same strong relationship holds for speakers of other languages. Under these circumstances, it is hardly surprising that immigrants concerned with the economic well-being of their offspring would encourage them to learn English. This encouragement, however, has typically gone hand in hand with reduced efforts to maintain the native language. There is something of a hydraulic pattern in the dynamics of the two languages. The two languages appear to be competing for limited linguistic space, so that the primary outcome is displacement.

Part of the hydraulism can be traced to aggressive policy decisions to eradicate non-English languages from the public schools, most vividly witnessed at the height of nationalism and xenophobia during the First World War. Bearing the brunt of this policy were the German-Americans, nine million strong in 1910, who had been struggling to maintain their language on American soil through religious and community organizations, German-language newspapers, and German schools.

Until this period, there had been considerable tolerance of instruction in German in both public and private schools. Beginning with Wisconsin in 1854, a number of states had passed laws preventing school authorities from interfering with the use of German (or, in many cases, any foreign language) in the public schools. These included Illinois, Iowa, Kansas, Minnesota, Indiana, and Nebraska. Erosion of this tradition of tolerance for German had begun by the late 1880s, and with the rise of anti-German feelings peaking in 1919, these permissive laws were repealed; German was barred not just from many private and public schools but also from public meetings, telephone communications, and the streets. The scene became positively ugly (Kloss 1966).

These laws prohibiting the use of foreign languages in the schools were declared unconstitutional by the U.S. Supreme Court in 1923, but the damage had been done. The effects of the legislation in eradicating German from the public schools can be seen dramatically by comparing statistics on the percentage of students in high school who were enrolled in German classes. In 1915, 24 percent of the students were enrolled in German classes. By the time of the next set of figures, in 1922, the number had dropped to one-sixth of one percent. German in the public schools had been dealt a severe blow whose impact can be seen to the present day.

As Glenn Gilbert (1981), who compiled these statistics, has remarked, "The concerted and speedy action to drop German, which was taken in unison by independent local and state school boards across the country, is truly frightening. An educational decree issued from a centralized dictatorship could have hardly done it better" (p. 262). Through such institutional processes, coupled with the highly negative value placed on the language, the German-speaking immigrants had been subdued into a tiny linguistic minority. Kloss noted that "no other nationality group of equal numerical strength and living in one country has ever been so wellnigh completely assimilated" (p. 249).

The Germans were not the only group to suffer from linguistic repression. Other notable examples include the Japanese-Americans, who were moved to internment camps during the Second World War and whose Japanese-language schools were closed down, and Hispanics, who until the 1960s were commonly punished for using Spanish in school (Laosa, in press). Linguistic repression has not been the only agent of rapid language shift in the United States, however. In fact, as students of the history of immigrant languages have observed, the United States policy toward immigrant languages has generally been one of benign neglect. Fishman noted that "by and large, more linguistic and cultural treasures have been buried and eroded due to permissiveness and apathy than would ever have been the case had repression and opposition been attempted" (1966, p. 30).

Another reason for the rapidity of the loss of the native language in the United States has been the work of the educational psychologists, whom we closely scrutinized in chapter 2. It will be remembered that they gave bilingualism a bad press and buttressed the advice of school authorities who urged parents to give up the non-English language at home. It was not until the 1960s that the habit-learning view of second-language acquisition, tied to the contrastive analysis movement and discussed in chapter 5, began to be questioned. In this view of language learning, the suppression of native-language habits was thought to facilitate the acquisition of English.

It is evident that the notion of a trade-off between the native language and English is a popular conception of bilingualism. For example, in surveying the language use of Italian-Americans in San Francisco, Correa-Zoli (1981) found that the most common reason the respondents offered for not maintaining Italian was "to learn English quickly and be Americans" (p. 252).

Yet another reason for the American hydraulism, perhaps the most powerful of all, involves the close relationship between language and values and social identity. For obvious reasons, evidence of this relationship can be found only in detailed personal accounts such as autobiographies. One such is the story of Richard Rodriguez (1982), the son of Mexican immigrants who settled into a primarily white neighborhood in the Sacramento area of California. Rodriguez grew up speaking only Spanish at home. His autobiography describes his painful experiences not only in learning English but also in leaving the security of his ethnic home to become a member of American society.

Rodriguez paints a sharp distinction between the two spheres of his life, the private and the public, and the place of language in each of them. One sphere centered around the language of his home (Spanish) and the other around the language of his public persona (English). Spanish was family, protection, intimacy. English was the outside, the public, the unfamiliar. As young Rodriguez progressed through school, he went through a transformation from a Spanish to an English identity. "Nights when relatives visited and the front rooms were warmed by Spanish sounds," he wrote, "I slipped quietly out of the house" (p. 51). This shift was encouraged by his parents, who despite their own lack of control of English accepted the advice of the Catholic nun teachers at his school to make every effort to speak English at home. Dinner-table conversation ceased as his parents mumbled their English. The parents were even willing to take the scorn of their intimates to let "Ricardo" become "Richard."

When Richard transformed himself from a private Spanish identity to a public English one, language was not the only thing that changed. Richard had detached himself from his Mexican society. His lack of fluency in Spanish was seen by relatives and family friends as a rejection of their society and values. Rodriguez tells of one recurring encounter:

A long-time friend of my father from San Francisco would come to stay with us for several days in late August. He took great interest in me after he realized that I couldn't answer his questions in Spanish. He would grab me as I started to leave the kitchen. He would ask me something. Usually he wouldn't bother to wait for my mumbled response. Knowingly, he'd murmur: *"Ay Pocho, Pocho, adónde vas?"* And he would press his thumbs into the upper part of my arms, making me squirm with currents of pain. Dumbly, I'd stand there, waiting for his wife to notice us, for her to call him off with a benign smile. I'd giggle, hoping to deflate the tension between us, pretending that I hadn't seen the glittering scorn in his glance. (Pp. 29–30)

In viewing his own cultural identity, Rodriguez sees the development of his public identity to be at the expense of a private one; in his world, there is insufficient space for both. He is bewildered by the suggestion of advocates of bilingual education that students can learn school skills essential for public success while at the same time preserving their cultural (and private) identity:

Behind this screen there gleams an astonishing promise: One can become a public person while still remaining a private person. At the very same time one can be both! There need be no tension between the self in the crowd and the self apart from the crowd! Who would not want to believe such an idea? Who can be surprised that the scheme has won the support of many middle-class Americans? If the barrio or ghetto child can retain his separateness even while being publicly educated, then it is almost possible to believe that there is no private cost to be paid for public success. (Pp. 34–35)

Rodriguez uses his own experience to blast away at bilingual education (more on this in the next chapter). But must one's values be hydraulically set? It would seem, rather, that there are conditions under which a hydraulic value system could be adaptive, and others under which a non-hydraulic, additive bilingualism could be adaptive.

A glimpse at differences among individual value systems can be seen in a study by Irvin Child (1943), who conducted a classic investigation of acculturation among second-generation Italian-American men in New Haven. Child found three types of reactions to the conflict between their identities as Italians and as Americans. The rebel reaction sought active acceptance as an American; the in-group reaction maintained active ties with the Italian community; and the apathetic reaction was characterized by avoidance of situations that created conflict between the two systems.

Among the rebels, Child found avoidance of the use of Italian, as evidenced in the following comment by one subject:

For two Italian-Americans to speak together in Italian would be considered ill-advised, ill-bred, and ill-educated. . . . [Why do you avoid speaking Italian?] As I said before, I have no occasion to do so, no opportunity. And I'm not going to speak it to entertain other people, because I want to be an American. And as long as I can dissociate the Italian in me, I want to do so at all times. (P. 101)

Among the rebels, Italian was seen as acceptable when it carried high social prestige. The various nonstandard Italian dialects spoken by the group in New Haven were seen by this group to be stigmatized. Some subjects interviewed by Child found Italian to be useful for entry into social clubs that were very largely American, but only if it was standard Italian, not the local dialect: "Truthfully, I'd like to speak Italian, but not the dialect. We're a low class of people and all have the dialect" (p. 102).

Those characterized by the in-group reaction tended to value their Italian and used it actively. This group expressed interest in having their children learn Italian: "I wouldn't like them to forget the Italian nationality or the Italian language" (p. 142). The attitudes of the apathetic group were reflected in their views about the preservation of Italian. As Child wrote, "In general, the apathetic informants do not express pride in their ability to speak Italian as a mark of membership in the Italian group, nor do they feel they should hide this skill in order to gain acceptance in the American group" (p. 176).

In seeking the sources of these different types of reactions, Child offered the suggestion that "various individuals adopt a particular type of reaction because of quite different determinants in their own life histories" (p. 193). For example, he noted the source of one individual's rebel reaction:

This informant was from early childhood unusually submissive to authority. His parents encouraged his transferring to his teachers his submissiveness to their own authority by, for example, urging him to respect and obey his teachers just as he did them. Partly through the cooperation of his parents he became highly responsive to the wishes of his teachers, and adopted rather early in life many goals derived from his perception of them and other Americans. When, after graduation from high school, he obtained a job in which his associates and his superiors were non-Italian, his accustomed submissiveness to authority increased the reward-value for him of conforming to their norms; in addition, the early training by his parents reduced the amount of anxiety that he felt in rebelling against them so long as he was still conforming to authority." (Pp. 192–93)

The personal accounts found in Rodriguez's autobiography and Child's observations illustrate the competing value systems of the two cultures of the immigrant, the old world and the new world, and how the languages associated with them can be part of the individual's life choices.

The tensions between the use of the mother tongue and English may be viewed as a series of stages related to social mobility. At first, according to Donald Taylor (1980), members of the new immigrant group relate their disadvantaged status to their own personal characteristics, including motivation, intelligence, and basic abilities, and to their social status in their country of origin. We have seen, in chapter 2, that members of the majority can take an active role in reinforcing this belief, by denigrating genetic quality and bilingualism. At this stage, members of the minority will learn English for economic reasons, but not with the belief that it will improve their social status. They are poorly motivated to speak English as a native does. At this point, too, there are comparatively greater rewards for maintaining the ethnic language, since individuals are jockeying for better positions within the minority group. This period constitutes the first stage of upward mobility and is characteristic of the first generation of an immigrant group.

Taylor's second stage comes when some people in the group begin to show upward social mobility by identifying with the advantaged majority. These individuals continue to attribute their social position to their own internal characteristics, but now they are highly motivated to learn English, expecting improvement in their social status. They consciously avoid speakers of the native language. At this stage, the two languages are competitive, and the native language is in fact seen to be a personal liability for upward mobility.

The third stage, which Taylor calls "consciousness raising," comes about as the minority group realizes that all but its most extreme assimilationists are prevented by the majority group from continued upward social mobility. At this point, group members dramatically change their explanation of social status, from internal characteristics to discrimination by the powerful majority. They come to realize that mobilization of the group as a whole is crucial to a rise in status for themselves, and they attempt to raise the consciousness of the entire group. The ethnic language can play a large role in mobilizing the group, the most notable recent example being the movement among Hispanic Americans to maintain their Spanish. At this point, the two languages are no longer seen as being in a competitive relationship but rather an additive one.

Despite these sorts of explanations, the rapidity of the language shift in the United States remains a deep mystery. After all, immigrants have come from so many different places, language groups, social classes, and educational backgrounds, and at so many different times, that a shift of such massive proportions in the direction of monolingualism would not seem fated. But the puzzle must remain a puzzle, at least given our present state of knowledge.

Some Other Bilingual Communities

When we talk about the relationship of language to social life, we are in the domain of sociolinguistics, populated by a motley group of scholars with backgrounds in sociology, political science, anthropology, and linguistics. They make a profession of digging out and displaying those relationships, and their research is not only widely scattered in many professional journals but widely diverse in methodology and questions asked.

The best way to describe the work in this area is to sample it. I have selected four examples, including research among the tribes of the Northwest Amazon, the inhabitants of Oberwart, Austria, and the Puerto Ricans of Jersey City, New Jersey, as well as a large-scale depiction of bilingualism in Canada. The cases provide a good sense of the intriguing and unusual linguistic phenomena brought to light by sociolinguists, and they illustrate the eclectic set of instruments through which we can look at the problems of policies regarding bilingualism in society.

THE NORTHWEST AMAZON

There is an area along a tributary river to the Amazon, spanning the border of Brazil and Colombia, where at least twenty-five different languages are spoken in a region no larger than New England. Oddly, perhaps, a dense concentration of languages such as this does not always assure bilingualism. If groups are separated by sharp geographical features and/or hostility, they tend to be linguistically isolated and monolingual; when contact must be made, such as for trade, they use a variety of language known as "pidgin," which normally consists of extremely simple rules and words borrowed from each of the languages involved. This is not the case in the Northwest

Amazon, however, according to anthropologist Arthur Sorenson (1967), who spent several summers of research there. Sorenson found that the population in this area has rampant multilingualism.

The customs surrounding identity and marriage are central to the linguistic situation. Individuals are identified by their native language, but social conditions necessitate bilingualism. To communicate with members of other tribes, most individuals must learn another language, Tukano (one of the tribal languages), which has come to be accepted as the lingua franca. Intertribe communication is common, because the tribes are not hostile and the culture of the region is quite homogeneous. Perhaps the strongest factor leading to multilingualism is a rule barring marriages between persons who have the same mother tongue and thus belong to the same tribe. The Indians consider marriage within the same language group to be incestuous. In fact, they express astonishment when told of the Western practice of marriage within the same linguistic group.

In courting a prospective bride, a young man must learn the language of her tribe. Upon marriage, the bride moves into her husband's tribal unit and must learn its language. Their children start by learning the mother's language but soon also learn the father's tribal language, the language by which they are identified. By adolescence, most children are trilingual in their mother's language, their father's language, and the lingua franca.

The multilingualism does not stop there. Because there are women from many different tribes in any given tribal unit, the children are exposed to even more languages. Sorensen writes,

I observed that as an individual goes through adolescence, he actively and almost suddenly learns to speak these additional languages to which he has been exposed, and his linguistic repertoire is elaborated. In adulthood he may acquire more languages; as he approaches old age, field observation indicates, he will go on to perfect his knowledge of all the languages at his disposal. (P. 678)

The Indians here consider it odd to be asked how many languages they know. Multilingualism is a way of life in this unusual community.

What is particularly striking about Sorenson's account is the observation that languages serve as markers of one's familial-tribal origin but that no particular language seems to be specialized for particular social situations. The choice of what language to use appears to be quite casual. As Sorenson noted,

Each individual initially speaks in his own father-language during such a conversation in order to assert his tribal affiliation and identification, but after a while the junior persons change, without comment, to the [language of the tribal unit where the conversation takes place], to Tukano as the lingua franca, or to another language, whatever one is most convenient for the others. (P. 678)

The multilingualism of the Northwest Amazon appears to be founded on an egalitarian basis. Although the lingua franca, Tukano, is a language identified with a tribe, there is no cultural significance attached to this fact. It is even reported that native speakers of Tukano resented the fact that missionaries found their language to be the only one worth learning (Jackson 1983). Cases such as this are important in showing that institutionalized bilingualism is not necessarily related to deep social divisions and conflicts, a fear expressed by many critics of bilingualism.

OBERWART, AUSTRIA

Another well-described community of bilinguals, this one showing considerably more change over time than the situation just described, can be found near the present-day border of Austria and Hungary, about sixty miles directly south of Vienna, in the city of Oberwart (Gal 1979). Oberwart's long history, described in captivating detail by Gal, dates back a full thousand years, when it was settled as an agricultural community where Hungarian was spoken. Its geographical location has played a key role in its linguistic character. The Turkish invasion of the region in the 1500s forced most of the Hungarians in the surrounding communities to flee, but the Oberwarters remained. After the invasion, the area was resettled by people who were ethnically and linguistically German, making Oberwart an isolated Hungarian-speaking community. In the mid-1800s, however, the town had a large influx of German-speakers, attracted by its growing role as a commercial and railroad center. Unlike the resident Hungarian-speakers, the German-speakers were not farmers. They came as merchants, artisans, and bureaucrats. Thus Oberwart became socially stratified along linguistic lines. As the character of Oberwart changed from agricultural to commercial, the language of prestige increasingly came to be German.

The strength of German was magnified at the end of the First World War, when the territory including Oberwart was transferred from Hungary to Austria and German became the official language. The rise of the Third Reich led to the official banning of Hungarian in the schools. The isolation of the Oberwarters from Hungary was symbolically completed at the end of the Second World War, as the Hungarian border was sealed off from Austrian Oberwart. As Gal describes it, "on the Hungarian side, a barbed wire fence, armed sentries in a string of look-out towers, and a mine field mark the boundary" (p. 55).

The postwar economic boom changed the character of the labor force among the Hungarian-speaking Oberwarters. By 1964, less than 20 percent were full-time farmers and over one-third were employed in business and industry (Gal, p. 56). As the Hungarian-speakers entered the mainstream German-speaking economy, the language of the home, Hungarian, has come to assume an increasingly restricted role. Gal summarized it as follows:

It would not be too extreme to say that Hungarian spoken mostly by peasants and former peasants symbolizes the old way of life, the old forms of prestige of the peasant community. These values are now being rejected by all but the oldest bilingual Oberwarters. In contrast, the educated upperclass of Oberwart consists of German monolinguals. The world of schooling, of employment, and of material success is a totally German-speaking world. The language itself has come to symbolize the higher status of the worker and the prestige and money that can be acquired by wage work. While Hungarian is the language of the past and of the old, German is seen as the language of the future, of the young people who are most able to take advantage of the opportunities that Oberwarters feel exist in the German-speaking world. (P. 106)

Gal spent a great deal of time living among the bilingual Oberwarters and documented the conditions under which the two languages are used. The main determinants are who is speaking to whom and whether anyone else is present.

In one household a young man of about twenty-five and his thirteen-year-old niece were joking together in the kitchen speaking German to each other. The man's mother was also there cooking. When the young man, in the midst of his conversation with the niece, asked his mother something, he said it in Hungarian, the language in which he always addressed his mother. The addressee was the only factor that had changed in this situation. (P. 122)

Apparently, the presence of monolingual Germans invariably results in a switch to German, regardless of where the conversation takes place. The women always pray in Hungarian, although they vary in the amount of German they normally use otherwise. Younger members of the community tend toward greater use of German with most interlocutors, although there is much variation.

Most differences between individuals can be accounted for by their social relationships. For example, János Vonatos and Sándor Ács were both in their early thirties. They were from similar peasant backgrounds, and both had skilled jobs. Vonatos worked at the railroad station, switching tracks and hooking trains. Ács was the foreman at the county's water control department. Both men worked primarily with monolinguals. The main difference was in their social network.

Vonatos liked to spend his leisure hours drinking and playing cards at the inn at the railroad station, where most of his friends were monolingual police officers and office clerks. Vonatos had minimal contact with his relatives, even with his in-laws.

In sum, for [Vonatos] the only possible source of pressure to conform to peasant norms in language choice, despite his status, came from his in-laws, who were relatively far away and who, having long ago given their land to their daughter, were relatively powerless to influence him, at least through material inducements. Any pressure from other kin, work mates, and even neighbors would not have been toward peasant norms. These people had little reason to want or expect [Vonatos] to act in ways other than the worker they knew him to be, to use anything but German in most interactions. (Pp. 147–48)

Ács spent his moments of leisure at the inn near his residence, which was not frequented by his fellow workers. The patrons of the inn were primarily from a peasant background. His favorite companions were a peasant, an unskilled laborer who raised pigs, and a carpenter. They had all been friends since grade school. Ács lived in the same neighborhood as his mother and brothers, and they frequently helped each other out. Gal summarized Ács's situation as follows:

They lived in the same neighborhood, depended on each other for help and drank together. The symbol of solidarity and trust for these people was Hungarian, especially in black market transactions. If for some reason the carpenter had rejected his linguistic symbol, which most of his contacts expected of him, I suspect they would have interpreted it as a rejection of them and of their values. Had they collectively labelled him untrustworthy, pretentious, or unsociable, he would have been left nearly alone socially. (P. 150)

Language in this bilingual town of Oberwart, then, is strongly related to social ties of individuals and their identification with distinct value systems associated with German and Hungarian.

THE PUERTO RICAN COMMUNITY IN JERSEY CITY

Joshua Fishman and his colleagues from Yeshiva University rented an apartment in Jersey City, New Jersey, in the heart of the Puerto Rican community in this highly urbanized city. The apartment provided the home base for an ambitious study of the bilingual community (Fishman, Cooper, and Ma 1971). In the midst of rapid loss of non-English languages in the United States, this community served as an example of apparently stable bilingualism. Several of the team members lived in the apartment during the four months of the project, participating in the life of the Puerto Rican community and observing the conditions under which Spanish and English were used.

The bilinguals of this community had a conscious awareness of the alternating uses of the two languages, reflecting the values embedded in the languages. Consider the following account by a young man of the time he told his father about a scholarship he had received from a Hispanic youth organization:

In Spanish I told him . . . I approached him in Spanish because I knew what would happen. So I, no, but I was expecting to have a favorable reaction, not an unfavorable, and I said, "Papi, me dieron la beca para asistir a un colegio en Massachusetts." And he said, "Oh, sí, y cuánto cuesta eso?" Right away, you know, "How much does it cost?" I said, "Well, they're giving me a scholarship." Le dije que era una beca, and you know, I explained about the scholarship, in Spanish, and he says, ". . . You can't go away." And I said, "Why not?" "Because you have no,"—this he said in English, which surprised me—"there's no supervision. You have no supervision if you go away." I said, "What do you mean? Do you think I'm still a child? I'm eighteen years old. I have nothing, you know, to hide from you and you know who I am, and you should have a little trust in me." "Pero"—and he starts in Spanish

—"no, eso no es la cosa, que tú siempre no entiendes las cosas. . . ."
(P. 262)

From careful observations and interviews such as these, Fishman arrived at a list of five "domains," in each of which either Spanish or English was consistently used: family, friendship, religion, employment, and education. These domains, he felt, were anchor points of distinct value systems that in turn are related to the alternating use of English and Spanish.

To confirm that each of these domains carried with it different expectations for whether Spanish or English would be used, Fishman and his colleagues conducted several studies. In one study, they constructed hypothetical conversations that differed in terms of their interlocutors, place, and topic. The combination of these factors determined the congruence of the conversation in terms of what language would be expected. For example, a highly congruent conversation would be a conversation with a priest, in a church, about how to be a good Christian. Highly incongruent would be talking with your employer at the beach about how to be a good son or daughter.

High school students were asked to imagine themselves in hypothetical conversations, where two of the three components of the situation mentioned above were given. The subjects were asked to provide the missing third component. They might be asked, "You are talking to someone in your place of work about how to do your job in the most efficient way. To whom would you most probably be talking?" (p. 631). They found that the subjects tended overwhelmingly to provide congruent answers for any given domain. Furthermore, when they were asked to rate the probable language in which they thought the hypothetical conversation would take place, they were consistent. The most likely place for Spanish was the family domain, followed by friendship, religion, employment, and education.

In another study to validate the concept of domains, Fishman analyzed the results of a "language census" that he conducted with everyone living in the neighborhood of his Jersey City apartment. The effort was important because the questionnaire followed a method akin to that used in official censuses that include questions about language (such as the United States census mentioned earlier), but Fishman was able to ask considerably more questions that specifically addressed language use. As predicted, Fishman found that there were several clusters of language use to which Spanish and English were differently related. Spanish was associated with home and religion, while English was associated with work.

These attempts to find evidence for the existence of domains of language use are by no means infallible. One suspects, for example, that responses to questionnaires of the sort used by Fishman are influenced by the respondent's perceptions of what the investigator is after. Self-report data are notorious for not matching up to actual behaviors. Nevertheless, the effort is laudable in its attempt to link the levels of institutional categories such as education and religion with actual behavior.

A COUNTRY CALLED CANADA

Canada has done a good job of keeping track of the linguistic composition of its residents. Information is available on their mother tongue and their current ability to speak the two official languages, French and English. Such information provides grist for the analytic machinery of demographers. They can create indices of bilingualism and of mother-tongue retention and see what demographic and institutional forces are related to them. Stanley Lieberson (1970) has made extensive use of these official data to look at patterns of bilingualism and of language shift (and retention) among the bilinguals.

Lieberson's analyses take cities as their unit of analysis. For example, for each city, it is possible to compare the percentages of those who become bilingual among those whose mother tongue is English with those whose mother tongue is French.

The results show that bilingualism among both of these groups is related to the city's proportion of other-tongue speakers. For both groups, the more they were a linguistic minority in the city, the more likely they were to become bilingual.

There were, however, differences in the amount of pressure exerted on English- and French-mother-tongue groups. Apparently, it takes a greater concentration of French speakers to induce bilingualism in English natives than it does English speakers to induce French natives to become bilingual. For example, in cities that have 50 percent or more English-mother-tongue individuals, most of the French natives become bilingual. On the other hand, even in cities where French is the mother tongue of 80 to 90 percent of the residents, less than 50 percent of the English-speaking natives become bilingual. This pattern is a strong indication of the dominance of English over French in the overall linguistic composition of Canada.

Much of the pressure toward bilingualism in both groups can be seen as occupational. Overall there is a greater rate of bilingualism among men than among women, largely because of the greater participation of men in the labor force, a labor force that is highly English-dominant (Lieberson supports this contention with analyses of other data, such as the Yellow Pages of telephone directories of the various communities).

The picture is sharpened when the difference in bilingualism between men and women is compared with the linguistic composition of the community. In both English- and French-mother-tongue groups, the sex difference increases as a function of the increased percentage of residents in the overall community with French as the mother tongue. For the French-mother-tongue group, this means that when their language group is in the minority, everyone must become bilingual, so the sex differences are minimal. With an increase in French speakers, however, the pressure to learn English decreases, but less so for those participating in the labor force. For the English-mother-tongue group, when they are in the majority, most remain monolingual, and since the occupational demands for French are minimal, the sex difference is negligible. With increasing French composition, the occupational pressure to learn French, over and above the overall community pressure, results in a larger proportion of bilingualism in men. (Since the data were collected in 1961, when women participated in the labor force less than at present, it would be illuminating to compare these results with current figures.)

The community pressure toward bilingualism apparently has little impact during early childhood. The index of bilingualism becomes more responsive to community pressure during the school years, but the pattern of the sex difference mentioned above does not appear until early adulthood.

Simple logic suggests that bilingualism per se is a necessary but not sufficient condition for mother-tongue shift. For example, populations will not shift from French to English as mother tongue without some intervening period of bilingualism, and language choice results in greater use of English. Lieberson investigated factors associated with mother-tongue shift, which could be estimated for individual cities over time. French was retained across generations as a function of bilingualism in the French-mother-tongue group. There are two striking features in the data. First, there is almost 100 percent retention of French in cities where less than 80 percent of the French-mother-tongue population is bilingual (and thus can speak English). Retention of French drops rapidly in cities with over 80 percent bilinguals, resulting in language shift to English. And second, dramatic as the result may seem, there is tremendous variation in retention of French in cities where more than 80 percent is bilingual.

Lieberson points to a number of other factors that chip away at the large variation in French retention among the different cities. These include the mother-tongue composition of the city and the neighborhood; whether schooling is available in French; the type of employment available (which results in differential pressure to learn English); mating patterns; and the communication utility of the languages.

From the demographer's seat, sifting through the vast quantities of information collected by the government, Lieberson has drawn a rich and dynamic picture of bilingualism and language shift in Canada on a grand scale.

The Micro and Macro Levels of Sociolinguistics

The linguistic communities just described are in states of relatively stable bilingualism that apparently depend on different factors. It would be instructive to speculate about the elements that would be required for changes to occur in the linguistic circumstances of these four communities.

For the Indians of the Northwest Amazon, whose multilingualism is based on the marriage system and on values attached to language itself, change would involve changes in deeply rooted customs and taboos and in the individual's very sense of identity. For the Oberwarters, change would also involve changes in the values attached to the two languages. It might take a movement (analogous, say, to the "back to the land" movement of the United States in the 1960s), with Hungarian reflecting the new value system, to bring about changes in the relative positions occupied by German and Hungarian.

Bilingualism in the Puerto Rican community of Jersey City, on the other hand, seems to hinge on the concept of domain of language use. The establishment of institutional boundaries between languages is what preserves the bilingualism of the community. Thus change would come about with the breakdown of these institutional separations of language. The use of English at home and Spanish in school and at work would dissolve the distinctiveness of the two languages in terms of their uses, leading toward monolingualism. Similarly, in Canada a shift in bilingualism would be expected with changes in occupational demands for either language or with changes in the demographic composition of cities with respect to their concentration of language groups.

It is instructive to note that distinct levels of discussion are used in the descriptions of the relative stability of bilingualism in these communities. On one level, the emphasis is on the values attached to particular languages in the construction of an individual's social identity. This is the case with the Northwest Amazon and Oberwart. Another level emphasizes larger social institutions, such as schools and occupations and cities, which appear to impose conforming uses of the two languages. These can be witnessed in the studies of Jersey City and Canada.

Emphasis on either level—the micro and macro levels of sociolinguistics, as they are called—is commonly related to the disciplinary and philosophical inclinations of the investigator. Anthropologists and ethnographers commonly engage in micro-level investigations of bilingualism, sociologists and demographers in macro-level studies.

Sociolinguists of the micro-level persuasion believe that institutional categories are irrelevant to their goal. They want to be able to explain bilingual behavior by demonstrating relationships between a person's choice of language and its expression of the person's values and communicative needs. They are impatient with the abstractions of the macro-level sociolinguists, who claim the importance of sociological categories without explaining how they might arise. They are more sympathetic with the view of human action as motivated by the search for meaning in a world full of chaos and conflict—a view that has led sociologists Stanford Lyman and Marvin Scott (1970) to name the enterprise after Camus, as "a sociology of the absurd." For them, social order arises out of values expressed through language use, much as in the realm of language acquisition grammar is seen to arise out of discourse patterns.

Macro-level sociolinguists, on the other hand, believe that institutional boundaries are vital and that they impose constraints on individual behavior. While the macro-level sociologists concede individual variation within institutional categories, they consider this abstraction necessary to form broader generalizations about culture.

To appreciate the divergence in views between the macro and micro levels, consider a particular type of macro-level sociolinguistic description called *diglossia* (Ferguson 1959). (Although originally used to describe the differential use of two varieties of a single language—a "high" and a "low" variety—depending on the situation, the term has been extended to the two languages of the bilingual situation.) Macro-level sociolinguists, such as Joshua Fishman, consider diglossia to be an important condition for the existence of stable bilingualism—a situation that can be found in contemporary Paraguay (Rubin 1968) and Tanzania. According to Fishman, without diglossia bilingualism is unstable and usually results in a shift to monolingualism in the more prestigious language:

Under what circumstances do the speech varieties of languages involved lack clearly defined or protected separate functions? To answer briefly, such circumstances are those of rapid social change, of great social unrest, of widespread abandonment of earlier norms before the consolidation of new ones. In such circumstances, children typically become bilingual at a very early age, while still largely confined to home and neighborhood, since their elders (children of school age and adults alike) carry into the domains of intimacy a language learned outside its confines. (1971, p. 547)

This is a situation—bilingualism without diglossia—that might be considered typical of bilingualism as commonly found in the United States. English rapidly becomes the language of the home, and unless the immigrant language is protected through some other institutional means, such as through an ethnic language school or a church, there will be a shift to English monolingualism.

Micro-level sociolinguists, such as John Gumperz, reply that such institutional separation of languages, while reported by individuals, does not hold up under observation. For example, in a bi-dialectal town in northern Norway, informants told him, as expected from diglossic theory, that "everyone in our town speaks only village dialect, except in school, church or in some formal meetings" (1982, p. 62). Yet his examination of actual tape recordings, sentence by sentence, showed considerable switching into the standard dialect even outside of these institutional boundaries. Gumperz claims to have found similar discrepancies in the Puerto Rican community in Jersey City reported by Fishman.

What is more important, Gumperz contends, is that valuable information is lost when data are aggregated into domains in macro-analysis. For example, bilinguals differ widely in the degree to which they use either of their languages consistently, even in similar situations with the same people. Further, and more interestingly, people switch languages for metaphorical purposes even within a given utterance. None of this, he contends, is captured by the abstract methods of the sociologist.

The scuffles between the macro- and micro-level sociolinguists may appear to the outsider to be a petty argument among academics, having to do with a particular *method* of investigation rather than with substantive theory (Fishman 1983). Actually, the issue is of utmost theoretical importance—how to parcel out the causal chain of events in bilingual societies. The macro-level approach emphasizes the importance of societal institutions and thus makes individual behavior a consequence of forces operating at this abstract level. The micro-level, on the other hand, sees individual interactions as the basis for social order. In terms of social change, then, the macro-level approach would advocate changes in structure at the institutional level that would filter down to individual behaviors, while the micro-level approach would prescribe change in individual behaviors, to be followed by larger social change.

An Integrative Approach

One response to such divergence between the micro and the macro levels is to say that both are legitimate scholarly activities and should be viewed as two parallel enterprises operating in different dimensions, one the individual and the other the societal. That, however, begs the question of the relationship between the individual and society.

A more exciting prospect would be to bring some of the societal (supposedly abstract) factors into the domain of human thinking that guides individual behavior. That is to say, the macro-level forces can be seen not only to affect the environment but to influence individual behavior directly. For example, the policies that various states took to ban German from the schools resulted in an environment without German, which had its own set of consequences on the extent to which bilinguals maintained the language. In addition, however, the macro level, by acting as a symbolic concept, would influence the way in which a German speaker builds meaning from interaction with other German speakers. Under these circumstances, the use of German in public indeed would symbolize the building of solidarity against an unfair form of persecution.

As another example of how macro-level factors can influence the bilingual in these two ways, consider a recent declaration by the liberal World Council of Churches (1972) taking a symbolic posture with respect to language. In a position paper titled "The Threat of Monolinguism to the World Council of Churches," the body noted the alarming tendency towards English monolingualism in the Church and the political implications:

Every language carries with it a particular history, culture, philosophy, and ultimately an ideology. To reduce the interchange of ideas in the Ecumenical Movement to a single language is to reduce its opportunity to escape the confines of a particular historical tradition. . . . Progress and creativity depend on confrontation of ideas, cultures, ideologies, etc. . . . Monolinguism tends to eliminate such necessary conflict. (P. 4)

This declaration could have two effects. First, it could result in a policy that encouraged the use of non-English languages, thereby providing an environment where other languages would be used. And second, the declaration itself could take on a symbolic role in the minds of the individual members and directly influence their behavior.

To drive the point home, let us look at another symbolic example. President Kenyatta of Kenya issued a decree on July 4, 1974, making Swahili, a language not indigenous to the country, the national language of Kenya. His motivation was to unite a nation consisting of about sixty distinct ethnic communities and many different languages under a common language (thereby avoiding the use of ethnic languages that are reflected differentially in various sectors of the government): "A nation without culture is dead, and that is why I decreed that Swahili would be the national language" (Harries 1976, p. 155). This decree had an immediate impact on the language of the official channels of government, but it also, in and of itself, acted as a symbol such that use of Swahili in individual interaction would signal the speaker's advocacy of national unification.

As a final example, to anticipate the topic of the next chapter, let us take bilingual education in the United States. The most significant thing about bilingual education is not that it promotes bilingualism—it does not, as we shall soon see—but rather that it gives some measure of official public status to the political struggle of language minorities, primarily Hispanics.

The task for anyone interested in an integration of the macro and micro approaches is to find out if and under what conditions societal concepts, such as language group, educational opportunity, group cohesiveness, social mobility, and so forth —that is, the kinds of terms thrown about by sociologists who talk about language maintenance—have psychological reality as concepts in bilingual individuals, and how they might affect behavior. This approach has been advocated to some implicit degree by Fishman (1966, p. 450) and by Giles, Bourhis, and Taylor (1977). It falls under a general class of problems, faced by students of social behavior, concerning the relationship between thought and behavior. The match between the two is not perfect—as imperfect as the relationship between attitudes and second-language learning, or between conscious knowledge of grammar and actual speech—but we do know that they are two facets of the same phenomenon. Knowing that, we must continue our commitment to charting their relationship.

Chapter 8

Bilingual Education

RALPH ROBINETT is director of bilingual/foreign language education in Dade County, Florida, where he supervises the education of more than ten thousand students who have been identified by the school system as LM/LEPs—members of a "language minority" (non-English-speaking) group who are "limited in English proficiency." These students are taught in their native language—overwhelmingly, Spanish—with gradual increments of English until they can survive in English-only classrooms.

Funded by the federal government and consistent with its policy, the program is aimed at transition to English. It does not support the native language of LM/LEP students beyond helping them keep their heads above water in their other courses. Such a transitional program is in sharp contrast to the experimental bilingual program Robinett originally helped to establish in Dade County in 1963. There the goal was to create functional bilinguals, who would maintain both languages through their school years. Confusion of goals—maintenance versus transition—has contributed much to the controversy swirling around bilingual education.

Considering the controversy and publicity surrounding bilingual education, it is surprising how little we know about the extent and nature of bilingual instruction in the United States. Systematic information is scarce even on fundamental aspects of bilingual education, such as the exact nature of activities in different kinds of bilingual education programs. What I shall provide, then, is but a collage, beginning with Robinett's original maintenance program, the roots of the contemporary bilingual education movement.

The Origins of Recent Bilingual Education

With the influx of Cuban refugees into Florida in the late 1950s and early 1960s, the Ford Foundation saw the need for an experimental program in bilingual education, and it set up such a program in Dade County in 1963.* Heading the project was Pauline Rojas, former director of the English Program in Puerto Rico. She in turn asked Ralph Robinett to direct the program's curriculum development; Rojas knew the Kansas-born Robinett from his work in Puerto Rico as a specialist in English as a Second Language (ESL).

The goal was ambitious: to include children from both Cuban and English-speaking homes and make them into functional bilinguals. The Cuban children would achieve as much in Spanish as they would in a monolingual Spanish program, and they would attain equal proficiency in English. The English-speaking children would not suffer in their acquisition of English skills, and at the same time they would attain appropriate levels in Spanish. The program, in short, was oriented toward enrichment of the child's linguistic and cultural experiences; it was not compensatory.

*The discussion in this section was derived primarily from conversations with Robinett and from Mackey and Beebe's (1977) rich description of the program.

Out of the 150 elementary schools in the Miami area, the Coral Way Elementary School was selected as the first site for the project. The demographics were right. The community consisted of an equal proportion of families of English- and Spanish-speaking backgrounds. The income levels of both groups were in the comfortable middle-class range. And the principal of the school showed an interest in the project. The logistics of implementing the program now had to be worked out. These included developing a curriculum, obtaining community support for the program, and staffing the program.

In developing the curriculum, Robinett and Rojas were joined by educators who had had extensive experience in Cuba (one of them, Rosa Inclan, had directed a training program for ESL teachers at the University of Havana; another, Hermina Cantero, had been supervisor of ESL in elementary and secondary schools in Cuba). Robinett recalls that in the initial planning phases, he instructed this high-powered group to read "everything and anything having to do with bilingual education."

Robinett has told me that he looked into the early literature on bilingualism and intelligence testing and was "sickened by the false scientism." On the other hand, he was impressed with Leopold's study of Hildegard, which symbolized to him that language grows in a systematic way and that "things aren't always the same, and that systems are fluid." (So taken was Robinett by Leopold's study that when he and his wife had their first son, he made systematic tape recordings of the child's language development.) In the end, however, Robinett and the group based their decisions not on the literature but on their own, more valuable experiences with bilingual education elsewhere.

In broad outline, the program was set up in the following way. In the mornings, students from the same first-language group received instruction in that language in language arts and other subjects. In the afternoons, they switched over to their second language. At midday, the two groups were encouraged to mix at lunch and in programs in art, music, and physical education. During the midday lunch break the English and Spanish counterpart teachers exchanged information on the students' progress and coordinated instruction, so that the afternoon activities in the second language could extend and reinforce the morning lessons. English-language curriculum materials were of course already available, but the Spanish materials had to be assembled in a variety of ways, mainly by being brought in from Spanish-speaking countries.

The principal of the school, Joseph Logan, played the primary role in convincing the parents of the value of this bilingual curriculum. The Spanish-speaking parents were almost unanimous in their approval, particularly at the idea that their children could maintain their Spanish language and cultural ties. The English-speaking parents were not as enthusiastic, but they respected the judgment of the principal. As Mackey and Beebe (1977) note:

If the school principal believed that all of the children would sharpen their general ability to think by working in two languages and not become confused, these parents were confident that this would prove to be true. Although the parents understood that their young children would be required to move to a number of different classrooms during the school day like older students in junior and senior high schools, they also knew that their children would have the opportunity to learn from the "cream of the crop" of Cuban refugee teachers. (P. 65)

Some of the teachers in the school expressed resentment of the bilingual program. All English-speakers, they were aware that the program ultimately would require half the teachers to be Spanish-speakers. It worked out, however, that after some teachers voluntarily transferred to other schools, the right number of teachers remained to participate in the bilingual program. Their Spanish-speaking counterparts were not difficult to find. The influx of Cuban refugees brought with it a number of talented teachers, who readily received state certification through the Cuban Teacher Retraining Program. Robinett and his group worked with their team of teachers during the summer of 1963, and on September 3 they opened shop to 350 first-, second-, and third-graders participating in the first resurrection of bilingual education in the United States in recent history.

Subsequent evaluations of the bilingual program at Coral Way supported the common observation that, in most respects, it had been a success. Both language groups showed steady progress in their first-language reading test scores. The English-speaking students compared favorably on English reading with students who attended monolingual English schools. They did not, however, reach Spanish reading scores comparable to their ability in reading English. The Spanish-speaking students, on the other hand, attained equivalent levels in both languages. In retrospect, this difference between the two groups was not unexpected, since the predominant language of the environment is English. Another measure of the success of the program was the observation by teachers and administrators that students were learning equally well whether English or Spanish was used as the medium of instruction and that "they were broadening their understanding of other people, and they were being prepared to live satisfying lives and to contribute to their bicultural community and their country" (Mackey and Beebe 1977, p. 81).

Once the feasibility of bilingual education was demonstrated at Coral Way, other schools in the Dade County system, particularly those with high concentrations of Cubans, began setting up their own programs. The expansion was not just to other elementary schools but to junior high and high schools as well (see the excellent account of this expansion in Mackey and Beebe [1977]). In 1974, a decade after the beginning of the program in Coral Way, there were 3,683 students in bilingual programs in the elementary schools (including 2,608 Spanish-speakers) and approximately 2,000 in the secondary schools. In these programs, students continued to show progress in their native language comparable to that of students in monolingual programs, although the differences between English- and Spanish-speakers with respect to reading ability in their second language persisted.

The increase in the number of students enrolled in bilingual schools in Dade County was impressive, but the educational opportunity was still available to only a limited segment of the population. In 1975, the school system identified 16,406 students who were considered of non-English-speaking or limited-English-speaking ability (Mackey and Beebe 1977, p. 123). Most of these students were not in bilingual education but in ESL programs. It was at this point that bilingual education in Dade County, which had been developed mostly through local initiative, came into contact with the efforts of the federal government in bilingual education, which had begun seven years earlier.

The Federal Role in Bilingual Education

The passage of the Bilingual Education Act of 1968 (Title VII, an amendment to the 1965 Elementary and Secondary Education Act) heralded the official coming of age of the federal role in the education of persons with limited English-speaking ability. Seven and a half million dollars were appropriated for the 1969–1970 fiscal year, to support experimental programs responsive to the "special educational needs of children of limited English-speaking ability in schools having a high concentration of such children from families . . . with incomes below $3,000 per year" (Bilingual Education Act, 1968).

Title VII appropriations saw a steady annual increase over the years. Within three years, the budget had tripled to 25 million dollars, and by 1980 (the last year of the Carter administration), it had peaked at 191.5 million dollars. In 1984, the appropriation was 139.4 million dollars.

The original 1968 bill was passed in the wake of the Black civil rights movement that had culminated in the Civil Rights Act of 1963. Chicano organizations in the Southwest were demanding equal opportunity programs and bilingual education for the large numbers of Chicano children who were failing in English-only schools. (Blanco 1978). In 1966, Senator Ralph Yarborough of Texas, in response to such pressures, set up a special Bilingual Education Subcommittee that held hearings in California, Texas, and New York, states with high concentrations of children who would benefit from bilingual instruction. Apparently, politicians quickly saw the political advantage in the advocacy of bilingual education, and forty-three separate bilingual education bills were introduced in the House of Representatives (Stoller 1976).

The House debated and whittled down these bills and, on May 24, 1967, voted for the legislation. The Senate soon followed suit, and the final legislation took shape in conference on December 15, 1967, and was approved January 2, 1968. The goal of the legislation was to recognize the "special education needs of a great many students whose mother tongue is other than English" (quoted in Stoller 1976, p. 50). School districts eligible for aid were those that had substantial numbers of children of limited English-speaking ability who were from low-income families. The bill established an Advisory Committee on the Education of Bilingual Children (later called the Office of Bilingual Education and Minority Language Affairs) in the Office of Education to help establish regulations and policy.

The intent of the Act was to stimulate innovative programs that would eventually be supported through local and state funds. Stoller points out that during the first few years (1968–1973), the emphasis was on elementary school education (about 86 percent of the programs were in this category). Over the years, increasing emphasis was placed on secondary school, adult education, dropout programs, and vocational/trade

199

school bilingual education, but the major emphasis continues to be in the early years of schooling.

Although opportunities for experimentation with bilingual programs became available through Title VII, local school systems were under no legal obligation to use them. The primary instrument for the spread of bilingual education in the United States came in the form of litigation. In a famous 1974 decision, Lau v. Nichols, the U.S. Supreme Court overturned an earlier decision by the federal district courts in a class action suit brought by Chinese public school students against the San Francisco Unified School District in 1970. The plaintiffs argued that no special programs were available to meet their specific linguistic needs and that they consequently suffered educationally since they could not benefit from instruction in English. The Supreme Court ruled that "there is no equality of treatment merely by providing students with the same facilities, textbooks, teachers, and curriculum; for students who do not understand English are effectively foreclosed from any meaningful education" (quoted in Teitelbaum and Hiller 1977, p. 7).

The plaintiffs had argued on the basis of both their constitutional rights (the equal protection clause of the Fourteenth Amendment) and Title VI of the Civil Rights Act of 1964, which ruled that "no person in the United States shall, on the ground of race, color or national origin, be excluded from participation in, be denied the benefits of, or be subjected to discrimination under any program or activity receiving Federal financial assistance" (quoted in Teitelbaum and Hiller 1977, p. 6). The Supreme Court avoided the constitutional issue altogether and used Title VI as the basis for their decision. "It seems obvious that the Chinese-speaking minority receives fewer benefits than the English-speaking majority from respondents' school system which denies them a meaningful opportunity to participate in the educational program—all earmarks of discrimination banned by the regulations" (quoted in Teitelbaum and Hiller 1977, p. 8).

Although bilingual education was the remedy originally requested by the plaintiffs, by the time the case reached the Supreme Court, the specific request had been dropped. The Court, consistent with earlier decisions that specific educational remedies should be left to the local school boards, wrote: "No specific remedy is urged upon us. Teaching English to the students of Chinese ancestry who do not speak the language is one choice. Giving instructions to this group in Chinese is another. There may be others. Petitioners ask only that the Board of Education be directed to apply its expertise to the problem and rectify the situation" (quoted in Teitelbaum and Hiller 1977, p. 8). In a consent decree, the San Francisco Board of Education provided for a bilingual-bicultural program for the Chinese, Filipino, and Spanish language groups who made up over 80 percent of the students with little or no English in the district. For the remaining groups, ESL was offered.

The Lau decision had an impact on a number of other cases that resulted in court-mandated bilingual programs, such as Serna v. Portales Municipal Schools and Aspira of New York, Inc. v. Board of Education of the City of New York. In addition, it provided fuel for expansion of the Bilingual Education Act, which was amended in 1974 to broaden eligibility (the poverty requirement was eliminated) and the range of services offered. In addition, it provided impetus for the passage of state legislation mandating bilingual education (which followed the precedent set by Massachusetts in 1971 and Illinois and Texas in 1973).

The Lau decision was translated into federal policy when the U.S. Office of Education recruited a group of experts to develop informal policy guidelines for school districts judged to be out of compliance with Title VI and the Lau decision. In their document, "Task Force Findings Specifying Remedies Available for Eliminating Past Educational Practices Ruled Unlawful Under Lau v. Nichols" (commonly called the "Lau Remedies"), school boards were directed to identify students with a primary or home language other than English and to assess their relative proficiency in English and their native language. Elementary school students were to be instructed in their dominant language until they were able to benefit from instruction exclusively in English (Birman and Ginsburg 1983).

The significance of the Lau Remedies was that they prescribed a transitional form of bilingual education and specifically rejected ESL as a remedy for elementary school students: "Because an ESL program does not consider the affective nor cognitive development of students . . . and time and maturation variables are different [for elementary school students], an ESL program is *not* appropriate" (U.S. Department of Health, Education and Welfare 1975, Section III.1.A).

By 1978, when the Bilingual Education Act came up for reauthorization, a large number of school systems around the country had followed the Lau Remedies and set up bilingual education programs. The great expansion of federal subsidy of education that began in the early 1960s meant that a large number of school systems were receiving various sorts of federal aid, and continuation of that aid was now contingent on following the Lau guidelines. The amendments of 1978 greatly expanded the programs overseen by the Office of Bilingual Education and Minority Language Affairs, as can be seen in the list of programs in table 8.1. Funds are available not just for the development and implementation of programs, but also for the training of future teachers and administrators of bilingual education programs. In ten short years, proponents of bilingual education had managed to pass legislation allowing a rather broad foundation for the addition of a new group to the ranks of the teaching profession.

TABLE 8.1
Programs Supported by Title VII

1. *Basic Bilingual Programs.* Provides financial assistance to local school systems to implement educational programs designed to assist children of limited English proficiency to improve their English language skills; provides supplementary activities to parents of children in programs and to teachers in the program.

2. *Demonstration Projects.* Demonstrates outstanding programs of bilingual education. Priorities for funding have been given to projects serving recent immigrants, projects with exemplary community or parental involvement activities, and projects with outstanding approaches to including the participation of children whose language is English.

3. *Bilingual Vocational Training Program.* Provides bilingual vocational training to persons whose dominant language is not English and who are either unemployed or underemployed because of their limited English-speaking ability.

4. *Bilingual Vocational Instructor Training Program.* Provides training to persons to improve their skills and qualifications as vocational education instructors to limited-English-proficient persons.

5. *State Educational Agency Projects for Coordinating Technical Assistance.* Assists bilingual education programs within the state by disseminating information, facilitating information exchanges among programs, and by aiding in general program planning.

6. *Bilingual Education Service Centers.* Provides training in bilingual education to persons working in a bilingual education program and to parents of children in a bilingual program.

7. *Evaluation, Dissemination, and Assessment Centers.* Assesses, evaluates, and disseminates bilingual education materials to be used in bilingual education programs.

8. *Materials Development Centers.* Develops instructional and testing materials to be used in bilingual education programs.

9. *Training Projects.* Trains existing or future bilingual teachers, parents, and others in bilingual education.

10. *School of Education Projects (Dean's Grants).* Provides programs at accredited universities or colleges leading to degrees in bilingual bicultural education.

11. *Fellowship Programs.* Provides financial assistance to full-time graduate students who are preparing to become bilingual teacher trainers.

12. *Refugee Education Assistance Act of 1980.* Awards financial assistance to state educational agencies for distribution among local schools providing supplementary education services to refugee children enrolled in public and private schools.

13. *Bilingual Desegregation Support Programs.* Provides financial assistance to local school systems to help meet the educational needs of children from non-English-speaking homes and who lack equal educational opportunity because of language and culture.

14. *Research Agenda.* Provides funds for research in bilingual education.

NOTE: National Clearinghouse for Bilingual Education, *Bilingual education information packet* (Rosslyn, Va.: National Clearinghouse for Bilingual Education, n.d.).

The Impact of the Federal Initiatives

In 1975, the United States Civil Rights Task Force took a close look at Dade County (as it did at many other school systems around the country receiving federal assistance). It declared that the constitutional rights of 10,803 elementary school students who were not receiving bilingual education were being violated. The Lau remedies had specifically ruled out ESL as unacceptable.

Threatened with the loss of all federal funds to the school system (which at that time were estimated at forty million dollars annually), Ralph Robinett, who had now become the Director of Bilingual Programs, was charged with the formidable task of providing bilingual education to all non-English-speaking and limited-English-speaking students in Dade County. The list of languages to be taught, originally just Spanish, grew to include Haitian-French, Vietnamese, Chinese, Italian, Hebrew, Portuguese, German, Arabic, Greek, and Korean.

Unlike the model of bilingual education that developed out of Coral Way, the aim of which was to maintain students' native language while they learned the second language, the model prescribed by the federal government was to be judged ultimately on its success in creating students proficient in English. The native language was to be a transitional tool—a medium of instruction only until the student learned enough English to profit from instruction entirely in English. The native language would be phased out. (Dade County has continued to provide maintenance in the form of a voluntary program offering instruction in Spanish regardless of the student's English skills, but by comparison this program is small.) Under the model created by Robinett, the first year of the program began with 42 percent of the instruction provided in the native language and 58 percent in English. By the end of the third year, only 8 percent was in the native language. And by the fourth year, the students were mainstreamed into monolingual, English classes.

Despite the growth of Title VII over the years, the actual number of limited-English-proficient students who receive bilingual education in the United States is not as large as is commonly thought. O'Malley (1982) conducted a survey in the spring of 1978 that represented all states except Texas (which had a low LEP response rate). Out of an estimated 1.7 million LEP students aged five to fourteen years, 23 percent were in bilingual programs, 11 percent were in English classrooms with ESL, and 58 percent were in English-medium instruction, which included remedial English. Thus while bilingual education had made considerable headway since federal involvement began in 1968, ten years later it had reached less than a quarter of the population for which it was intended.

More recent estimates of the extent of bilingual education from data gathered in 1983 suggest that bilingual instruction has remained an important—but by no means the singular—method for instruction of LEP students. Although the full report is yet to be released, the preliminary findings of a federal study show that among LEP first-grade pupils—the grade level in which the highest proportion of students receive bilingual instruction—40 percent receive services classified as "movement from native language content course instruction toward all-English instruction" (National Clearinghouse for Bilingual Education 1985, p. 3). Only a negligible proportion of schools attempt to maintain the native language of the children. Furthermore, over half of the schools do not provide any content area instruction in the native language of the children.

A Scrapbook of Opinions

"Nothing I've ever written has drawn a larger response," wrote Stephen Rosenfeld of the *Washington Post* (1974b) referring to his column about bilingual education (1974a); "about four to one against, by the way," he added.

The budget for bilingual education has been very small, even in its bumper years. For example, it made up less than one percent of the total United States federal education budget of 15.4 billion dollars in 1984. Yet, as Rosenfeld's observation indicates, bilingual education has received a disproportionate amount of public horn-locking by politicians, educators, and ordinary citizens alike. This has been the story of bilingual education ever since its beginning. The mismatch between the funding level and the amount of controversy generated is not surprising, however, for at stake are issues that strike at the heart of American identity.

Rosenfeld's unofficial count of four-to-one against bilingual education squares with my own informal tally of letters to the editor I have seen over the years. Opponents are vociferous; in contrast, proponent views are often defensive efforts in response to a negative letter or editorial. Witness these excerpts from disapproving letters to the editor that I have collected from the *New York Times:*

No historical basis for bilingualism exists in New York. The United States, through the Port of New York, received immigrants from every country of the globe. Each wave of immigration brought new languages and new cultures to this city; however, these groups realized that their goals could only be accomplished through participation in the mainstream of economic and social life. They were able, for the most part, to maintain their chosen cultural identity while finding adequate upward mobility achieved through the medium of a common language. To subsidize a system of bilingual education is obviously in direct contradiction of historical precedent, and weakens the ability of the city to function as a cohesive economic unity. (September 13, 1974)

In 1913 I was assigned to an English class of about thirty boys, most of whom spoke only Yiddish or Polish. Although the total of non-English-speaking students in New York City was greater than the present number of Spanish-speaking children, we had no bilingual classes at that time. We sat totally non-English-speaking students alongside those who knew some English and permitted personal translations when necessary. I believe that students can learn faster that way. The bilingual method is probably more confusing than helpful to many. Exposure to English throughout the day results in more rapid and more effective progress than dilution in a bilingual process. (November 3, 1976)

It was just 42 years ago this month that, at age 9, I left Germany with my family and came to New York, speaking two words of English: yes and no. I was put in the fourth grade, and I remember now with amusement that I was given an I.Q. exam during my first week in school. . . . My experience and that of my contemporaries was that after half a year of regular schooling we were almost indistinguishable from our native American peers—this despite the fact that most of our parents spoke very little English. I am convinced a bilingual education would have impeded my integration into American society. (January 18, 1981)

President Reagan also has concerns about bilingual education, which led him to depart from his prepared text in speaking to a group of mayors.

It is absolutely wrong and against American concept to have a bilingual education program that is now openly, admittedly dedicated to preserving their native language and never getting them adequate in English so they can go out into the job market (*New York Times,* March 3, 1981).

What is evident from these remarks, which do not necessarily represent the views of all Americans but certainly represent some vocal segments of society, is that bilingual education is seen as a maintenance concept, rather than transitional. As such it is regarded as a threat to the status of English and to the ideals of the Americanization of immigrants that English represents. These arguments have been sharply put forth in debates conducted at the level of policy makers.

The Policy Debate on Bilingual Education

In 1983, President Reagan mobilized to slash the federal budget for bilingual education and to relax regulations on the methods that local school districts may choose to use in educating limited-English-proficient students. Bilingual education was costing the federal government $138 million, and it was undergoing close scrutiny in Congress. Two organizations were called to testify: the National Association for Bilingual Education (NABE), an organization of bilingual education professionals, mostly teachers and administrators, and U.S. English, an organization founded by former Senator S. I. Hayakawa to lobby for a constitutional amendment making English the official language of the United States.

NABE'S ARGUMENTS FOR CONTINUED BILINGUAL EDUCATION

In testimony before the Senate Appropriations Subcommittee on Labor, Health and Human Services, and Education, NABE pointed to the accomplishments of the Title VII programs. The gains made, they claimed, "include improved academic achievement test scores, reduced rates of school dropout and student absenteeism, increased community involvement in education, and enhanced student self-esteem" (*Youth Policy,* June 1983, p. 17). They pointed to a figure of 3.5 million LEP students in the nation's schools and emphasized that the federal government bore a responsibility to improve their educational opportunities.

NABE's argument that federal support should supplement local and state efforts was based on four considerations. First, they appealed to Title VI of the Civil Rights Act of 1974, the basis for the Supreme Court decision in Lau v. Nichols. Second, they claimed that both present and past federal policy was responsible for the presence of a large part of the LEP popula-

208

tion in the United States, through the acquisition of territory (such as Puerto Rico) and through foreign wars (such as Vietnam). Third, they argued that improvement of education is imperative for the future economic productivity of the United States as a whole. And fourth, they pointed to the value of developing the "natural linguistic resource" provided by the LEPs for reasons of national security and economic health, noting that bilingual education should be used "as the foundation for a national program to expand the linguistic competencies of all Americans" (*Youth Policy*, p.19).

U.S. ENGLISH'S ARGUMENT AGAINST BILINGUAL EDUCATION

U.S. English testified before the comparable committee in the House. Its representatives began their testimony by pointing to the "serious misgivings" that the American people have about bilingual education. They further argued that "at the very least, bilingual education retards the acquisition of English language skills, and the integration of the student into the American mainstream" (*Youth Policy*, p. 18). Public schools, by conducting instruction in the students' home language, could lead parents to the wrong conclusion that "English is perhaps not essential after all." This problem is compounded by the segregation of the bilingual students from their American peers, so that the bilingual students are "doomed to remain forever strangers in their new country" (*Youth Policy*, p. 18).

Appropriations for Title VII should be substantially reduced, they claimed, pointing to evaluation studies that failed to show bilingual education to be more effective than alternative (and less costly) methods, including English as a Second Language. Furthermore, referring to an internal document by a policy analyst at the Department of Education (Barnes, later published in 1983), they argued that the original estimate of 3.6 million children requiring services was a gross overcount and that the actual number is more like a third the original figure; they recommended that the budget be trimmed in direct proportion to these figures.

Based on these observations, U.S. English recommended that alternative methods of education for LEPs be developed and that funds thus saved be reallocated "for improved and greatly expanded foreign language programs for American students at all levels—elementary, secondary, and university" (*Youth Policy*, p. 20).

The Charges and Their Rebuttals

The excerpts from letters to the editor and from the congressional testimony suggest the following charges against the bilingual education establishment: that there is no historical precedent for bilingual education; that most existing programs follow the maintenance model; that there is no popular support for bilingual education; that young children learn a second language in a very short period of time, so not much time is lost if they are placed in English-only classes; that education in the native language takes away valuable time that would otherwise be spent in English; that bilingual education is not effective; and that the number of eligible students is far smaller than originally estimated. There is research evidence that bears on all these points, evidence with which all too few of those who voice their opinions are familiar.

There is no historical basis for bilingual education. Appeals to history can be elegant, but they are largely irrelevant for purposes of passing judgment on bilingual education. If for emotional reasons and for perspective one would like to appeal to history, however, one could point to non-English language instruction provided in the 1800s in Pennsylvania, Ohio, and New York, mostly for immigrants from German, Scandinavian, and French

backgrounds (see chapter 7; Heath 1977; Kloss 1977; Schlossman 1983).

Historian Steven Schlossman presents an account of the debate surrounding the use of German in the public schools of
Cincinnati and Milwaukee, much of which is reminiscent of the
debate today. Bilingual instruction was seen as an instrument
for luring German families into public education. Illustrative is
the following argument made by the president of the school
board in Milwaukee, in favor of German:

The real opposition to the German language does not arise from the
amount of money expended upon it, but rather from fear on the part
of many citizens, that the children of German parents will be *Ger-
manized,* as they express it, by making the study a part of their school
education. No greater mistake was ever made. In banishing the German language from our Public Schools, the very object will be accomplished which they seek to avoid. They will drive from the schools
three-fourths of all the children of German parentage, who will be sent
to private German schools, where a good German education can be
secured, but where the facilities to acquire good English education are
limited; they will keep such pupils away from association with pupils
of American birth, and create a clannish spirit among German children;
in a word they will furnish the best means conceivable to *German-
ize* them. (Quoted in Schlossman [1983], p. 170)

The goals of current American bilingual education can also be
seen as directed toward assimilation of the non-English-speaking children. One of the original concerns that led to bilingual
education, it will be recalled, was the alarmingly high dropout
rates among minority students. By retaining these students in
the school system for as long as possible, we can better hope to
achieve the goal of drawing them into the mainstream of
American society.

Bilingual education lacks popular support.   Letters to the editor are
not random samplings of public opinion. In an attempt to approach the question of public opinion scientifically, my stu-

dents and I sampled the attitudes toward bilingual education in New Haven, Connecticut (Hakuta 1984a). The New Haven Public Schools have a modest-sized bilingual education program (to be described in more detail later) that serves Spanish-speaking students, most of them from Puerto Rico. The local newspaper is not sympathetic to bilingual education and has published editorials claiming that children in these programs do not learn English and that the principal beneficiaries of bilingual education are its teachers and administrators.

In December 1983, I took advantage of having an exceptionally talented and eager group of students taking my course on bilingualism at Yale, and we conducted a telephone survey of local attitudes toward bilingual education. Most of the 179 respondents we contacted (they were selected randomly from the telephone directory) described themselves as "not knowledgeable" about bilingual education, but they were willing, often eager, to express their sentiments about it.

The attitudes among this sample were mostly favorable to bilingual education. Seventy percent felt that bilingual education was the best way for a Spanish-speaking child to learn English, and only 18 percent felt that funding for bilingual education classes should be decreased (while a full 50 percent felt that it should be increased). There was even considerable support for the notion that bilingual programs should maintain the Spanish language and culture of the children (58 percent).

The most interesting aspect of the results was in the background characteristics of the respondents who were against bilingual education. Three characteristics were important. First, men were more likely than women to oppose bilingual education. Second, men and women aged fifty or older tended to be more opposed. And third, men and women who had grown up using a non-English language at home were more opposed. These three effects were additive, so that among men in their fifties who had grown up using a non-English language (mostly Italian), there was overwhelming opposition.

The spontaneous opinions offered by some of our respondents were reminiscent of what we find in letters to the editor:

No one taught me in my own language. I had to learn the hard way and it took less than a year even though I spoke my own language at home. This is an English-speaking country; if the parents want their kids to speak Spanish, they should teach them at home like I taught my kids.

There's too many people coming here from other countries. My parents came from Italy—they didn't get any help. These people, they want everything for nothing. I wish it would go back to the old time. It was beautiful.

They spend too much time being Spanish and not enough time being American.

I have very strong feelings about these Puerto Ricans coming in here. They should learn to speak the American language . . . CLICK

It was evident that, although the majority supported bilingual education, the most strongly held sentiments were the negative ones.

In another survey conducted in October 1982, Cole found, in a nationwide sample, considerable support for some form of bilingual education. Only 33 percent said that Hispanic students should be in all-English programs. The most interesting finding of the study was that most people associate bilingual education with maintenance efforts for the native language. Respondents who thought that the United States would be better off if immigrants stopped speaking their native language and learned English were less likely to support bilingual education. In addition, support was related to general political attitudes, with support coming primarily from those identified with liberal ideology. And finally, as in the New Haven study, there was a generation effect, with the older respondents showing less support for bilingual education.

Cole also drew a second sample from Hispanics in the New York and Los Angeles areas. There was in general slightly stronger support for bilingual education among this group (28 percent felt that Hispanic students should be in all-English programs), although it was not overwhelmingly different from the nationwide sample. Among the Hispanics, the biggest determinant of attitude was their language orientation toward English or Spanish (this index was created by their responses concerning which language they used in various situations), with the most support among those with high Spanish orientation. Cole found that this index of language orientation was also related to education and income, with those of high English orientation coming from relatively high education and income levels. The Hispanic data suggest, not surprisingly, that the greatest support for bilingual education is found among those whose children are most likely to be served by the program.

In presenting the New Haven findings at professional meetings of bilingual educators, I have been struck by the reactions I have encountered. Educators have questioned whether surveys of their own communities would show similar results, because they have become accustomed to the strong negative opinions voiced in editorials and other public forums. They even express concern that negative opinion arising from such a survey might do more harm than good for their cause. The results of the surveys that have been done, however, indicate that such fear needs to be empirically attacked, and I believe that further studies will continue to turn up majority sympathy for bilingual education. My own feeling is that public opinion should be monitored by local bilingual educators, and that the most important information to be obtained through such study is not whether people support it or not but how that support varies according to the respondent's background. That information could be very useful in planning for advocacy and for educating the public.

Most bilingual programs are not transitional but maintenance models. The American Institutes for Research (Danoff et al. 1977, 1978), commissioned to study the effectiveness of bilingual instruction, reported an incidental finding that alarmed many Americans. They found evidence for a proliferation of maintenance bilingual programs, rather than the mandated transitional programs. Of the thirty-eight Title VII projects that they investigated, school authorities reported that less than a third of the students in these classrooms were there because of their limited English-speaking ability. The project directors who were interviewed were openly proud of their maintenance programs, and only 5 percent of them said that Spanish-dominant students were transferred to an English-only classroom once they had learned enough English to function in school.

Unfortunately, the study only told us what the project directors told the researchers. We do not know, for example, how the conduct of the interview itself might have influenced their responses. A more accurate basis for the survey would have been the program's policies regarding student entry into and exit from the bilingual program. How many years has the average student spent in the bilingual program? What determines the length of stay in the program? Such information is currently lacking, but it is critical in estimating the relative mix of programs with transitional and maintenance policies.

In New Haven, most children are in the bilingual program for two to three years. In fourth- and fifth-grade bilingual classes, about half the students are exited into mainstream classrooms annually. It is a full-blooded transitional program. Yet I can imagine that depending on the way the question were asked, a survey could elicit an answer suggesting that it is a maintenance-type program. For example, it is in fact true that while the students are in the bilingual program, they are provided with maintenance of Spanish language and culture.

Information on the goals of bilingual education programs is sparse, but what indications there are suggest that they are mainly transitional in nature, of the sort New Haven has and Ralph Robinett runs in Dade County. O'Malley (1982) compared the amount of English-language instruction that the av-

erage LEP elementary student in a bilingual program receives
with the amount that an LEP in an English-medium classroom
receives and found no difference. Furthermore, he reported a
sharp drop in the percentage of LEP children receiving bilingual
instruction from elementary school (54 percent) to middle
school (17 percent), which is attributable mostly to mainstreaming. And finally, he estimated that between 70 and 80
percent of the students in Title VII programs could be correctly
classified as LEPs. He concluded that "the types of bilingual
education provided either through Federal or State support do
not appear to be focused on maintaining the children's non-
English language, and do not appear to draw instructional time
away from learning English" (p. 31). Similarly, a preliminary
report of a federal study conducted in 1983 found that "in
almost all cases, the goal of the special services was to enable
LEP students to function in an all-English classroom. Only a
small proportion of the schools attempted to maintain and enhance the students' proficiency in the native language" (National Clearinghouse for Bilingual Education 1985, p. 3). In
short, the claim that the American bilingual education programs
are aimed toward maintenance of the native language and culture finds little support in systematic data.

Young children learn a second language quickly anyway. The argument here is that young children have little difficulty in learning
a second language, so that even if children are placed in English-
only classrooms, they quickly pick up English. Studies of child
second-language acquisition, such as those described in chapter
5, would appear to support this position.

Actually, what those studies show is that it is possible for
some children to acquire a second language rapidly. Studies of
children such as Uguisu definitely demonstrate this. But it
doesn't follow that this finding can be extended to all children.
At the end of chapter 5, I noted Evelyn Hatch's observation that
not all children find it so easy. Policy must take into consideration the incidence of children who do not acquire a second
language easily.

Furthermore, the individual case studies are usually from a population different from that from which students in bilingual education programs are drawn. Case studies usually look at children from middle-class, often academic, families—home environments particularly well suited for language development. Children in bilingual education, at least in the United States, come primarily from homes with low income (and, concomitantly, less support for the development of language skills). While we know very little about social class differences in second-language ability, extreme caution is warranted in generalizing conclusions across different groups.

We've noted before the widespread belief that young children have some magical quality that enables them to learn a second language. Noel Epstein (1977), for example, claims that if conditions are right children can acquire a basic proficiency in English in "a matter of weeks" (p. 25). Yet research evidence (though once again not from the population served by bilingual education programs) tends to suggest that there are few qualitative differences between younger and older second-language learners and that, if anything, the older learner might pick up the second language more rapidly (with the exception of accent).

And finally, before information related to age and second-language acquisition can be useful for applications to bilingual education, we have to construct a more refined notion of what it is that we mean by "proficiency in English." At the end of chapter 5, I argued for the importance of a distinction between different functions of language. We called them contextualized and decontextualized language use. Jim Cummins has vociferously argued for the importance of this distinction between language that is fundamentally communicative and contextual and language that is removed from context and more useful for academic-type skills. Intuitions of observant teachers suggest that there are some students who quickly pick up glib use of contextual language (on the playground, for example) but who take considerably longer to use the language in school-related skills. This distinction may account for why some students are considered by their bilingual teachers to be proficient in English (that is, they can use it in context) yet have difficulty when they are transferred to monolingual English classrooms and have to pick up academic skills in English.

Valuable time for learning in English is wasted. Obviously, the more hours that are spent in instruction in Spanish, the fewer hours are available for instruction in English. This is the basis for the concern of many who believe that if the ultimate goal of the bilingual program is to increase proficiency in English, then as much instruction as possible should be given in English.

Perhaps the single largest assumption in bilingual education, whether it is a transitional or a maintenance model, is that skills taught in one language are transferred to the other language. If you teach concepts in one language, they do not need to be retaught (at least completely) in the other language. The assumption certainly played a large role in winning the acceptance of the parents of the students in the bilingual program at Coral Way in Dade County (Mackey and Beebe 1977, p. 68), and it has done so elsewhere as well.

What is remarkable about the issue of transfer of skills is that despite its fundamental importance, almost no empirical studies have been conducted to understand the characteristics or even to demonstrate the existence of the transfer of skills. (One could offer the studies of linguistic interdependence from studies of adult bilinguals that I reviewed in chapter 4, particularly in the section on educational psychology.) There are, however, many incidental reports attesting to its existence from Canadian studies of bilingual education (Lambert and Tucker 1972; Stern, Swain, and McLean 1976; Genesee, Polich, and Stanley 1977; Swain 1978; Genesee 1979).

Perhaps this neglect in research comes from the fact that transfer of skills is such an obvious phenomenon. Teachers in bilingual classrooms know that it goes on. For example, I recently spoke to a group of teachers in New Haven about a study

I wanted to do with transfer of skills from Spanish to English. (In New Haven, bilingual instruction is conducted most frequently by pairs of teachers. One teaches in Spanish and the other in English, and they rotate cohorts of students between them.) They validated the fact that transfer occurs and even expressed puzzlement as to why one would want to do research on something so obvious. My answer was twofold. First, for reasons of policy, one wants to document it as "hard fact," so that the standard objections to bilingual education can be realistically evaluated. And second, transfer is likely to occur more rapidly in certain kinds of school skills than in others, and we need to understand this in order to improve curriculum (Chamot 1983) as well as for strictly scientific reasons.

Bilingual education is not effective. There is a sober truth that even the ardent advocate of bilingual education would not deny. Evaluation studies of the effectiveness of bilingual education in improving either English or math scores have not been overwhelmingly in favor of bilingual education. To be sure, there are programs that have been highly effective, but not very many. In a short monograph titled "Research Evidence for the Effectiveness of Bilingual Education," for example, Rudolf Troike (1978) listed about a dozen of them. An awkward tension blankets the lack of empirical demonstration of the success of bilingual education programs. Someone promised bacon, but it's not there.

Demand for evaluation of the effectiveness of Title VII in attaining its goals began mounting in the early 1970s. In response to these demands, the Office of Planning, Budgeting and Evaluation of the Office of Education contracted for such a study to be conducted by the American Institutes for Research. The study (Danoff et al. 1977, 1978), briefly mentioned earlier, is commonly known as the AIR Report. It compares the English reading and math test performance of elementary students from thirty-eight school districts receiving Title VII funds with those of a comparison sample of students who were not in bilingual classrooms. The students were observed over a period of time, some for five months and others over almost two years of schooling.

The AIR Report is bulky and technical. It consists of three volumes filled with tables and statistical analyses plus an appendix—a large amount of technical information that few people would care to lift, let alone read. The main conclusion, however, can be found in a single sentence in the final pages of the report: "While there were instances of Title VII impact in some subjects in some grades, the overall across-grade Total Title VII student analyses showed that Title VII does not appear to be having a consistent significant impact in meeting its goals as set forth in the legislation" (1978, IV: 6). I have read the document quite thoroughly; it is technically a good, workmanlike job. To be sure, there are flaws here and there: I would like to have seen additional analyses, and there are some interpretations of data that I would not have made. But all in all, if I had been given the data to analyze, I probably would have derived the same conclusion.

Criticisms of the report were expected, and there were many (Cardenas 1977; O'Malley 1978; Swain 1979; Gray 1981). Broadly, they came in two types. The first type was methodological and internal to the study. Experienced researchers can guess what the criticisms were: the reliability and validity of measures, subject selection, confounding of the treatment variable (Title VII with non–Title VII) with other factors such as the socioeconomic status of the students.

Such methodological criticisms are important. But to me the fury of such protests was misplaced, considering the second type of objection. The study had taken bilingual education to mean a homogeneous intervention, rather than an experimental approach to develop innovative ways of teaching language-minority students. Whatever was funded by Title VII was considered bilingual education, but depending on the school district, there were different manifestations of the program.

Consequently, critics rightly pointed out the insensitivity of the study to the heterogeneous nature of the programs that were evaluated. "If nothing else," Cardenas wrote, "the AIR study substantiates one imperative need in bilingual education, namely, the need for leadership in developing, implementing and monitoring the federal Title VII investment in bilingual education" (1977, p. 75).

Another way in which the study was insensitive to the broader goals of bilingual education was in restricting the criteria for a program's success. Achievement in English and in math are certainly important, but not all-important. As Christina Bratt Paulston (1980) wrote,

It makes a lot more sense also to look at employment figures upon leaving school, figures on drug addiction and alcoholism, suicide rates, and personality disorders, i.e., indicators which measure the social pathology which accompanies social injustice rather than in terms of language skills. . . . The dropout rate for American Indians in Chicago public schools is 95 percent; in the bilingual-bicultural Little Big Horn High School in Chicago the dropout rate in 1976 was 11 percent, and I find that figure a much more meaningful indicator for evaluation of the bilingual program than any psychometric assessment of students' language skills. (P. 41)

Such indicators were not included in the AIR study, nor are they commonly reported in evaluation studies.

More recently, Keith Baker and Adriana de Kanter (1983), in an internal OPBE report, raised another flurry of controversy as they surveyed a large number of evaluations of individual bilingual education projects. Their findings continue to support the conclusion that when achievement in English and math are used as criteria, bilingual education attains equivocal results. (And again, the same kinds of criticisms are heard concerning their method for selecting studies for analysis as were voiced about the AIR report.) But AIR stands as the only major effort to date to collect original data to assess the effectiveness of bilingual education.

In retrospect, I believe that the reactions to the AIR Report (and to the Baker-deKanter document) were far more valuable than the contents of the reports themselves. Bilingual educators became aware that they could not continue to blame poor programs on the lack of trained staff. The days of their fledgling status were numbered and this awareness has stimulated professionalization. The point that bilingual education is a heterogeneous set of programs also came to be firmly established as an effective defense against blanket criticism. For bilingual education to be meaningfully evaluated, the variation in existing program characteristics will have to be thoroughly understood.

Documenting program characteristics thus seems to be the focus of the U.S. Department of Education at present. It recently funded a study to look at characteristics of bilingual classrooms that were judged by school authorities to be effective (National Clearinghouse for Bilingual Education, 1984). Currently, it is funding large-scale surveys to document the kinds of services that schools and school districts provide to LM/LEPs. Whatever the complex set of motives behind these studies, they are a welcome move in the direction of finding out what is really going on in the programs, rather than narrowly focusing on outcomes as measured by standard paper-and-pencil tests of performance.

There are not as many LEPs as expected. U.S. English, the organization founded to promote English as the national language, likes to cite the figure of 1.2 million as the size of the population eligible for bilingual education (Barnes 1983). NABE, on the other hand, finds strength in a recent estimate of 6.6 million (Waggoner 1984). The original estimate from a study mandated by Congress and conducted in 1978 put the figure at 3.6 million (O'Malley 1981).

Why the disparities? After all, the definition of the limited-English-speaker, defined by legislation, is clear enough:

The terms limited English-speaking ability when used with reference to an individual means—(A) individuals who were not born in the United States or whose native language is a language other than English; and (B) individuals who come from environments where a language other than English is dominant . . . and by reason thereof, have difficulty speaking and understanding instruction in the English language. (Section 703a1, quoted in O'Malley 1981, p. 7)

One reason for the differences is that different data bases have been used. For example, Waggoner used the 1980 census, while both O'Malley and Barnes used the 1974 Survey of Income and Education. Other reasons have to do with the definition of what it means to have difficulty speaking and understanding instruction in English. For example, should it include children who are dominant in the non-English language but can nevertheless progress competitively in mainstream classes? The estimates are based on self-report information on language use in the home, both by household members and by the child in question. There would be little argument in including children who speak primarily the non-English language at home. But depending on the definition, there are differences in how much weight should be assigned to those whose parents report that their children primarily use English.

Perhaps the most important set of reasons has to do with the purpose of the studies. O'Malley's congressionally mandated study was "part of a systematic attempt to estimate the number of LEP children requiring special services now and in the future" (Ulibarri 1982, p. 14). Barnes's study was conducted not under the Title VII effort but rather by OPBE, "to estimate the size of the eligible language minority population under the proposed rules so that the cost and service requirements could be determined" (Ulibarri 1982, p. 15). Barnes (1983, p. 13) therefore argued that the estimate should not include children who were either not enrolled in school or enrolled in private schools.

The "estimate" aspect of population estimates of LEPs cannot be overemphasized, for the reasons noted above. These numbers should be treated with great respect, however, not for their accuracy but because once the numbers find their way onto paper, they have a way of becoming fact, and facts are powerful with Congress and the press. With a few turns of the screw, be it a shift in definition or a change in assumptions, the estimates —now facts—can be altered dramatically.

An unfortunate consequence of the emphasis on making accurate and tightly defined head counts is that they detract attention from community-level factors that would provide a far more accurate picture of the needs of LEP students. The sociolinguistic circumstances surrounding an LEP youngster in a city with low concentrations of LEP students will undoubtedly differ from those of someone in an environment with high concentrations. Yet the individual-level head counts do not differentiate between the two. A more accurate picture of the magnitude of the needs of LEP students in the United States would be gained by studies of the numbers and kinds of different linguistic communities rather than of individuals.

Having said all this about the numbers game, I will end this section with an estimate that could be regarded (at least conceptually) as independent of the absolute number of LEPs. A study by Oxford et al. (1980) tried to estimate changes in the LEP population in the United States through the year 2000. The estimates, as always, should be treated with caution, because they rely on various assumptions and also because they exclude the flow of illegal immigration. It is, however, noteworthy that they project a 35 percent increase in LEPs by the year 2000, using 1976 estimates as a base figure.

Bilingual Education in Perspective

All too frequently I have occasion to respond to criticisms of bilingual education, and I pull out the various research-based answers that I have detailed in the last section. When I hear that bilingual education has no historical basis, and that the story of immigrants has been a sink-or-swim experience, I point out if one considered historical precedence to be a criterion for current policy (which I do not), in fact bilingual schools existed in various parts of the country in the 19th century. When I am told that current bilingual programs are for maintenance, I note that in fact they very closely follow the policy of mainstreaming children into English-only classes as quickly as possible. When someone says that the American people are against bilingual education, I tell them about public opinion surveys indicating considerable support for bilingual education as a method of education for language-minority students. Being told that children pick up English in a matter of weeks if they're thrown into regular classrooms, I deliver a lecture on the wisdom of providing instruction in the native language for a considerable length of time, since children are not the instantaneous second language learners painted in our folklore, and since it may take them even longer to learn the kinds of language necessary to perform well in school. When the point comes up that there is no logic to teaching them in Spanish if we want them to learn in English, I argue that there is considerable transfer of skills across languages, so that subject matter taught in one language does not have to be retaught in the other. As for the effectiveness issue, I can only point to the flaws of the studies that fail to show effectiveness and express dismay at the lack of systematic research using broader and more long-term notions of program effectiveness, such as drop-out rates and quality of life. However, I do point out that there is tremendous variation in the quality of bilingual programs, just as there is in the quality of regular school programs, and that the goal should be to learn from characteristics of the effective bilingual programs.

Still, my data-based monologues aimed at critics usually elicit some comment indicating deference to the scholar and his research, followed by an affirmation of the importance of English in the United States, followed by a criticism of bilingual education. To me, this pattern indicates that while research findings are publicly acknowledged as an important basis upon which decisions are to be made—the sure signs of a technological society—critics of bilingual education will continue to use other criteria for their personal opinions. Perhaps it is the residue of infrequent but salient instances of encounters with individuals of separatist persuasions. Or it may be the strong identification of "bilingual" with "Hispanic," and the consequent association of bilingual education with the political mobilization of Hispanics. (I vividly recall an unusual but illustrative incident at a recent meeting of bilingual education researchers in which one speaker rose for his presentation and said, "Since this is a meeting of bilingual researchers, I assume that everyone speaks Spanish" and proceeded to deliver his paper in Spanish.) Whatever it may be, the point is that bilingual education, regardless of the reality that it is assimilationist in its orientation, carries with it the burden of a societal symbol. Bilingual education openly acknowledges the legitimacy of non-English languages in a centrally important public institution, and it appears to threaten the status of English. That is what critics are reacting to. Were it not for the symbolic status of bilingual education, one could easily imagine the assimilationists applauding the goals of the current bilingual education programs.

In other words, the public acceptance of an educational program that uses more than one language has much to do with what the public perceives as its goal. Is the program seen as an instrument for the advancement of the status of the language-minority groups? Is it a way of rapidly assimilating the group into the mainstream of society? Is it part of an educational movement that caters to the specialized group of teachers who are from the various language-minority groups? Or is it a means by which the elite minorities enhance their social status at the expense of the less powerful members of their group? As Christina Bratt Paulston (1980) pointedly asked,

Who stands to gain, where "gain" can be operationalized as an indicator of which group benefits in the power struggle. The literature on bilingual education is noticeable for the almost complete absence of such questions. The pious assumption is of course that the children are the ones who stand to gain, with indicators like standardized test scores on school achievement and self-concept. (P. 57).

The particular methodologies adopted by the different factions assume an importance because they serve as the public turf upon which some of this battle occurs. The debate over whether language minority students are best served by bilingual education programs (in which the teachers "happen to be" largely of the ethnolinguistic group of the students and belong to an organization called the National Association for Bilingual Education) or by English as a Second Language programs (in which the teachers "happen to be" largely native English-speakers and belong to an organization called Teachers of English to Speakers of Other Languages) is cloaked in what Paulston calls "a pervasive technocratic concern with methods, techniques, curriculum, and teacher training" (1980, p. 23), yet it can equally well be understood in terms of social conflict, for at stake are jobs and prestige.

The Future of Bilingual Education

This social-conflict perspective helps clarify one of the more recent debates over the possibility of importing the method of bilingual education developed in Canada, called "immersion."

This method is frequently offered as an alternative to the current model of bilingual education. By all accounts, French immersion programs in Canada have been a great success story. This story began in St. Lambert, a comfortable suburb of Montreal, in the 1960s. The program was created in response to demands by English-speaking parents, who were concerned that their children, to function successfully in a bilingual society, would have to learn French. The traditional French language instruction in the schools was ineffective, and they wanted a radical change.

In a typical French immersion program, children who are monolingual English-speakers are placed in a classroom in which, from day one, only French is used. The teachers are themselves bilingual (most often, native speakers of French from continental Europe), and they make the children fully aware that they know English, but they always use French. In second grade, the children are introduced to English language arts for approximately an hour a day. Over subsequent years, the mix of English is increased, until by sixth grade the two languages are used in roughly equal proportions.

Evaluations of French immersion programs are positive. The children do not fall behind in English and math achievement in comparison with peers instructed exclusively in English, and their French, although behind that of their peers from French-speaking backgrounds, is respectably good (Lambert and Tucker 1972; Swain and Barik 1978). This type of bilingual program is living up to expectations, and its proliferation in Canada attests to its popularity.

Can such a program be successfully imported to the United States? It actually has been, in Culver City, California (Cohen 1974). Monolingual English-speaking children were immersed in Spanish, and the program yielded positive results. The Culver City program replicates St. Lambert, not just in the curriculum but also in the social group from which the students were drawn. In both cases, they were from the dominant language group learning the language of a substantial minority group.

Critics of bilingual education have looked at the success of these programs and called for adapting the immersion model to the language-minority population in the United States (see, for example, Epstein 1977; Baker and de Kanter 1983). Students in these programs would be exposed only to English in the classroom. The advocates of immersion for language minorities in the United States are careful to point out that this would not be the old sink-or-swim method, in that all the non-English-speaking children would be placed in separate classes. They argue that the method holds promise since it has been shown to work in Canada and even in the United States.

In the long run, it would appear that the most important determinant of whether such a program will become widely implemented in the United States will be the political power of the current bilingual educators and how sensitive the advocates of the immersion program are to their concerns. Naturally, the debate will center on progress that the students make on the traditional yardsticks by which program success is measured. In my opinion, neither of the presently available alternatives— bilingual education in its the present form or some variant on the immersion method—avoids the stigma of compensatory programs in which the native language of the student is seen as a deficit to be overcome. Consequently, I very much doubt that either of them will ever turn out to be a resounding success in turning out high achievers, bilingual or monolingual.

Perhaps the rosiest future for bilingual education in the United States can be attained by dissolving the paradoxical attitude of admiration and pride for school-attained bilingualism on the one hand and scorn and shame for home-brewed immigrant bilingualism on the other. The goals of the educational system could be seen as the development of all students as functional bilinguals, including monolingual English-speakers. The motive is linguistic, cognitive, and cultural enrichment

—the creation of citizens of the world. In this ideal society, speakers of immigrant languages would be seen as holders of a valuable natural resource to be developed, and they in turn would help in the efforts of monolingual English-speakers to learn their language. At the same time, the English-speakers would be seen as resources for the non-English-speakers. School programs based on such an "interlocking" concept for creating functional bilinguals from both language groups are currently being piloted in several American school districts, such as San Diego. In many ways, considering the rate of shift in mother tongue toward English in the United States, it would be only modest hyperbole to say that the linguistic and cultural pluralism of the country depends on the success of such programs.

Chapter 9

Reflections on Bilingualism

THE LANDSCAPE of research in bilingualism surveyed in this book is wide and varied, covering the entire domain of the social sciences. Not surprisingly, understanding of the subject is far from complete. Yet "experts" are constantly pressed to draw general conclusions. And if they do not, somebody else with less knowledge about the field will. It is with this unhappy alternative in mind that I offer the following working conclusions about the state of the art in research on bilingualism. They follow, by and large, the order of topics presented in this book.

• Bilingualism, all other things being equal, has little or no influence on general intellectual abilities in childhood. If any effects are to be found at all, I would predict that they would be positive effects in areas closely related to language, such as in metalinguistic abilities. However, bilingualism is frequently associated with other social factors that might relate to performance on tests of general intellectual abilities. To the extent that bilingualism is associated with the more prestigious social classes, it correlates positively with measures of intellectual functioning in school. The reverse is true where bilingualism is associated with groups with less social prestige.

- Children who grow up in middle-class homes where two languages are spoken initially treat the two languages as a single system (thereby appearing to confuse them), but they rapidly separate the two languages. The commonly held fear that early simultaneous bilingualism causes retardation in language finds little support in data.

- The bilingual uses his or her two languages as an interdependent system. Knowledge that is acquired in one language readily transfers to the other. However, the bilingual is also able to remember the particular language in which events occurred.

- The type of environment in which a person becomes bilingual does not seem to affect the structure of his or her cognitive system. There is little evidence to support the notion that different kinds of bilinguals are produced by different kinds of exposure. Research efforts are better directed at discovering whether there are different ways of storing linguistic information *within* particular individuals, rather than focusing solely on differences *between* individuals.

- Children demonstrate a remarkable ability to acquire a second language spontaneously in the absence of explicit instruction. Their initial statements are tied to the context of conversations and tend to be "prefabricated" in that they do not display use of grammatical structure. Structure is gradually acquired through still undetermined processes that I suspect are largely attributable to an innate capacity to acquire language.

- There are large individual differences in the rate at which children acquire a second language. Variation may be attributable to personality and social factors, as well as to individual differences in verbal ability. It is probably a myth that children find the process of second-language acquisition "painless." Their success at the task notwithstanding, there are a number of reports that suggest emotional stress concomitant with second-language acquisition.

- There is no evidence for a biologically determined critical period for second-language acquisition, with the possible exception of accent. The developmental patterns of second-language grammar are similar for adults and children. During the initial phase of learning, adults and older children are faster at learning the second language than younger children. In the long run, however, children are more successful learners of a second language. The superiority of children is probably due to attitudinal, motivational, and situational factors, rather than to biological factors present only in childhood.

- Learners of different native-language backgrounds, both children and adults, tend to learn a given second language in the same way. Evidence is sparse that the learner uses the grammar of his or her native language as a crutch for second-language acquisition. Most of the "action" in second-language acquisition consists of mastering the complexities of the target language. Evidence for transfer from the native language provides a fascinating avenue for the study of language universals and linguistic relativism, however, and should not be ignored.
- Bilingualism can be found in a large variety of societal contexts around the world, and in many societies it takes on social and political significance. The two languages often represent different social networks and associated value systems, and the choice of language can come to symbolize an individual's identification with either system.
- Bilingualism will be most stable when there are societal norms that govern differential use of the two languages depending on the situation. Bilingualism without diglossia will result in monolingualism.
- Societal institutions that govern the use of language influence the individual in two distinct ways: by setting the language environment and by acting as a symbol that can guide choices about language.
- The debate over bilingual education in the United States is framed in terms of curriculum, effectiveness, and other traditional educational criteria. Answers to many of the objections about bilingual education are available, and research largely supports the contentions of the advocates of bilingual education. Objective data on bilingual programs are ineffective in resolving the underlying issue of the debate, however. Most of the emotional heat over bilingual education is generated by the official recognition of ethnicity as a special status in public education. The conflict can be resolved either by convincing the public of the pedagogical value of bilingual education or by diluting its association with ethnicity and making functional bilingualism the goal for all students.

The Mirror of Bilingualism

Throughout this book, I have harped on the theme that the tensions found in research on bilingualism are quite general in nature. Apart from the broader theoretical questions, the facts by themselves are of limited interest and utility. Why do we care, at face value, about the fact that Spanish speakers learn the English articles *a* and *the* more readily than do Koreans? Does it make a difference to know that immigrants from southern and eastern Europe performed poorly on IQ tests because they had difficulty with English? What will we do with our understanding that the thought processes of the bilingual operate on the two languages as an interdependent system? These facts are interesting and useful primarily because they serve to confirm or modify our beliefs about the nature of language, mind, and society, and these beliefs in turn influence our decisions about things like whether to fund bilingual education or whether to raise our children with two languages.

Yet as scholars, preoccupied with our daily routines of specialized research, we rarely ponder the larger issues. To give a personal example, I am often asked whether I am a researcher of "first-language acquisition" or of "second-language acquisition," a parochial distinction that exists only because the former happens to be studied by the more academic disciplines such as psychology and linguistics, the latter by the more applied ones such as education. When the definitions of a discipline become so narrow, one may become expert in an area without realizing that the conflicts in that area are only specific instances of more general tensions. I now turn to some of these general tensions as a way of integrating the topics covered in this book.

RIGIDITY VERSUS PLASTICITY OF SYSTEMS

The malleability of the system has long been a favorite issue among scholars, whether the system is the mind, language, or society. The best-known battle has concerned the relative roles of nature and nurture in determining IQ. We have encountered many instances of this tension between rigidity and plasticity, beginning with the debate between the hereditarians and environmentalists on the nature of the language handicap in bilinguals. The hereditarians interpreted it as the product of the unmalleable and inferior genetic qualities of the immigrants. The environmentalists treated it as the outcome of the confusion that resulted from bilingualism.

The issue of malleability showed up again in our discussions of the theorists of language and thought in chapter 4. The computer metaphors of the Chomskyan mind hardly leave room for shaping by culture and the environment, while the Marxist psychologist Vygotsky envisioned a sweeping role for culture and technology in shaping thought. In the same chapter, we witnessed one extreme consequence of the assumption made by information-processing psychologists in considering the mental topography of the bilingual. Boldly, in a way that only those who assume rigidity of mental structures would, they took for granted that independence or interdependence of the two languages were mutually exclusive possibilities.

In reviewing the issue of individual differences in second-language learning, we stumbled again into the divide between rigid and plastic accounts. Those who emphasize aptitude and personality as important determinants of the extent of second-language learning are implicit subscribers to the rigid view. By contrast, an emphasis on attitudes and situational characteristics is an endorsement of plasticity.

Finally, the tension between micro-level and macro-level sociolinguistics reflects a difference in the malleability dimension. Since the micro-level emphasis is on individual interaction and the social meanings that each interaction creates, the social status quo is constantly being redefined. On the other hand, in the macro-level approach, societal norms and institutions exert a demanding influence on individual behavior, even though the individuals themselves may be relatively malleable in their behavior potentials.

INTERNAL VERSUS EXTERNAL SOURCES OF REGULARITIES

The factors that cause patterns of behavior to exhibit regularity can be either internal or external to the individual. For example, the massive language shift to English that took place among American immigrants could be attributed to both internal and external influences. On the one hand, the need for an American social identity induced many immigrants to shun their native language. At the same time, external influences such as the mass persecution of foreign elements following the First World War played an equally large role.

Second-language acquisition poses a classic problem of internal versus external sources of regularity. The internal view sees it as the expression of an innate language-acquisition capacity that requires minimal external input in order to be activated. An example of this approach is the emphasis on grammar as the primary accomplishment of language acquisition. By contrast, the discourse and communication approach to language acquisition stresses the social foundations of language that only gradually become internalized.

UNIVERSAL VERSUS PARTICULAR TRUTHS

An account of the language shift to English among immigrant groups in the United States that was limited to factors universally affecting all immigrant groups would strike most people as weak. The history of immigration is full of particular experiences of particular groups. This tension, between general statements and case studies of localized circumstances, permeates social science generally. For example, the conflict between micro- and macro-level sociolinguistics is in large part a reflection of this tension. The ethnographers are bounded by the situation and eschew statements that go beyond the particular. The sociologists want to make generalizations about cities and countries, as did Lieberson in the studies I described in chapter 7. The flare-ups between these two camps are predictable and nasty (see, for example, Pedraza, Attinasi, and Hoffman 1980; Fishman 1983).

In the area of bilingual cognition, the issue is whether the research focuses on universal characteristics of bilinguals or differences between them. The bilingual autonomy studies asked the universalistic question of how bilinguals store their two languages. The question of bilingual typology—whether different kinds of bilinguals are distinguishable—is an example of a particularistic orientation.

The tension between universal and particular can also be seen in the issue of whether the particular native language of the second-language learner influences the pattern of acquisition. Those interested in the universal aspects of second-language acquisition have emphasized the similarities between learners of different language backgrounds learning the same target language. On the other hand, those interested in particulars have focused on the evidence of transfer specific to the learner's native language structure.

Finally, there is the problem of the nature of adult second-language acquisition. I argued for the view that there are common processes among adults in the way in which they acquire a second language, although the extent to which they learn it may differ depending upon various determinants. On the other hand, those who are interested in the determinants of differences between individuals obviously lean toward the particular.

THE EXTENT OF ABSTRACTION

Bilingualism, like any other social or individual phenomenon, can be described with varying degrees of abstractness. Werner Leopold and Madorah Smith, for example, hailed from empiricist traditions in which the goal was to construct a science based purely on observable data. Their scholarship was an exercise in concreteness. Chomsky's attack on the empiricist position was built on the inadequacies of purely concrete descriptions and on the strength of abstract models that can characterize rational intuitions about language. Chomsky's influence on the study of language acquisition enabled researchers to speculate about abstract mental entities that were not necessarily supported by observation.

Similarly, tension abounds in sociolinguistics in the degree with which it tolerates abstraction. The debate over Fishman's sociological notion of domains of language use in bilinguals is criticized by ethnographers like Gumperz as an abstraction that bears little relation to the realities of behavior. On the other hand, the defender of abstractions can argue that societal institutions will never coincide perfectly with individual behavior, but that idealizations of their correspondence are necessary to uncover greater generalities that extend across different bilingual societies.

An issue related to the extent of abstraction is that of formal systems. Formal systems are a nemesis for some people and a joy for others. The role of formal models is nowhere more salient than in the analysis of second-language acquisition, where it serves to illustrate the advantages and disadvantages of an obsession with such systems. The view that a second-language learner is progressing toward a mature state that can be characterized by a formal grammar leads to a concentration on just this aspect of development. Such a focused analysis can lead to important insights about grammar and keep the researcher from getting overwhelmed by the complexities of the entire process. On the other hand, aspects of the learner that do not reveal information about grammar will tend to be ignored. By contrast, a more functionalist, less formal, communication-oriented perspective holds the promise of capturing important insights about language development that might otherwise be overlooked.

THE STATUS OF APPLIED RESEARCH

If we consider the study of bilingualism to be a mirror of the tensions in the different disciplines of the social sciences, bilingual education might be the mirror of bilingualism. It should be an exciting area of research activity, where theories about bilingualism could be tested and refined in an applied setting. Yet bilingual education in the United States has not succeeded in attracting the kind of research talent and enthusiasm one might expect of an area with such potential richness and importance.

A primary reason for this lack of interest can be found in the minority status of students in such programs. The contexts of the research in bilingual education in Canada provides an instructive comparison, because the healthy research tradition there (as can be judged from the more respectable treatment accorded this topic in mainstream journals and textbooks) goes hand in hand with the fact that much of the bilingual education there involves students from middle-class and majority backgrounds. In the United States, most researchers must overcome differences in social class and ethnic group membership (Hakuta, in press).

A related reason is the marginal status of bilingual education in the United States. Its goals, success, and political status are dubious at best. As we saw in the previous chapter, it remains primarily a compensatory program whose track record is mixed even in its goals of transition to monolingual English instruction. Researchers reflect the general societal trend of flocking around winners, and the negative image of bilingual education has not helped in attracting them.

Also prominent are prejudices against applied research in general. There is a prevalent assumption that social science is like the physical sciences, and that phenomena should be studied in their "purest" uncontaminated states before any additional complexities are figured in. Thus the inclination is to understand the process of first-language acquisition in monolingual children before trying to understand untutored second-language acquisition and to understand both of these before trying to understand second-language acquisition in bilingual education classrooms. The flaw in this reasoning is that it is an unproven assumption that second-language acquisition is more complicated than first-language acquisition. In many ways, it would be more plausible that second-language acquisition is less complicated, because it does not occur simultaneously with all the other developing capacities of the young child. In fact, second-language acquisition in the context of a bilingual education classroom with controlled settings for learning and observation might even be considered a simpler problem for the researcher than first-language acquisition. The point, however, is that "pureness" of a phenomenon is a subjective term that in practice refers to something with which the researcher is more familiar.

Ironically, bilingual education research in the United States turns out to be a mirror, but not one that reflects the wondrously complex phenomenon of bilingualism that I have treated in this book. Rather, its marginal status in research reflects the fact that social scientists are, after all, human and are thus subject to the same set of prejudices as those held by other members of their society. Two factors would change the neglected state of research in bilingual education in the United States: first, larger numbers of researchers of language-minority backgrounds, and second, the involvement of students of majority, native-English-speaking backgrounds in the sorts of bilingual programs discussed at the end of chapter 8. Each of these alternatives should be pursued aggressively for its intrinsic merits; together their institution would have the effect of greatly enlivening research in bilingual education. In the meantime, however, social scientists of all disciplinary backgrounds should consider the rich opportunities for understanding cultural and linguistic variation afforded by bilingual education programs. The essence of the relationship of language, mind, and society can be found thriving in this microcosm.

References

Albert, M. L., and L. Obler. 1978. *The bilingual brain: Neuropsychological and neurolinguistic aspects of bilingualism.* New York: Academic Press.

Anastasi, A. 1980. Anne Anastasi. In *A history of psychology in autobiography.* Ed. G. Lindzey. Vol. 7. San Francisco: W. H. Freeman.

Anastasi, A., and F. Cordova. 1953. Some effects of bilingualism upon the intelligence test performance of Puerto Rican children in New York City. *Journal of Educational Psychology* 44: 1–19.

Asher, J., and G. Garcia. 1969. The optimal age to learn a foreign language. *Modern Language Journal* 38: 334–41.

Austin, J. L. 1975. *How to do things with words.* Cambridge, Mass.: Harvard University Press.

Ayres, L. P. 1909. *Laggards in our schools.* New York: Russell Sage Foundation.

Bachi, R. 1956. A statistical analysis of the revival of Hebrew in Israel. *Scripta Hierosolymitan* 3: 179–247.

Bailey, N., C. Madden, and S. Krashen. 1974. Is there a "natural sequence" in adult second language learning? *Language Learning* 21: 235–43.

Bain, B. 1974. Bilingualism and cognition: Toward a general theory. In *Bilingualism, biculturalism, and education: Proceedings from the conference at College Universitaire Saint Jean,* ed. S. T. Carey. Edmonton: University of Alberta Printing Department.

Bain, B., and A. Yu. 1980. Cognitive consequences of raising children bilingually: "One parent, one language." *Canadian Journal of Psychology* 34: 304–13.

Baker, K. A., and A. A. de Kanter, eds. 1983. *Bilingual education: A reappraisal of federal policy.* Lexington, Mass.: Lexington Books.

Balkan, L. 1970. *Les effets du bilinguisme français-anglais sur les aptitudes intellectuelles.* Bruxelles: Aimav.

Barnes, R. E. 1983. The size of the eligible language-minority population. In *Bilingual education: A reappraisal of federal policy,* ed. K. A. Baker and A. A. de Kanter. Lexington, Mass.: Lexington Books.

Bellugi, U. 1967. *The acquisition of negation.* Ph.D. dissertation, Harvard University.

References

Ben-Zeev, S. 1977a. The influence of bilingualism on cognitive strategy and cognitive development. *Child Development* 48: 1009–1018.

———. 1977b. The effect of bilingualism in children from Spanish-English low economic neighborhoods on cognitive development and cognitive strategy. *Working Papers on Bilingualism* 14: 83–122. Also available as ERIC Document ED148106.

Bilingual Education Act. 1968. *United States Statutes at Large,* vol. 81:817.

Birman, B. F., and A. L. Ginsburg. 1983. Introduction: Addressing the needs of language-minority children. In *Bilingual education: A reappraisal of federal policy,* ed. K. A. Baker and A. A. de Kanter. Lexington, Mass.: Lexington Books.

Blanco, G. 1978. The implementation of bilingual/bicultural education programs in the United States. In *Case studies in bilingual education,* ed. B. Spolsky and R. Cooper. Rowley, Mass.: Newbury House.

Bloom, A. H. 1981. *The linguistic shaping of thought: A study in the impact of language on thinking in China and the West.* Hillsdale, N.J.: Lawrence Erlbaum Associates.

Bloom, L. M. 1970. *Language development: Form and function in emerging grammars.* Cambridge, Mass.: MIT Press.

Bolinger, D. 1976. Meaning and memory. *Forum Linguisticum* 1:1–14.

Brigham, C. C. 1923. *A study of American intelligence.* Princeton, N.J.: Princeton University Press.

Brown, R. 1968. The development of *wh* questions in child speech. *Journal of Verbal Learning and Verbal Behavior* 7:279–90.

———. 1973. *A first language: The early stages.* Cambridge, Mass.: Harvard University Press.

Brown, R., and U. Bellugi. 1964. Three processes in the child's acquisition of syntax. *Harvard Educational Review* 34: 133–51.

Cancino, H., and K. Hakuta. 1981. *The acquisition of English by working class adult speakers of English.* Final report, National Institute of Education.

Cancino, H., E. Rosansky, and J. Schumann. 1978. The acquisition of English negatives and interrogatives by native Spanish speakers. In *Second language acquisition: A book of readings,* ed. E. Hatch. Rowley, Mass.: Newbury House Publishers.

Cardenas, J. A. 1977. Response I. In *Language, ethnicity, and the schools: Policy alternatives for bilingual-bicultural education,* ed. N. A. Epstein. Washington, D.C.: Institute for Educational Leadership, George Washington University.

Carroll, J. B. 1956. Introduction to *Language, thought and reality: Selected writings of Benjamin Lee Whorf,* ed. J. B. Carroll. Cambridge, Mass.: MIT Press.

Carroll, J. B., and J. B. Casagrande. 1958. The function of language classification. In *Readings in social psychology,* 3d ed., ed. E. E. Maccoby, T. M. Newcomb, and E. L. Hartley. New York: Holt, Rinehart and Winston.

Carroll, J. B., and S. M. Sapon. 1958. *Modern Language Aptitude Test.* New York: The Psychological Corporation.

Chamot, A. U. 1983. How to plan a transfer curriculum from bilingual to mainstream instruction. *Focus,* no. 12. Rosslyn, Va.: National Clearinghouse for Bilingual Education, October, 1983.

Child, I. L. 1943. *Italian or American? The second generation in conflict.* New Haven: Yale University Press.

Chomsky, N. 1957. *Syntactic structures.* The Hague: Mouton.

———. 1965. *Aspects of the theory of syntax.* Cambridge, Mass.: MIT Press.

Cohen, A. 1974. The Culver City Spanish Immersion Program: The first two years. *Modern Language Journal* 58: 95–103.

Cole, M., and S. Scribner. 1978. Introduction to *Mind in society*, by L. S. Vygotsky, ed. M. Cole, V. John-Steiner, S. Scribner, and E. Souberman. Cambridge, Mass.: Harvard University Press.

Cole, S. 1982. Attitudes towards bilingual education among Hispanics and a nationwide sample. Final report, Center for the Social Sciences, Columbia University.

Corder, S. P. 1971. Idiosyncratic dialects and error analysis. *International Review of Applied Linguistics* 9: 147–60.

Correa-Zoli, Y. 1981. The language of Italian Americans. In *Language in the U.S.A.*, ed. C. A. Ferguson and S. Brice Heath. Cambridge: Cambridge University Press.

Cummins, J. 1976. The influence of bilingualism on cognitive growth: A synthesis of research findings and explanatory hypothesis. *Working Papers on Bilingualism* 9: 1–43.

————. 1980. The cross-lingual dimensions of language proficiency: Implications for bilingual education and the optimal age issue. *TESOL Quarterly* 14: 175–87.

————. 1981. The role of primary language development in promoting educational success for language minority students. In *Schooling and language minority students: A theoretical framework*, California State Department of Education. Los Angeles: Evaluation, Dissemination and Assessment Center, California State University.

————. 1982. Linguistic interdependence among Japanese and Vietnamese immigrant children. In *The measurement of communicative proficiency: Models and applications*, ed. C. Rivera. Washington, D.C.: Center for Applied Linguistics.

Cummins, J., and M. Gulutsan. 1974. Bilingual education and cognition. *Alberta Journal of Educational Research* 20: 259–69.

d'Anglejan, A., and G. R. Tucker. 1975. The acquisition of complex English structures by adult learners. *Language Learning* 25: 281–96.

Danoff, M. N., G. J. Coles, D. H. McLaughlin, and D. J. Reynolds. 1977, 1978. *Evaluation of the impact of ESEA Title VII Spanish/English Bilingual Education Program.* 3 vols. Palo Alto, Calif.: American Institutes for Research.

Darsie, M. L. 1926. The mental capacity of American-born Japanese children. *Comparative Psychology Monographs* 3 (15): 1–89.

de Villiers, J. G., and P. A. de Villiers. 1978. *Language acquisition.* Cambridge, Mass.: Harvard University Press.

Diaz, R. 1983. Thought and two languages: The impact of bilingualism on cognitive development. *Review of Research in Education* 10: 23–54.

Diebold, A. 1968. The consequences of early bilingualism in cognitive development and personality formation. In *The study of personality: An interdisciplinary appraisal*, ed. E. Norbeck, D. Price-Williams, and W. A. McCord. New York: Holt, Rinehart and Winston.

Diller, K. 1970. "Compound" and "coordinate" bilingualism: A conceptual artifact. *Word* 26: 254–61.

Dulay, H., and M. K. Burt. 1972. Goofing: An indicator of children's second language learning strategies. *Language Learning* 22: 235–52.

————. 1973. Should we teach children syntax? *Language Learning* 23: 245–58.

————. 1974. Natural sequences in child second language acquisition. *Language Learning* 24: 37–53.

Duncan, S. E., and E. A. De Avila. 1979. Bilingualism and cognition: Some recent findings. *NABE Journal* 4: 15–50.

Duskova, L. 1969. On sources of errors in foreign languages. *International Review of Applied Linguistics* 7: 11–36.

Edelsky, C., S. Hudelson, B. Flores, F. Barkin, B. Altwerger, and K. Jilbert. 1983. Semilingualism and language deficit. *Applied Linguistics* 4: 1–22.

Epstein, N. 1977. *Language, ethnicity, and the schools: Policy alternatives for bilingual-bicultural education.* Washington, D.C.: Institute for Educational Leadership, George Washington University.

Ervin, S. 1964. Language and TAT content in bilinguals. *Journal of Abnormal and Social Psychology* 68: 500–507.

Ervin, S., and C. Osgood. 1954. Second language learning and bilingualism. *Journal of Abnormal and Social Psychology,* Supplement, 49: 139–46.

Ervin-Tripp, S. 1967. An Issei learns English. *Journal of Social Issues* 23: 78–90.

———. 1974. Is second language learning like the first? *TESOL Quarterly* 8: 111–27.

Fathman, A. 1975. Language background, age, and the order of English structures. Paper presented at the TESOL Convention, Los Angeles, California.

Ferguson, C. A. 1959. Diglossia. *Word* 15: 325–40.

———. 1965. Preface to *The grammatical structures of English and Spanish,* by R. Stockwell, D. Bowen, and J. Martin. Chicago: University of Chicago Press.

Fillmore, L. W. 1979. Individual differences in second language acquisition. In *Individual differences in language ability and language behavior,* ed. C. Fillmore, D. Kempler, and W. Wang. New York: Academic Press.

Fishman, J. A., ed. 1966. *Language loyalty in the United States.* The Hague: Mouton.

———. 1977. The social science perspective. In *Bilingual Education: Current Perspectives,* vol 1. Arlington, Va.: Center for Applied Linguistics.

———. 1982. Whorfianism of the third kind: Ethnolinguistic diversity as a worldwide societal asset (The Whorfian Hypothesis: Varieties of validation, confirmation, and disconfirmation II). *Language in Society* 2: 1–14.

———. 1983. Epistemology, methodology and ideology in the sociolinguistic enterprise. *Language Learning* 33: 33–47.

Fishman, J. A., R. L. Cooper, and R. Ma, eds. 1971. *Bilingualism in the barrio.* Bloomington, Ind.: Indiana University Press.

Fishman, J. A., and J. E. Hofman. 1966. Mother tongue and nativity in the American population. In *Language loyalty in the United States,* ed. J. A. Fishman. The Hague: Mouton.

Fodor, J. A., T. G. Bever, and M. F. Garrett. 1974. *The psychology of language.* New York: McGraw-Hill.

Gal, S. 1979. *Language shift: Social determinants of linguistic change in bilingual Austria.* New York: Academic Press.

Galloway, L. 1980. *The cerebral organization of language in bilinguals and second language learners.* Ph.D. dissertation, University of California at Los Angeles.

Galton, F. 1890. Remarks on mental tests and measurements, by R. Cattell. *Mind* 15: 380–418.

Galziel, T., L. Obler, S. Benton, and M. Albert. 1977. *The dynamics of lateralization in second language learning: Sex and proficiency effects.* Paper presented at the Boston University Conference on Language Development.

Gardner, R. C. 1980. On the validity of affective variables in second language acquisition: Conceptual, contextual, and statistical considerations. *Language Learning* 30: 255–70.

————. 1983. Learning another language: A true social psychological experiment. *Journal of Language and Social Psychology* 2: 219–39.

Gardner, R. C., and W. E. Lambert. 1972. *Attitudes and motivation in second-language learning.* Rowley, Mass.: Newbury House.

Gazzaniga, M. S. 1983. Right hemisphere language following brain bisection: A 20-year perspective. *American Psychologist* 38: 525–37.

Genesee, F. 1979. Scholastic effects of French immersion: An overview after ten years. *Interchange* 9: 20–29.

Genesee, F., J. Hamers, W. E. Lambert, L. Mononen, M. Seitz, and R. Starck. 1978. Language processing in bilinguals. *Brain and Language* 5: 1–12.

Genesee, F., E. Polich, and M. H. Stanley. 1977. An experimental French immersion program at the secondary school level—1969 to 1974. *The Canadian Modern Language Review* 33: 318–32.

Gilbert, G. 1981. French and German: A comparative study. In *Language in the U.S.A.,* ed. C. A. Ferguson and S. B. Heath. New York: Cambridge University Press.

Giles, H., R. Y. Bourhis, and D. M. Taylor. 1977. Towards a theory of language and ethnic group relations. In *Language, ethnicity and intergroup relations,* ed. H. Giles. New York: Academic Press.

Glanzer, M., and A. Duarte. 1971. Repetition between and within languages in free recall. *Journal of Verbal Learning and Verbal Behavior* 10: 625–30.

Gleitman, H. 1981. *Psychology.* New York: W. W. Norton.

Gleitman, L., and E. Wanner, eds. 1982. *Language acquisition: the state of the art.* New York: Cambridge University Press.

Goddard, H. H. 1917. Mental tests and the immigrant. *Journal of Delinquency* 2: 243–77.

Goodenough, F. 1926. Racial differences in the intelligence of school children. *Journal of Experimental Psychology* 9: 388–97.

————. 1940. New evidence on environmental influence on intelligence. In *The thirty-ninth yearbook of the National Society for the Study of Education. Intelligence: Its nature and nurture. Part 1: Comparative and Critical Exposition.* Bloomington, Ill.: Public School Publishing Company.

————. 1946. The measurement of mental growth in childhood. In *Manual of child psychology,* ed. L. Carmichael. New York: John Wiley and Sons.

Gould, S. J. 1981. *The mismeasure of man.* New York: W. W. Norton.

Graham, V. T. 1926. The intelligence of Chinese children in San Francisco. *Journal of Comparative Psychology* 6: 43–71.

Gray, T. 1981. Challenge to USOE Final Evaluation of the Impact of ESEA Title VII Spanish/English Bilingual Education Programs. Arlington, Va.: Center for Applied Linguistics.

Grosjean, F. 1982. *Life with two languages.* Cambridge, Mass.: Harvard University Press.

Guiora, A. Z., R. Brannon, and C. Dull. 1972. Empathy and second language learning. *Language Learning* 22: 111–30.

Gumperz, J. J. 1982. *Discourse strategies.* Cambridge: Cambridge University Press.

Hakuta, K. 1974. Prefabricated patterns and the emergence of structure in second language acquisition. *Language Learning* 24: 287–97.

————. 1976. A case study of a Japanese child learning English. *Language Learning* 26: 321–51.

————. 1984a. Bilingual education in the public eye: A case study of New Haven, Connecticut. *NABE Journal* 9: 53–76.

References

————. 1984*b*. *The causal relationship between the development of bilingualism, cognitive flexibility, and social-cognitive skills in Hispanic elementary school children.* Final Report, National Institute of Education.

————. (in press). Why bilinguals? In *Development of language and language researchers (Essays presented to Roger Brown),* ed. F. Kessel. Hillsdale, N.J.: Lawrence Erlbaum Associates.

Hakuta, K., and H. Cancino, 1977. Trends in second-language-acquisition research. *Harvard Educational Review* 47: 294–316.

Hakuta, K., and R. Diaz. 1984. The relationship between bilingualism and cognitive ability: A critical discussion and some new longitudinal data. In *Children's language,* vol. 5, ed. K. E. Nelson. Hillsdale, N.J.: Lawrence Erlbaum Associates.

Harries, L. 1976. The nationalization of Swahili in Kenya. *Language in Society* 5: 153–64.

Harris, Z. 1951. *Methods in structural linguistics.* Chicago: University of Chicago Press.

Hatch, E. 1978*a*. Discourse analysis and second language acquisition. In *Second language acquisition: A book of readings,* ed. E. Hatch. Rowley, Mass.: Newbury House.

————, ed. 1978*b*. *Second language acquisition: A book of readings.* Rowley, Mass.: Newbury House.

Haugen, E. 1953. *The Norwegian language in America.* Philadelphia: University of Pennsylvania Press.

————. 1970. Discussion of Macnamara. In *Bilingualism and language contact,* ed. J. E. Alatis. Washington, D.C.: Georgetown University Press.

Heath, S. B. 1976. A national language academy? Debate in the new nation. *International Journal of the Sociology of Language* 11: 9–43.

————. 1977. Social history. In *Bilingual Education: Current Perspectives,* vol. 1. Arlington, Va.: Center for Applied Linguistics.

Hinofotis, F., J. Schumann, M. McGroarty, M. Erickson, T. Hudson, L. Kimball, and M. L. Scott. 1982. Relating ILR oral interview scores to grammatical analysis of the learner's speech. Unpublished paper, English Department, University of California at Los Angeles.

Huang, J., and E. Hatch. 1978. A Chinese child's acquisition of English. In *Second language acquisition: A book of readings,* ed. E. Hatch. Rowley, Mass.: Newbury House.

Ianco-Worrall, A. 1972. Bilingualism and cognitive development. *Child Development* 43: 1390–1400.

Jackson, J. E. 1983. *The fish people.* Cambridge: Cambridge University Press.

Jakobovits, L. 1970. *Foreign language learning: A psycholinguistic analysis of the issues.* Rowley, Mass.: Newbury House.

Jones, Maldwyn A. 1960. *American immigration.* Chicago: University of Chicago Press.

Kamin, L. J. 1974. *The science and politics of I.Q.* New York: John Wiley and Sons.

Kelly, F. J. 1923. Review of K. Young, *Mental differences in certain immigrant groups. Journal of Educational Research* 7: 255–56.

Kessler, C., and M. E. Quinn. 1980. Positive effects of bilingualism on science problem-solving abilities. In *Current issues in bilingual education,* ed. J. E. Alatis. Washington, D.C.: Georgetown University Press.

Kinsbourne, M. 1975. The ontogeny of cerebral dominance. In *Annals of the New*

York Academy of Sciences, 263 *(Developmental psycholinguistics and communicative disorders),* ed. D. Aaronson and R. W. Reiber. Pp. 244–50.

Kintsch, W., and E. Kintsch. (1969). Interlingual interference and memory processes. *Journal of Verbal Learning and Verbal Behavior* 8: 16–19.

Klein, W., and N. Dittmar. 1979. *Developing grammars: The acquisition of German syntax by foreign workers.* New York: Springer-Verlag.

Kloss, H. 1966. German-American language maintenance efforts. In *Language loyalty in the United States,* ed. J. A. Fishman. The Hague: Mouton.

————. 1974. Linguistic composition of the nations of the world. Quebec: Presses de l'Université Laval.

————. 1977. *The American bilingual tradition.* Rowley, Mass.: Newbury House.

Kolers, P. 1963. Interlingual word association. *Journal of Verbal Learning and Verbal Behavior* 2: 291–300.

————. 1965. Bilingualism and bicodalism. *Language and Speech* 8: 122–26.

————. 1978. On the representations of experience. In *Language Interpretation and Communication,* ed. D. Gerver and H. Sinaiko. New York: Plenum Press.

Kolers, P. A., and E. Gonzalez. 1980. Memory for words, synonyms, and translations. *Journal of Experimental Psychology: Human Learning and Memory* 6: 53–65.

Krashen, S. 1973. Lateralization, language learning, and the critical period. *Language Learning* 23: 63–74.

————. 1981. *Second language acquisition and second language learning.* Oxford: Pergamon Press.

Krashen, S., and P. Pon. 1975. An error analysis of an advanced ESL learner: The importance of the monitor. *Working Papers on Bilingualism* 7: 125–29.

Lado, R. 1964. *Language teaching: A scientific approach.* New York: McGraw-Hill.

LaLonde, R. N., and R. C. Gardner. 1984. Investigating a causal model of second language acquisition: Where does personality fit in? *Canadian Journal of Behavioral Science* 16: 224–37.

Lambert, W. E., and E. Anisfeld. 1969. A note on the relationship of bilingualism and intelligence. *Canadian Journal of Behavioral Science* 1: 123–28.

Lambert, W. E., and S. Fillenbaum. 1959. A pilot study of aphasia among bilinguals. *Canadian Journal of Psychology* 13: 28–34.

Lambert, W. E., J. Havelka, and D. Crosby. 1958. The influence of language-acquisition contexts on bilingualism. *Journal of Abnormal and Social Psychology* 66: 239–43.

Lambert, W. E., M. Ignatow, and M. Krauthamer. 1968. Bilingual organization in free recall. *Journal of Verbal Learning and Verbal Behavior* 7: 207–14.

Lambert, W. E., and G. R. Tucker. 1972. *Bilingual education of children: The St. Lambert experiment.* Rowley, Mass.: Newbury House.

Laosa, L. M. 1984. Ethnicity, race, language, and American social policies toward children. In *Child development research and social policy,* ed. H. H. Stevenson and A. Siegel. Chicago: University of Chicago Press.

Larsen-Freeman, D. 1976. An explanation for the morpheme acquisition order of second language learners. *Language Learning* 26: 125–34.

Lashley, K. S. 1951. The problem of serial order in behavior. In *Cerebral mechanisms in behavior: The Hixon symposium,* ed. L. A. Jeffress. New York: John Wiley and Sons.

Lenneberg, E. H. 1967. *Biological foundations of language.* New York: John Wiley and Sons.

Leopold, W. F. 1939. *Speech development of a bilingual child: A linguist's record.* Vol. 1,

Vocabulary growth in the first two years. Evanston, Ill.: Northwestern University Press.

———. 1947. *Speech development of a bilingual child: A linguist's record.* Vol. 2, *Sound-learning in the first two years.* Evanston, Ill.: Northwestern University Press.

———. 1948. The study of child language and infant bilingualism. *Word* 4: 1–17.

———. 1949a. *Speech development of a bilingual child: A linguist's record.* Vol. 3, *Grammar and general problems.* Evanston, Ill.: Northwestern University Press.

———. 1949b. *Speech development of a bilingual child: a linguist's record.* Vol. 4, *Diary from age 2.* Evanston, Ill.: Northwestern University Press.

Lieberson, S. 1970. *Language and ethnic relations in Canada.* New York: John Wiley and Sons.

Lieberson, S., G. Dalto, and M. E. Johnston. 1975. The course of mother-tongue diversity in nations. *American Journal of Sociology* 81: 34–61.

Liedtke, W. W., and L. D. Nelson. 1968. Concept formation and bilingualism. *Alberta Journal of Educational Research* 14: 225–32.

Lightbown, P. 1977. French L2 learners: What they're talking about. Paper presented at the First Los Angeles Second Language Research Forum, University of California, Los Angeles.

Lopez, M., and R. Young. 1974. The linguistic interdependence of bilinguals. *Journal of Experimental Psychology* 103: 981–83.

Lyman, S. M., and M. B. Scott. 1970. *A sociology of the absurd.* New York: Appleton-Century-Crofts.

McCarthy, D. 1946. Language development. In *Manual of child psychology,* ed. L. Carmichael. New York: John Wiley and Sons.

Mackey, W. F. 1967. *Bilingualism as a world problem/Le bilinguisme: phenomene mondial.* Montreal: Harvest House.

Mackey, W. F., and V. N. Beebe. 1977. *Bilingual schools for a bicultural community: Miami's adaptation to the Cuban refugees.* Rowley, Mass.: Newbury House.

MacNab, G. L. 1979. Cognition and bilingualism: A reanalysis of studies. *Linguistics* 17: 231–55.

Macnamara, J. 1966. Bilingualism and primary education. Edinburgh: Edinburgh University Press.

———. 1970. Bilingualism and thought. In *Bilingualism and language contact,* ed. J. E. Alatis. Washington, D.C.: Georgetown University Press.

———. 1976. Comparison between first and second language learning. *Die Neueren Sprachen* 2: 175–88.

McCormack, P. D. 1974. Bilingual linguistic memory: Independence or interdependence: Two stores or one? In *Bilingualism, biculturalism and education,* ed. S. T. Carey. Edmonton, Alberta: University of Alberta Printing Department.

———. 1977. Bilingual linguistic memory: The independence-interdependence issue revisited. In *Bilingualism: psychological, social, and educational implications,* ed. P. A. Hornby. New York: Academic Press.

McLaughlin, B. 1984. *Second-language acquisition in childhood.* Vol. 1, *Preschool children.* 2d ed. Hillsdale, N.J.: Lawrence Erlbaum Associates.

Marler, P. 1970. Birdsong and speech development: Could there be parallels? *American Scientist* 58: 669–73.

Mead, M. 1927. Group intelligence tests and linguistic disability among Italian children. *School and Society* 25: 465–68.

References

Miller, G. A. 1962. Some psychological studies of grammar. *American Psychologist* 17: 748–62.

Miller, G. A., E. Galanter, and K. H. Pribram. 1960. *Plans and the structure of behavior.* New York: Holt, Rinehart and Winston.

Mitchell, A. J. 1937. The effect of bilingualism in the measurement of intelligence. *Elementary School Journal* 38: 29–37.

Naiman, N., M. Frolich, and H. H. Stern. 1975. *The good language learner.* Toronto: Ontario Institute for Studies in Education.

National Clearinghouse for Bilingual Education. 1984. Significant bilingual instructional features study completed. *FORUM* 7 (3): 1–4.

———. 1985. Descriptive phase of national longitudinal study released. *FORUM 8* (3): 1–3.

———. (n.d.). *Bilingual education information packet.* Rosslyn, Va.: National Clearinghouse for Bilingual Education.

National Society for the Study of Education. 1928. *The twenty-seventh yearbook of the National Society for the Study of Education. Nature and nurture, Part I: Their influence upon intelligence.* Bloomington, Ill.: Public School Publishing Company.

———. 1940. *The thirty-ninth yearbook of the National Society for the Study of Education. Intelligence: Its nature and nurture.* Bloomington, Ill.: Public School Publishing Company.

Nemser, W. 1971. Approximative systems of foreign language learners. *International Review of Applied Linguistics* 9: 115–23.

Newby, R. W. 1976. Effects of bilingual language system on release from proactive inhibition. *Perceptual and Motor Skills* 43: 1059–64.

Newmeyer, F. J. 1980. *Linguistic theory in America: The first quarter-century of transformational generative grammar.* New York: Academic Press.

Obler, L. 1979. Right hemisphere participation in second language learning. In *Individual differences and universals in language learning aptitude,* ed. K. Diller. Rowley, Mass.: Newbury House.

Ojemann, G. A., and H. A. Whitaker. 1978. The bilingual brain. *Archives of Neurology* 35: 409–12.

Oller, J., and K. Perkins, eds. 1980. *Research in language testing.* Rowley, Mass.: Newbury House.

Olson, D. 1977. From utterance to text: The bias of language in speech and writing. *Harvard Educational Review* 47: 257–81.

O'Malley, J. M. 1978. Review of the Evaluation of the Impact of ESEA Title VII Spanish/English Bilingual Education Program. *Bilingual Resources* 1: 6–10.

———. 1981. *Children's English and services study: Language minority children with limited English proficiency in the United States.* Rosslyn, Va.: InterAmerica Research Associates.

———. 1982. *Children's English and services study: Educational and needs assessment for language minority children with limited English proficiency.* Rosslyn, Va.: InterAmerica Research Associates.

Oxford, R., L. Pol, D. Lopez, P. Stupp, S. Peng, and M. Gendell. 1980. *Projections of non-English language background and limited English proficient persons in the United States to the year 2000.* Rosslyn, Va.: InterAmerica Research Associates.

Oyama, S. 1976. A sensitive period for the acquisition of a nonnative phonological system. *Journal of Psycholinguistic Research* 5: 261–85.

———. 1978. The sensitive period and comprehension of speech. *Working Papers on Bilingualism* 16:1–17.

References

Paivio, A., and A. Desrochers. 1980. A dual-coding approach to bilingual memory. *Canadian Journal of Psychology* 34: 388–99.

Paivio, A., and W. E. Lambert. 1981. Dual coding and bilingual memory. *Journal of Verbal Learning and Verbal Behavior* 20: 532–39.

Paradis, M. 1977. Bilingualism and aphasia. In *Studies in neurolinguistics*, vol. 3, ed. H. A. Whitaker and H. Whitaker. New York: Academic Press.

——. 1980. Language and thought in bilinguals. In *The Sixth LACUS Forum*, ed. W. McCormack and H. J. Izzo. Columbia, S.C.: Hornbeam Press.

——. 1981. Neurolinguistic organization of a bilingual's two languages. In *The Seventh LACUS Forum*, ed. J. E. Copeland and P. W. Davis. Columbia, S.C.: Hornbeam Press.

Patkowski, M. 1980. The sensitive period for the acquisition of syntax in a second language. *Language Learning* 30: 449–72.

Paulston, C. B. 1980. *Bilingual education: theories and issues.* Rowley, Mass.: Newbury House.

——. 1982. *Swedish research and debate about bilingualism. A report to the National Swedish Board of Education.* Stockholm: National Swedish Board of Education.

Peal, E. and W. E. Lambert. 1962. The relation of bilingualism to intelligence. *Psychological Monographs* 76 (27, Whole No. 546).

Pedraza, P., J. Attinasi, and G. Hoffman. 1980. Rethinking diglossia. Working Paper No. 9, City University of New York, Centro de Estudios Puertorriqueños.

Penfield, W., and L. Roberts. 1959. *Speech and brain mechanisms.* Princeton, N.J.: Princeton University Press.

Pfaff, C. W. 1981. Sociolinguistic problems of immigrants: Foreign workers and their children in Germany (a review article). *Language in Society* 10: 155–88.

Piaget, J. 1980. The psychogenesis of knowledge and its epistemological significance. In *Language and learning: The debate between Jean Piaget and Noam Chomsky*, ed. M. Piattelli-Palmarini. Cambridge, Mass.: Harvard University Press.

Piattelli-Palmarini, M., ed. 1980. *Language and learning: The debate between Jean Piaget and Noam Chomsky.* Cambridge, Mass.: Harvard University Press.

Pintner, R. 1923. A comparison of American and foreign children on intelligence tests. *Journal of Educational Psychology* 14: 292–95.

Richards, J. 1973. A non-contrastive approach to error analysis. In *Focus on the learner: Pragmatic perspectives for the language teacher.* ed. J. Oller and J. Richards. Rowley, Mass.: Newbury House.

Rist, R. C. 1979. Migration and marginality: Guestworkers in Germany and France. *Daedalus* 108: 95–108.

Rivers, W. 1964. *The psychologist and the foreign language teacher.* Chicago: University of Chicago Press.

Rodriguez, R. 1982. *Hunger of memory: The education of Richard Rodriguez.* Boston: David R. Godine.

Ronjat, J. 1913. *Le développement du langage observé chez un enfant bilingue.* Paris: Champion.

Rose, R. G., P. R. Rose, N. King, and A. Perez. 1975. Bilingual memory for related and unrelated sentences. *Journal of Experimental Psychology: Human Learning and Memory* 1: 599–606.

Rosenfeld, S. S. (1974a). Bilingualism and the melting pot. *Washington Post,* September 27.

———. (1974*b*). A second look at bilingualism. *Washington Post,* November 1.

Rubin, J. 1968. Bilingual usage in Paraguay. In *Readings in the sociology of language,* ed. J. A. Fishman. The Hague: Mouton.

Saer, D. J. 1924. The effect of bilingualism on intelligence. *British Journal of Psychology* 14: 25–38.

Samelson, F. 1975. On the science and politics of the IQ. *Social Research* 42: 467–88.

Schaie, K. W., and J. Geiwitz. 1982. *Adult development and aging.* Boston: Little, Brown.

Schaie, K. W., and C. R. Strother. 1968. A cross-sequential study of age changes in cognitive behavior. *Psychological Bulletin* 70: 671–80.

Schlossman, S. L. 1983. Is there an American tradition of bilingual education? German in the public elementary schools, 1840–1919. *American Journal of Education* 91: 139–86.

Schumann, J. 1975. Affective factors and the problem of age in second language acquisition. *Language Learning* 25: 209–35.

———. 1978. *The pidginization process: A model for second language acquisition.* Rowley, Mass.: Newbury House.

Selinker, L. 1972. Interlanguage. *International Review of Applied Linguistics* 10: 219–31.

Selinker, L., M. Swain, and G. Dumas. 1975. The interlanguage hypothesis extended to children. *Language Learning* 25: 139–52.

Simon, P. 1980. *The tongue-tied American: Confronting the foreign language crisis.* New York: Continuum.

Skutnabb-Kangas, T. 1978. Semilingualism and the education of migrant children as a means of reproducing the caste of assembly line workers. In *Papers from the first Scandinavian-German symposium on the language of immigrant workers and their children,* ed. N. Dittmar, H. Haberland, T. Skutnabb-Kangas, and U. Teleman. Roskilde, Denmark: Roskilde University ROLIG.

Skutnabb-Kangas, T., and P. Toukomaa. 1976. *Teaching migrant children's mother tongue and learning the language of the host country.* Helsinki: The Finnish National Commission for UNESCO.

Slobin, D. I. 1973. Cognitive prerequisites for the development of grammar. In *Studies of child language development,* ed. C. A. Ferguson and D. I. Slobin. New York: Holt, Rinehart and Winston.

———. 1977. Language change in childhood and in history. In *Language learning and thought,* ed. J. Macnamara. New York: Academic Press.

———. 1979. *Psycholinguistics.* 2d. ed. San Francisco: Scott Foresman.

Smith, F. 1923. Bilingualism and mental development. *British Journal of Psychology* 13: 271–82.

Smith, M. E. 1931. A study of five bilingual children from the same family. *Child Development* 2: 184–87.

———. 1939. Some light on the problem of bilingualism as found from a study of the progress in mastery of English among pre-school children of non-American ancestry in Hawaii. *Genetic Psychology Monographs* 21: 119–284.

Snow, C. E. 1983. Language and literacy: Relationships during the preschool years. *Harvard Educational Review* 53: 165–89.

———. 1984. Beyond conversation: Second language learners' acquisition of description and explanation. In *Second language acquisition in the classroom setting,* ed. J. Lantolf and R. DiPietro. Norwood, N.J.: Ablex.

Snow, C., and M. Hoefnagel-Hohle. 1978. The critical period for language acquisition: Evidence from second language learning. *Child Development* 49: 1114–28.

Snyderman, M., and R. J. Herrnstein. 1983. Intelligence tests and the Immigration Act of 1924. *American psychologist* 38: 986–95.

Soares, C., and F. Grosjean. 1981. Left hemisphere language lateralization in bilinguals and monolinguals. *Perception and Psychophysics* 29: 599–604.

Sorensen, A. P. 1967. Multilingualism in the Northwest Amazon. *American Anthropologist* 69: 670–84.

Stern, H. H., M. Swain, and L. D. McLean. 1976. *Three approaches to learning French.* Toronto: Ontario Institute for Studies in Education.

Stoddard, G. D., and B. L. Wellman. 1934. *Child psychology.* New York: Macmillan Company.

Stoller, P. 1976. The language planning activities of the U.S. Office of Bilingual Education. *International Journal of the Sociology of Language* 11: 45–60.

Swain, M. 1972. *Bilingualism as a first language.* Ph.D. dissertation, University of California, Irvine.

———. 1978. French immersion: Early, late or partial? *Canadian Modern Language Review* 34: 577–85.

———. 1979. Bilingual education: Research and its implications. In *On TESOL 79: The learner in focus,* ed. C. A. Yorio, K. Perkins and J. Schachter. Washington, D.C.: Teachers of English to Speakers of Other Languages.

Swain, M. and H. Barik. 1978. Bilingual education in Canada: French and English. In *Case studies in bilingual education,* ed. B. Spolsky and R. L. Cooper. Rowley, Mass.: Newbury House.

Taylor, D. M. 1980. Ethnicity and language: A social psychological perspective. In *Language: Social psychological perspectives,* ed. H. Giles, W. P. Robinson and P. M. Smith. Oxford: Pergamon Press.

Teitelbaum, H., and R. J. Hiller. 1977. The legal perspective. In *Bilingual Education: Current Perspectives,* vol. 3. Arlington, Va.: Center for Applied Linguistics.

Terman, L. M. 1916. *The measurement of intelligence.* Boston: Houghton Mifflin.

———. 1918. The vocabulary test as a measure of intelligence. *Journal of Educational Psychology* 9: 452–59.

———. 1926. *Terman group test of mental ability.* Yonkers-on-Hudson, N.Y.: World Book Company.

Thompson, G. G. 1952. *Child psychology.* Boston: Houghton Mifflin.

Troike, R. 1978. Research evidence for the effectiveness of bilingual education. Rosslyn, Va.: National Clearinghouse for Bilingual Education.

———. 1981. SCALP: Social and cultural aspects of language proficiency. Paper presented at the Language Proficiency Assessment Symposium, 15–17 March 1981, at Airlie House, Warrenton, Va.

Ulibarri, D. M. 1982. Limited-English proficient students: A review of national estimates. Report TN-10, November. Los Alamitos, Calif.: National Center for Bilingual Research.

U.S. Department of Health, Education and Welfare Office for Civil Rights. 1975. Task force findings specifying remedies available for eliminating past educational practices ruled unlawful under Lau v. Nichols.

Vaid, J. 1983. Bilingualism and brain lateralization. In *Brain functions and brain organization.* New York: Academic Press.

Veltman, C. 1979. *The assimilation of American language minorities: Structure, pace and extent.* Washington, D.C.: National Center for Education Statistics.

Vihman, M. M. 1982*a*. The acquisition of morphology by a bilingual child: A whole-word approach. *Applied Psycholinguistics* 3: 141–60.

————. 1982*b*. Formulas in first and second language acquisition. In *Exceptional language and linquistics,* ed. L. Obler and L. Menn. New York: Academic Press.

Vihman, M. M., and B. McLaughlin. 1982. Bilingualism and second language acquisition in preschool children. In *Progress in cognitive development: Verbal processes in children,* ed. C. Brainerd. New York: Springer-Verlag.

Volterra, V., and T. Taeschner. 1978. The acquisition and development of language by bilingual children. *Journal of Child Language* 5: 311–26.

Vygotsky, L. S. 1962. *Thought and language.* Cambridge, Mass.: MIT Press.

————. 1978. *Mind in society.* Ed. M. Cole, V. John-Steiner, S. Scribner, and E. Souberman. Cambridge, Mass.: Harvard University Press.

Waggoner, D. 1984. The need for bilingual education: Estimates from the 1980 census. *NABE Journal* 8: 1–14.

Wardaugh, R. 1974. *Topics in applied linguistics.* Rowley, Mass.: Newbury House.

Watson, J. B. 1930. *Behaviorism.* New York: W. W. Norton.

Weinreich, U. 1953. *Languages in contact: Findings and problems.* New York: Linguistic Circle of New York. Reprinted by Mouton, The Hague, 1974.

Werner, H., and B. Kaplan. 1963. *Symbol formation.* New York: John Wiley and Sons.

Whorf, B. L. 1956. *Language, thought and reality: Selected writings of Benjamin Lee Whorf.* Ed. J. B. Carroll. Cambridge, Mass.: MIT Press.

Williams, L. 1974. *Speech perception and production as a function of exposure to a second language.* Ph.D. dissertation, Department of Psychology and Social Relations, Harvard University.

World Council of Churches. 1972. The threat of monolinguism to the World Council of Churches. Document No. 15, Unit 3, Committee Meeting, Utrecht, August 5–11, 1972. Geneva, Switzerland: World Council of Churches Documentation Service.

Yoshioka, J. G. 1929. A study of bilingualism. *Journal of Genetic Psychology* 36: 473–79.

Young, K. 1922. *Mental differences in certain immigrant groups.* University of Oregon Publication, vol. 1, no. 11, July 1922. Eugene, Oregon: The University Press.

Young, R. K., and J. Saegert, 1966. Transfer with bilinguals. *Psychonomic Science* 6: 161–62.

Youth Policy (June 1983). Issue/Debate: Proposed fiscal 1984 reductions in bilingual education.

Zehler, A. M. 1982. *The reflection of first-language-derived processes in second language acquisition.* Ph.D. dissertation, University of Illinois at Urbana-Champaign.

INDEX

Acculturation: among Italian-Americans, in New Haven, CT, 171–73
Additive bilingualism, 42
Adult second-language acquisition, child second-language acquisition and, 141–44
Age: of becoming bilingual, 97–98; cerebral lateralization and, 138; of exposure, and second-language acquisition, 147–48
Age-related changes, in second-language acquisition, 145–46
AIR Report, on effectiveness of bilingual education, 219–22
Albert, M. L., 86
Alpha test, 20, 21, 25, 26; see also Binet test
Amazon, see Northwest Amazon
American anthropology, 74
American developmental psychology, 112
American immigrants, "old" and "new," 16–22
American linguistics, 68–69
American Sign Language, 3n
Anastasi, Anne, 31–32
Anisfeld, E., 39
Aphasia: in bilinguals, 86–87; in compound bilinguals, 95–97; in coordinate bilinguals, 95–97
Aptitude, see Language aptitude
Arabic, 204
Asher, J., 149, 150
Attinasi, J., 237
Attitude, see Language attitude
Attitude Motivation Index, 158
Austin, J. L., 132

Bachi, Roberto, 145–46, 147, 151
Bailey, N., 141
Bain, Bruce, 35, 36–38
Baker, K. A., 221, 222, 229
Balanced bilinguals, 34
Balkan, L., 35

Barik, H., 228
Barnes, R. E., 203, 209
Beebe, V. N., 194n, 196, 197, 198, 218
Belgium, separationist tendencies and bilingualism in, 7
Bellugi, Ursula, 110
Bengali, 4
Ben-Zeev, S., 35
Beta Test, 20, 21, 25; see also Binet test
Bever, T. G., 80–81
Bilingual acquisition: language awareness and, 67–68; period of undifferentiation in, 66–67
Bilingual education, 193–230; academic skills transfer and, 218–19; AIR Report on effectiveness of, 219–22; arguments against, 210–25; budget for, in United States, 206; in California, 200–201; in Canada, 94; community attitudes towards, among Hispanics, in Los Angeles, 213–14; community attitudes towards, among Hispanics, in New York, 213–14; community attitudes towards, in New Haven, CT, 8, 212–13; community attitudes towards, in United States, 213–14; in Dade County, FL, 215; dropout rate and, 221; ESL and, 202; Ford Foundation and, 194; future of, 227–30; in Illinois, 201; in Massachusetts, 201; in New Haven, CT, 215, 219; in New York, 201; origins, in United States, 194–98; policy on, in United States, 41, 208–10; program in Dade County, FL, 194–98; role of Federal Government in, 198–203; Spanish and English of Puerto Rican children in, 41; in Texas, 201; U.S. English and, 205–10; in United States, 7, 94, 191–92
Bilingual Education Act (1968), 198, 200–202, 205, 208, 209, 219
Bilingual mind, 73–105; educational psychology and, 93–94; information processing and, 89–93

Index